M000188541

THE PERIODIC SERVICE REVIEW

A Total Quality Assurance System
for Human Services and
Education

by

Gary W. LaVigna, Ph.D.
Clinical Director

Thomas J. Willis, Ph.D.
Associate Director

Julia F. Shaull, M.S.W.
Director of Supported Employment Services

Maryam Abedi, Ph.D.
Director of Supported Living Services

Institute for Applied Behavior Analysis
Los Angeles, California

and

Melissa Sweitzer, Ph.D.
Behavior Consultant
Irvine, California

·P A U L·H·
BROOKES
PUBLISHING Cº ®

Baltimore ▪ London ▪ Sydney

Paul H. Brookes Publishing Co.
Post Office Box 10624
Baltimore, Maryland 21285-0624
www.brookespublishing.com

Copyright © 1994 by Paul H. Brookes Publishing Co., Inc. All rights reserved.

"Paul H. Brookes Publishing Co." is a registered trademark of Paul H. Brookes Publishing Co., Inc.

Typeset by Brushwood Graphics, Inc., Baltimore, Maryland.
Manufactured in the United States of America by
Sheridan Books, Inc., Fredericksburg, Virginia.

Second printing, December 1997.
Third printing, March 2000.
Fourth printing, July 2003.

Library of Congress Cataloging-in-Publication Data
The Periodic service review : a total quality assurance system for human services and
    education / by Gary W. LaVigna . . . [et al.].
        p.   cm.
    Includes bibliographical references and index.
    ISBN 1-55766-142-1
    1. Human services—Management—Evaluation.   2. School management and
organization—Evaluation.   I. LaVigna, Gary W.
HV41.P42   1994
361'.006'5—dc20   93-39241
                                                                                              CIP

British Library Cataloguing-in-Publication data are available from the British Library.

We dedicate this book to our families, who support us and who cheer us on in the work we do.

· Contents ·

· Acknowledgments ·

There are many people who have supported us in writing this book. First and foremost is the Institute for Applied Behavior Analysis (IABA) management and supervisory team who use the Periodic Service Review (PSR) day in and day out as a primary strategy to assure the quality of our services. With our deepest appreciation for their commitment to excellence, we thank Heike Ballmaier, LeeAnn Christian, Stacy Daniels, Kathryn Edwards, Diane Feheley, Holly Hauff, Brian LaRue, Ayndrea LaVigna, Ellen Lewis, Ann Majure, Judy McGuire, Jonathan Mohn, Catherine Lichtenberger, Christopher Pellani, Cheryl Stroll Reisler, Diane Sabiston, Ihab Shahawi, Melissa Shapiro, Bob Shelton, and Angela Tippins. Although their names are too many to list, we also recognize and thank all of our direct service staff, who revel in providing the highest quality of service possible to the people we support, and who, with their suggestions, have helped us to improve the PSR over the years.

There are a number of people outside the IABA family whom we want to thank. Alice Prather, Steve Galindo, Rachelle Markley, Maria Marrero, and Dick Lynch played key roles in the development of the PSR and related materials for the behavior services unit, as did Lorraine Termini and Beth Forger in the development of the classroom PSR. We also thank Mark Katz and the staff at Therapeutic Living Concepts and the many managers and supervisors of other agencies who have attended our 1-day workshop on developing PSRs and/or with whom we consult in improving management systems as part of their continuous total quality process.

· About the Authors ·

Gary W. LaVigna, Ph.D., Clinical Director, Institute for Applied Behavior Analysis (IABA), 5777 West Century Boulevard, Suite 675, Los Angeles, California 90045-5673. Dr. LaVigna founded IABA, a psychological corporation, in 1982. A clinical psychologist, Dr. LaVigna is the author of numerous articles, the co-author of two books, *Alternatives to Punishment* and *Progress Without Punishment,* and an international lecturer.

Thomas J. Willis, Ph.D., Associate Director, Institute for Applied Behavior Analysis, 5777 West Century Boulevard, Suite 675, Los Angeles, California 90045-5673. Dr. Willis is cofounder with Dr. LaVigna of IABA, where he currently serves as Associate Director. Dr. Willis has worked as a behavioral consultant for more than 18 years, and has provided training to a wide variety of professional and paraprofessional groups across the United States and abroad.

Julia F. Shaull, M.S.W., Director of Supported Employment Services, Institute for Applied Behavior Analysis, 5777 West Century Boulevard, Suite 675, Los Angeles, California 90045-5673. Ms. Shaull is a licensed clinical social worker. She has developed services that include Systematic Training for Employment Program (STEP) and Community Behavioral Services Institute, which support about 200 adults with developmental disabilities in direct-pay employment in a three-county area in Southern California.

Maryam Abedi, Ph.D., Director of Supported Living Services, Institute for Applied Behavior Analysis, 5777 West Century Boulevard, Suite 675, Los Angeles, California 90045-5673. The services that Dr. Abedi directs at IABA include Social/Community Integration and Participation (SCIP) and Community Supported Living Arrangement (CSLA), which together support 60 adults with developmental disabilities to live in their own homes. Dr. Abedi has also worked as a behavioral consultant for 9 years, providing consultation in support of individuals who are challenged with developmental disabilities, and whose behavior can be a barrier to full social and community integration.

Melissa Sweitzer, Ph.D., Behavior Consultant, 6 Birdsong, Irvine, California 92714. Dr. Sweitzer is a licensed psychologist with over 15 years' experience working with individuals with challenging behaviors. Dr. Sweitzer served as Director of Clinical Services for IABA, before beginning her own private practice. She is currently a behavior consultant in Irvine, California, advising various agencies, and residential and day programs serving persons with developmental disabilities.

· Preface ·
THE CHALLENGE OF PROVIDING QUALITY

MANAGEMENT'S VIEW

Managers of human service and educational agencies have little trouble identifying areas within their agencies that should perform better in providing quality services. Moreover, the similarities between those areas that managers consider should be performing better are remarkable. When we ask managers and supervisors attending our management training seminars to identify negatives in their agencies that contribute to poor results they cite:

- *Not* spending enough time in the community
- *Not* providing enough systematic instruction to the individuals receiving services
- *Not* achieving satisfactory outcomes for the individuals being served; that is, not achieving a meaningful, positive impact on an individual's quality of life
- *Not* collecting data
- *Not* being consistent or accurate in data collection
- *Not* following agreed-upon procedures
- *Not* following the individualized service or education plan
- *Not* providing sufficient functional, age-appropriate activities
- *Not* respecting the individuals being served
- *Not* following schedules
- *Not* interacting positively with the individuals being served
- *Not* doing anything at all

When they try to explain why their agencies may fall short in some areas and in the quality of services they provide, managers and supervisors quickly point to what may seem to be obvious reasons. These reasons are also strikingly similar. They may include the following explanations, many of which are related.

- High staff turnover
- Poor staff motivation
- Poor wages
- Lack of staff training
- Lack of staff skills
- Lack of agreement in philosophy or effectiveness of strategies employed
- Too little time in the day
- Dislike of the individuals being served
- Lazy staff
- Lack of intelligent staff
- Not enough staff or other resources, and so forth

MANAGEMENT'S ROLE

A review of the literature, however, clearly shows that, although human service supervisors, managers, and administrators tend to blame low wages, bad attitudes, lack of skills,
poor communication, insufficient resources, and other factors outside their control for inconsistency and poor quality in the services provided, the real culprit seems to be *poor
management practice*. This point was well made by Reid, Parsons, and Green (1989a), who
observed:

> where pervasive problems in staff performance exist, the primary cause is ineffective supervi-
> sion and management. (p. 4)

Similarly, Christian and Reitz (1986) concluded:

> Management practice is the number one reason why there is a discrepancy between the develop-
> ment and implementation of treatment programs. (p. 24)

The Periodic Service Review (PSR) described in this book addresses this problem. It
was written to provide human service and educational agencies with a management system
for staff training and supervision based on proven principles and procedures. Such systems
enable agencies to meet their goals and objectives and to assure the quality of their services
and programs. Although many principles of effective management and supervision are
known, managers and administrators may not be able to translate them into a concrete system of practices and procedures applicable to their own agencies. In the following chapters,
we describe a procedural system that has succeeded in residential and educational settings
and in agencies that provide services to adults. The system has evolved from over a decade
of work at the Institute for Applied Behavior Analysis (IABA), and it is the result of our
efforts to solve the management and quality assurance challenges that we have dealt with
over that time.

EFFECT OF MANAGEMENT ON STAFF TURNOVER

We are often asked if the PSR can have a positive effect on staff turnover—a significant
problem in community-based service agencies. In fact, turnover is often cited as *the* major
barrier to delivering quality services and programs. Perhaps because of this inferred effect,
there has been a growing interest in identifying the causes of turnover. Most managers believe that high staff turnover is largely a function of the disparity between the wages and
benefits of direct service staff in public institutions versus wages and benefits of direct service staff working for service providers in the community (Braddock & Mitchell, 1992;
Lakin, 1988). The lower the wages, the higher the turnover (Braddock & Mitchell, 1992).

From this perspective, it is not hard to understand the call for higher wages for direct
service staff working in community-based agencies (Komar, 1992; Lakin, 1988). Nevertheless, it is unlikely that the disparity can be reduced soon. Significant improvement in the
wages of community staff did not occur during the economic boom of the 1980s, and it is
unlikely to occur in an austere economy when virtually every state is wrestling with its own
budget crisis.

What contribution can the PSR make toward solving the staff turnover problem? Although formal studies have not been carried out to answer this question, our experience is
that the contribution may be limited, but important. We have found that the PSR may not
significantly affect staff turnover; however, it is a system that can produce quality service,
even given the high turnover rate that, for the foreseeable future, is likely to remain characteristic of the field. Thus, the task of this management system is not to improve staff turn-

over rates but—given the realities of those rates—to provide a system whereby quality can be achieved despite them.

This is not an argument against advocating vigorously for increasing staff wages and benefits. The contributions and dedication of staff members to the field and to the individuals they serve demand nothing less than our best and continuing efforts to increase the wages and benefits of direct service staff. The human services field, however, is not the only service "industry" that must struggle to achieve quality within a workforce that, at its extremes, might be termed transitory. For example, such fast-food corporations and restaurant chains as McDonald's and Pizza Hut do not waste time and energy trying to solve their turnover rates, which seem even higher than our own. Instead, they take the high turnover rate as a given in their industry. Thus, they focus their energy and attention on training and quality assurance strategies to ensure a uniform level of quality in their corporate organizations, which span the nation and, increasingly, the globe.

To argue that producing a hamburger or a pizza to certain standards cannot be compared to providing community-based services sufficient to overcome the barriers to a good quality of life that many of our clients must confront on a day-to-day basis would miss the point. Providing high quality human services is assumed as a greater challenge. The point is, actually, that we cannot simply wait for a resolution of our turnover problems. We must go forward to assure quality services and programs in our agencies. It matters little if solutions to staff turnover eventually come from future improvement in wages and benefits, or from another strategy, or even if they remain elusive. What does matter is that our consumers cannot wait. We cannot continue to use high staff turnover as an excuse for poor quality. Quality must be today's agenda, and that agenda must be addressed within today's reality of high staff turnover.

· Introduction ·
DEVELOPMENT OF THE PSR

The Periodic Service Review (PSR) owes its language, structure, and inspiration to two approaches to management that might seem contradictory. The first is from the field of organizational behavior management (OBM); the second is from the work of Deming (1986) and the resulting movement toward Total Quality Management (TQM) in U.S. business and industry.

ORGANIZATIONAL BEHAVIOR MANAGEMENT (OBM)

Organizational behavior management is the explicit application of the operant principles and procedures of applied behavior analysis (Skinner, 1938, 1953) to problems in work settings (Crowell & Anderson, 1983; Luthans & Thompson, 1987; Mawhinney, 1992). These basic principles and procedures address, among other things, observable behavior, with its antecedents and consequences. Accordingly, OBM includes a clear definition of the work performances expected from staff (behavior), the training and other (antecedent) conditions under which these performances are to occur, methods for monitoring (observing) work performance, and provision of systematic feedback (consequences) to improve and maintain work performance. The A (antecedent)–B (behavior)–C (consequence) paradigm is central to OBM (Brethower, 1982).

It was natural that we would turn to the literature of organizational behavior management when we sought information to improve our management functions, especially since our services are rooted firmly within the framework of applied behavior analysis. What we found in our review of the *Journal of Organizational Behavior Management* was an impressive array of data showing the application of these principles of learning to a range of working environments.

For example, empirically proven principles of learning have been used in manufacturing plants (e.g., Frost, Hopkins, & Conard, 1982; Kempen & Hall, 1977; Wikoff, Anderson, & Crowell, 1983), retail settings (e.g., Luthans, Paul, & Taylor, 1986), office settings (e.g., Frederiksen, Riley, & Myers, 1985; Mankin, Bikson, & Gutek, 1985), hotels and motels (e.g., Anderson, Crowell, Sponsel, Clarke, & Brence, 1983), real estate and other sales offices (e.g., Anderson, Crowell, Sucec, Gilligan, & Wikoff, 1983; Miller, 1977), and almost every other setting where human performance is a factor. Similarly, these principles have been applied in a wide array of settings that provide human services (e.g., Frederiksen, Richter, Johnson, & Solomon, 1982; Frederiksen & Riley, 1983; Quilitch, 1978). Indeed, it should not be surprising that some of the most impressive contributions in the application of organizational behavior management to human services have come from professionals working in settings where the procedures of applied behavior analysis are also used in direct provision of clinical and educational services (Christian & Hannah, 1983;

Parsons, Schepis, Reid, McCarn, & Green, 1987; Reid, Parsons, & Green, 1989a; Reid & Whitman, 1983). It makes sense to extend procedures that have helped to meet the needs of our clients when we launch a quest to meet staff and organizational needs.

TOTAL QUALITY MANAGEMENT (TQM)

Although OBM has made an undeniable contribution to our understanding of the requirements for effective management, it has begun to acknowledge (Stowe, 1989) another approach to management that seems to have come from a different direction, and that has inspired a virtual revolution in the field of American business management. This revolutionary approach is based on the work of W. Edwards Deming (1986), who is credited with the rise to leadership of Japan's post–World War II economy. The attention given to the relationship of OBM to Deming's work (Mawhinney, 1987, 1992), as well as discussion in the literature of the opportunities that the TQM movement offers OBM (e.g., Redmon, 1992; Stowe, 1989), testifies to the unparalleled influence of TQM in the management field.

TQM emphasizes consumer satisfaction. High quality is defined as providing what the consumer of the product or service wants, at the best possible price. The TQM approach to management is to foster a culture within the management and staff of an enterprise that is totally focused and works together as a team to identify consumer desires and to satisfy those desires in the best and most cost-effective way possible. Many believe that U.S. business and industry will not be able to compete effectively in the global market without this approach. The basic principles of TQM have been summarized in 14 points (Deming, 1986, pp. 23–24). These points, shown in Table I.1, address the imperatives for unrelenting and ongoing efforts toward improvement of products and services, for management to assume leadership responsibility for change, for cost reduction through continual improvement of the systems of production and services, for staff training and education and self-improvement programs; and for teamwork.

In the same way that OBM has been applied in the field of human services (e.g., Christian & Hannah, 1983; Parsons et al., 1987; Reid et al., 1989a; Reid & Whitman, 1983), TQM and Deming's 14 points (1986) have been applied also (e.g., Albin, 1992; D.R. Jones,

Table I.1.   Deming's 14 Points for Total Quality Management

1.	Create and publish to all employees a statement of the aims and purposes of the company or other organization. The management must demonstrate constantly their commitment to this statement.
2.	Learn the new philosophy, top management and everybody.
3.	Understand the purpose of inspection, for improvement of processes and reduction of costs.
4.	End the practice of awarding business on the basis of price tag alone.
5.	Improve constantly and forever the system of production and service.
6.	Institute training.
7.	Teach and institute leadership.
8.	Drive out fear. Create trust. Create a climate for innovation.
9.	Optimize toward the aims and purposes of the company the efforts of teams, groups, staff areas.
10.	Eliminate exhortations for the work force.
11a.	Eliminate numerical quotas for production. Instead, learn and institute methods for improvement.
11b.	Eliminate M.B.O. Instead, learn the capabilities of processes, and how to improve them.
12.	Remove barriers that rob people of pride of workmanship.
13.	Encourage education and self-improvement for everyone.
14.	Take action to accomplish the transformation.

Reprinted from *Out of the Crisis* by W. Edwards Deming by permission of MIT and W. Edwards Deming, as revised. Published by MIT, Center for Advanced Engineering Study, Cambridge, MA 02139. Copyright 1986 by W. Edwards Deming.

1991). For example, Albin's work is particularly noteworthy in its attempt to apply Deming's recommendations to *Quality Improvement in Employment and Other Human Services* (1992). Albin's work reflects the *explicit* application of TQM to human services, but the PSR represents the *implicit* application of these principles in the development of a "concrete tool" that can be applied generally to improve the quality of services and programs across a variety of human service and educational settings. Because the system described in this book is presented in terms of the operationalized procedures of OBM, and because the relationship of this system to the principles of TQM may not be immediately apparent— and may indeed seem to conflict with TQM—congruence of the two approaches is analyzed in the final chapter.

To summarize, this book integrates the principles and procedures of both OBM and TQM. Our aim is to operationalize the findings and recommendations of both fields into a concrete and usable management system, capable of providing an agency with an ongoing process for assuring staff consistency and a high level of quality for its services and programs. The system was developed to be generic and applicable in any human service or educational setting.

ORGANIZATION OF THIS BOOK

The book is divided into seven chapters. Chapter 1 traces the background of our system, as we applied it to the challenges faced by the Institute for Applied Behavior Analysis. These include challenges we confronted as consultants to other agencies, where we did not have direct authority, as well as challenges we faced when providing our own direct services. The next four chapters discuss, in turn, each of the four components of the management system. In Chapter 2, we discuss the development of *performance standards* against which service quality can be measured. These performance standards address both processes and outcomes. In Chapter 3, we discuss *performance monitoring,* a critical feature of an effective management system. We devote much of this chapter to guidelines that ensure staff acceptance of the monitoring system. Discussing these guidelines is important because there is often resistance to the mere mention of monitoring. In Chapter 4, we discuss *performance feedback* based on the results of monitoring, to ensure ongoing improvement in and maintenance of service quality. Finally, in Chapter 5, we discuss the role and the limitations of *staff training.*

Chapter 6 is devoted to discussion of concrete steps you can follow to start developing and implementing the management system for your own agency. Rather than having to confront what could be a daunting and time-consuming task of translating and applying abstract principles to real-life circumstances, you will be relieved to see that the system is a very concrete one that can readily be adapted to your specific situation and the services your agency provides. We conclude, in Chapter 7, with a discussion of the management system as it relates to Deming's 14 points (1986) and the Total Quality Management movement, which is becoming widespread in U.S. business and industry and in the public and human service sectors, where we are privileged to serve.

THE
PERIODIC
SERVICE
REVIEW

· 1 ·

BACKGROUND

The Institute for Applied Behavior Analysis (IABA) was founded in 1981. One of the first services we provided was behavioral consultation to families, group homes, schools, and other service settings. As is the experience of many outside consultants without direct line authority within the client agency or setting, we began to experience problems. These included the sorts of things that other agencies report as problematic: poor data collection, lack of program implementation, nonfunctional and age-inappropriate activities, poor staff interaction with the people to whom they were providing services, and so forth. The overall problem was that, although the recommendations and services were set forth on paper, in the form of individual support plans and service designs, generally they remained there— inert and unimplemented.

Since that time, we have discovered through speaking to groups about management systems that our problems were typical. The same problems are experienced by professional consultants in Australia, Canada, Great Britain, Ireland, and across the United States. We—as they did—found that our recommendations often were met with expressions of acceptance, but at each weekly progress review, a different explanation was offered as to why these recommendations could not be implemented.

We had a snow storm and couldn't get out to do our community training.

Half of our staff were out with the flu, and the rest had to work double shifts. Data collection was impossible.

The office didn't send the petty cash check this week.

Our vehicle was in the shop for repairs all week.

We had to deal with behavioral crises all week. We couldn't carry out the scheduled instructional programs.

And so on, and so on, and so on.

Such were the explanations staff members gave to excuse the lack of quality in the services they were providing. As caring and sensitive professionals, we could not help but be understanding and sympathetic. However, this gridlock left us and our consulting staff extremely frustrated because week after week our recommendations were not initiated and needed services were not being provided. Because of these frustrations, an IABA task force was organized to address these problems. The task force included the authors and other consulting and management staff members of IABA.

MANAGEMENT PRACTICE

As the task force reviewed the literature, we began to realize that frustrations experienced by consultants in the field of human services reflect more fundamental and ubiquitous

1

problems than we had thought. As we describe in the Preface, this review revealed that the underlying problem was *poor management practice* (Christian & Reitz, 1986; Reid & Whitman, 1983).

It seems that agencies providing human services frequently are plagued with inconsistency and poor follow-through. These problems go beyond the mere failure to implement consultants' recommendations. They span the entire range of human services. Lack of follow-through results in service settings that fail to deliver meaningful services—rather they often offer nonfunctional and age-inappropriate solutions. Such poor services result in the persistence of interactional styles that are disrespectful of and/or frequently undignifying for the service recipients. Lack of follow-through and consistency frequently means that service recipients spend very little time in community/socially integrated settings; that helpful data are not kept at all or are collected inconsistently; that such agreed-upon services as behavior support plans and instructional sessions for critical skills are not carried out, or are not carried out as intended; that schedules are not followed; that reports are not completed; and so on. Yes, these are serious problems.

Why are human service managers unable to solve these problems? A quote from Peter Drucker (1974), a recognized leader in the field of business management, is revealing:

> . . . in the last analysis, management is practice. Its essence is not knowing but doing. Its test is not logic, but results. Its only authority is performance. (p. xiii)

In the human services field, however, we are promoted to our supervisory, managerial, and administrative positions not so much because of our abilities to produce results in this managerial sense, but because of what we *know* and because we have excelled in our different disciplines; that is, as psychologists, social workers, special education teachers, therapists, or direct service staff members. We have been neither trained nor prepared for the essential role of management; that is, the mobilization of staff resources toward achievement of selected goals and objectives. In fact, as human service professionals, we may avoid, and even feel uncomfortable with, the very idea of controlling other people, which is implicit in the managerial role. As managers, we want to be understanding, supportive, sympathetic, kind, and reflective. We seem to hope that if we create a nurturing work environment, our staff members will rise to the challenge and perform with energy and excellence. Regardless of our efforts, and even when we succeed in creating such nurturing work environments, the reality is that we remain unable to ensure high-quality and consistent service provision.

It is interesting to note that this lack of managerial competence is not unique to the human services field. In a study by Hogan, Curphy, and Hogan (in press), incompetence in U.S. business management was estimated at somewhere between 60% and 75%. They suggest that one reason for this level of incompetence is that, even in the business sector, people typically are thrust into management positions without formal training. This forces them to fall back on their own personal experiences and characteristics and the experiences and characteristics of the culture around them. Hogan et al. predict that improved managerial competence would rapidly produce such very desirable effects as decreased job stress, lowered overhead (e.g., absenteeism), fewer employee grievances, and increased productivity.

There is also growing awareness that a primary cause of the increasing gap between the vigor of the U.S. and Japanese economies is the difference in management competence between the two systems and their differing emphasis on quality assurance. In the U.S. system, blame for poor performance typically is laid at the feet of the American worker. In contrast, the Japanese blame the management and quality assurance systems, not the worker. This is ironic, because the Japanese approach to management and quality assurance was heavily influenced by Deming (1986), an American management consultant. Only in the past decade have Deming's work and the Deming (Japanese) approach to management received serious attention in the United States.

Poor management practice has taken its toll in areas beyond U.S. businesses and human services systems. Lack of managerial competence has affected such diverse elements of U.S. society as our national defense and local police; it can be seen in our research and science centers as well. For example, it is now generally recognized that managerial incompetence in the military was a major factor in the failure of the United States to prevail in Vietnam; this fact exists regardless of questions of whether or not we should have had an active military role there at all. It was no small admission for the military to have recognized that this was a major problem and to have spent the following 20 years rebuilding its managerial competence. This restructuring resulted in a performance in the Gulf War that led to the recognition that the U.S. armed forces have never been better trained and better managed.

A breakdown in management systems and practice was also cited as a major contributing factor in the Rodney King beating by the Los Angeles city police, the videotape of which was shown repeatedly on national television, to such an extent, indeed, that we would be hard put to find someone who hadn't seen it at least once. Perhaps this videotape is the most dramatic example of the devastation that can occur when quality assurance procedures break down in systems that affect people. The role of managerial negligence is not a mere secondary issue in this case, which some say led to the ultimate resignation of the Chief of Police, Darrell Gates. For example, it was reported that for some time prior to the King incident, quality control, which consisted of random field monitoring by Los Angeles Police Department (LAPD) sergeants of the arrests made by officers under their supervision, was terminated to save costs. Beyond the question of the guilt of the officers involved in the beating lies the greater question: Would the incident have happened at all, had the quality assurance strategy of random field checks not been discontinued? Perhaps the lesson will not be lost on the LAPD and police departments across the nation, and perhaps more attention will be given to improving their managerial competence and quality assurance systems.

Final examples of the costly effects of poor management practice are the recent tragedies and embarrassments in the NASA program. The deterioration of management practice and quality assurance systems was cited as the cause of the Challenger tragedy, as well as the Hubble Telescope debacle. Brilliant research and science can only be transformed into effective technology through a rigorous systems engineering approach; that is, a rigorous management system that focuses relentlessly on quality assurance. If cars cannot be built, wars cannot be fought, citizens cannot be protected, and space probes cannot be launched without good management, then it certainly must be true that quality—defined by Crosby (1979) as *conformance to a specified standard or group of standards*—in human services cannot be achieved without good management. In fact, the case can be made that the field of human services requires the most careful application of systems engineering, because quality services and good outcomes depend on the consistent application of incomplete technologies to the most challenging problems that people can have.

It behooves us, as external consultants, to remember that our recommendations often are made to agencies that lack the internal management structure or skills to follow through on their own plans and objectives, much less to follow our advice. Therefore, effective consultation must also aim toward improving agency management, as well as agency services.

This book describes a management system that we have found to be effective in improving agency operations in a variety of human service and educational settings. It is a management system that increases an agency's ability to mobilize staff, to maximize consistency in program implementation and service provision, and to meet its goals and objectives. Furthermore, human service managers who had felt uncomfortable with even the idea of a control system, express comfort with the system we recommend for two important reasons. First, it is designed explicitly as a two-way control system. True, it puts the manager in control of staff. However, it is designed as a bottom-up system that also gives staff members a large measure of influence over management. Second, the strategies for changing staff performance designed into the system are built strictly on the principles of positive reinforcement. They do not rely on the coercive strategies that characterize the stereotypic "take charge" manager.

In summary, human services agencies continue to have problems because their managers lack management training. However, these problems go beyond a simple lack of formal management training. They are complicated further by the reality that direct service staff members often lack the skills to carry out the difficult tasks they are assigned. This seems to present an interesting, perhaps even dangerous, paradox:

Those who
DON'T KNOW HOW TO MANAGE
are managing those
WHO DON'T KNOW WHAT TO DO

MANAGEMENT RESEARCH

The need for human services agencies to develop more effective management practices is more than clear; it is absolutely critical. What do we mean by "more effective management practices"? What does it involve? Where do you begin? The first step might be to review the literature. Reid, Parsons, and Green (1989b) did just that. Their literature review identified a number of essential elements for effective staff management in human service agencies. These include defining performance responsibilities and expectations, monitoring performance, teaching skills to staff, and changing performance.

Reid et al. (1989b) also point to some notable gaps in the presently available research. Specifically, they note that research to date is limited in scope, focusing on a small number of staff performance areas and accounting for a relatively small amount of staff time. For example, in Dyer, Schwartz, and Luce (1984), the objective was to increase the appropriateness of the activities provided to the residents of a small group home. Although the study reported a successful outcome, providing the opportunity for appropriate activities is only a small, albeit important, part of a staff person's job responsibilities. Numerous examples in the literature show that individual staff members' performances can be increased for a limited period of time during the day or week. But few or no examples describe an efficient strategy for increasing a broad range of staff performances across the entire working day and across shifts. Direct application of the results of all these diverse studies would be difficult, at the least. This "molecular," or piece-by-piece, approach would be an inefficient and impractical way of increasing staff performance and consistency.

A second crucial gap in the research literature is the general lack of maintenance studies (Reid et al., 1989b). There are demonstrations of management actions that can produce positive changes in staff performance, but there is little evidence that these changes are maintained. Obviously, we are not interested only in short-run change, such as that, for instance, to prepare us for a visit by a team of external monitors, or to remove identified deficiencies in order to retain certification or funding. Rather, we are interested in a management system that could be relied upon to produce permanent change, not only to achieve high-quality services for our agencies, but to maintain that high-quality service.

THE PERIODIC SERVICE REVIEW

The challenge, therefore, is to develop a management system that can improve a broad range of staff and agency performances—across the entire day, across shifts, and across time. Our answer to these challenges is the Periodic Service Review (PSR).[1] The PSR is both an instrument and a system. As an instrument, it is used to *assess* the quality of staff and their consistency in performing their responsibilities. It is also used to evaluate the implementation of a consultant's recommendations about providing individual services. The instrument (the PSR) can be customized to accommodate the specific standards of quality that apply to a service or program, including residential, educational, and adult day-care services. In addition, it can be adapted for use in community mental health settings, in-home support services, homeless shelters, substance abuse programs, hospital settings, and other settings in which human and health services are provided.

In addition to being used as an instrument to *assess* staff performance and the quality and consistency of the services provided, the PSR is also used as a total quality assurance system to *improve* staff performance and the quality of services. It not only incorporates research findings by including performance standards in the form of clearly specified and defined staff responsibilities, the monitoring of performance against these standards, supervisory and management feedback to improve and maintain quality, and staff training; it also efficiently addresses the challenge of staff consistency at the molar (overall) service unit level. It can be used to assess and increase a broad range of staff responsibilities and services across the entire day and across different shifts and locations. Furthermore, it has proved to be an effective way to maintain change and improvement. In the case of our own services, as described below, this improvement has endured and continued to increase for over 7 years.

Group Home Application

In order to understand the initial development of the PSR, it is important to understand the nature of the consulting services provided by IABA. In California, children and adults with developmental disabilities and challenging behaviors are frequently served in specialized residential programs run by private agencies or individual proprietors; for example, community-based group homes, each with six or fewer residents. Regulations require that these specialized service settings have access to behavioral consultants whose responsibility it is to perform behavior assessments, to design behavior support plans, to train staff to implement those plans, and to provide ongoing evaluations and recommendations. The consultants are hired by the agency or proprietor, but they have no direct line authority over direct service staff. Within this context, the PSR was developed in order to help our behavioral consultants deal with the week-to-week frustrations of seeing their recommendations remain unimplemented and services not provided as intended and agreed upon. The PSR was developed to provide a "Total Quality Assurance" system that integrates the research findings in this area, and gives our consultants an effective tool for improving the degree of implementation they could count on for their recommendations.

Figure 1.1 shows the results of one of our early applications of the PSR. The graph shows a group home's monthly percentage score of consistency in implementing the various elements of its service design, including our consultant's recommendations. The score is calculated by comparing the home's performance against a set of operationalized criteria, and the percentages of standards met are plotted on the PSR graph. As Figure 1.1 shows, this home's initial performance was at the 60% level—in other words, 60% of the standards were being met. In our experience, this is high for an initial evaluation. More typically, the

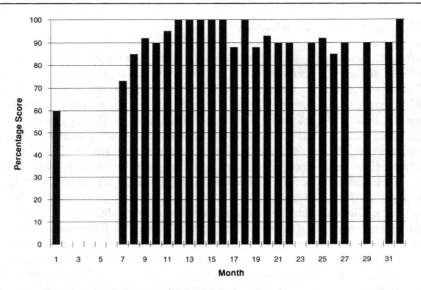

Figure 1.1.   Results of PSR system in a group home setting.

initial score is below 50%, even in an agency that considers itself to be doing well. Six months after the initial evaluation, the PSR management system was introduced, including clearly defined performance standards, monitoring, feedback, and staff training. Figure 1.1 shows steady improvement up to the 90% level or better and maintenance at that level for more than 2 years.

These performance scores reflect this group home's ability to remain consistent in the services they provided and to implement the consultant's recommendations, as measured against such standards as those listed on the score sheet, shown in Figure 1.2. Whether or not credit is earned during a given evaluation depends upon whether or not the criteria have been met. Each standard has operationally defined criteria, as illustrated by the sample standards abstracted in Figure 1.3. The PSR presently used for *behavior* management group homes is provided in Appendix A. The first part of Appendix A is the score sheet on which the group home's performance is scored against each of the individual standards. It is organized around three major headings. The first of these is *general program activities*, which includes performance standards having to do with the daily schedule of activities in the group home and with the instructional programs provided to develop further the skills of the individuals being served. The second heading addresses the *individual behavior support plans*, including the requirements for a behavior assessment, individualized service plan, accurate data collection, and so forth. The third category of performance standards addresses *staff development*. The second part of Appendix A spells out the operational definition for each standard. Clear operational definitions keep the process of monitoring objective and define how each standard should be evaluated.

It should be remembered that these standards reflect the philosophy, design, resources, and individuals served in these settings. It should also be remembered that no more than six people resided in each of the community-based homes, and there was a one-to-two, staff-to-resident ratio during all service delivery hours. The emphasis was on community-based, functional, chronological age–appropriate skill development, and use of strictly nonaversive behavioral support plans (LaVigna & Donnellan, 1986; LaVigna, Willis, & Donnellan, 1989).

Figure 1.4 illustrates the relationship between PSR scores and the behavioral incidents of an individual in a group home that adopted the PSR. As the graph shows, consistent

PERIODIC SERVICE REVIEW FOR
BEHAVIOR SERVICES GROUP HOMES

Score Sheet

Person's Name: _____   Date of Review: _____

Reviewer's Name: _____   Supervisor: _____

		Score	Possible	**Comments**
I.	**General Program Activities**			
A.	Daily Schedule of Activities			
	1. Individual schedule posted			
	2. Schedule spot check			
	3. Staff schedule posted			
	4. Staff schedule spot check			
B.	Skills Programs			
	1. Instructional protocols			
	2. Age-appropriate and functional			
	3. Datasheets			
	4. Summary graphs (optional)			
	5. Activity spot checks			
	6. Interobserver reliability			
	a. Program			
	b. Independent			
	7. Procedural reliability			
	a. Program			
	b. Independent			
II.	**Individual Behavior Support Plans**			
A.	Behavior Assessment			
B.	Individualized Service Plan			
C.	Quarterly Report			

(continued)

Figure 1.2.   A PSR score sheet.

Figure 1.2. (*continued*)

	Score	Possible	Comments

D. Behavior Protocols and Checklists

E. Program Implementation Knowledge

F. Raw Data

G. Reinforcement Charts

   1. Current

   2. Reliable

H. Program Implementation

I. Competing Contingencies

J. Data Summary Procedures

   1. Daily data summary

      a. Current

      b. Accurate

   2. Weekly data summary

      a. Current

      b. Accurate

   3. Monthly data summary

      a. Current

      b. Accurate

   4. Behavior graphs

      a. Current

      b. Accurate

K. Reliability Checks

   1. Interobserver

      a. Program

      b. Independent

   2. Procedural

      a. Program

      b. Spot check

(*continued*)

Figure 1.2. *(continued)*

	Score	Possible	Comments
L. Emergency Procedures			
1. Available			
2. Read by all			
3. Accurate			
4. Noted in raw data			

III. Staff Development

  A. Behavior Inservice Training

    1. 12-month record

    2. Average once a month

    3. Staff participants

    4. Competency tests

    5. Previous 4 weeks

  B. Scheduled Staff Meetings

IV. Other Areas

  A. Communication Logs

  B. Outcome Evaluation

	Total Earned	Total Possible	Percentage Score
SUMMARY SCORE			

Comments/Recommendations/Objectives:

performance at the 85%–90% level was associated with dramatic decreases in aggression, tantrums, and other behavior problems. However, these data should not be surprising. It should be obvious that more consistent application will produce better individual outcomes; these data merely confirm this (Greene, Willis, Levy, & Bailey, 1978). Indeed, it has been our experience that consistent quality assurance indicators (PSR scores) between 85% and 90%, and good individual outcomes, such as those in Figure 1.4, can be achieved with our consultant on site only one half day per week. We should also point out, once again, that these consultants are *external* to the group homes to which they are assigned, and as such, they have no direct authority over staff members.

Classroom Application

As a result of our early successful experience with the PSR, we presently install such management systems for all agencies to which we provide consultation. This enables both management and consultants to know how consistently an agency carries out its planned

---

B. Skills Programs

   1. Instructional protocols. Based on a review of an individual's records and *four* randomly selected skill programs, a + is given for each skills instructional protocol completed by the program supervisor, which is up-to-date and available to staff within 5 minutes of a request.

   2. Age-appropriate and functional. Based on a review of an individual's records and the *four* randomly selected skills programs selected in B.1., a + is given for each targeted skill that meets the criteria for "meaningful" activities engaged in by others of the same chronological age.

   3. Datasheets. Based on a review of an individual's daily/weekly/monthly data summaries, and the *four* randomly selected skills programs selected in B.1., a + is given for each skill for which a datasheet is available, and where the data were updated by the assigned staff within one training session (as indicated on individual's schedule).

   4. Summary graphs (optional). Based on a review of an individual's daily/weekly/monthly graphs, and the *four* randomly selected skills programs selected in B.1., a + is given for each skill for which a graph is available, and where the graph was updated by the program supervisor by the end of the shift on the previous Friday.

   5. Activity spot checks. Based on direct observation by the program consultant of two randomly selected individuals observed consecutively for periods of 5 minutes, a + is given for each person if the activities throughout the entire observation period meet the criteria for chronological age–appropriate and functional activities.

   6. Interobserver Reliability

     a. Program. Based on a review of observational reliability records, a + is given if the program supervisor has conducted at least one observational reliability check per individual during the quarter, and the results of the check have been entered as a percentage on the proper form, and this percentage is over 85%. The scores would be prorated for the months of the quarter. For the first month of the quarter, two checks would be expected; for the second month, four; and for the third month, six.

     b. Independent. Based on direct observation of one randomly selected skill program per month, of a randomly selected individual whose program is being run at the time that the PSR is conducted, a + is given if observational reliability exceeds 85%.

   7. Procedural Reliability

     a. Program. Based on a review of procedural reliability records, a + is given if the program supervisor has conducted at least one procedural reliability check per person during the quarter. The scores would be prorated for the months of the quarter. For the first month of the quarter, two checks would be expected; for the second month, four; and for the third month, six.

     b. Independent. Based on direct observation of one randomly selected skill training program per month, of a randomly selected individual whose program is being run at the time that the PSR is conducted, a + is given if the training procedures used match those specified by the skills training program (i.e., exceed 85%).

Figure 1.3.   Sample performance standards for a group home setting.

design and the consultant's recommendations, and it effectively establishes and maintains the level of staff consistency and quality assurance required to meet the program's outcome objectives. In addition to group homes, we have also installed PSR systems in classroom settings.

In one classroom situation, we were hired by a school district to help them upgrade the quality of services in one of their classrooms that had recently become the subject of a parent's complaint concerning the quality of educational services being provided. Although the complaint had already been settled, the district wanted to go beyond the settlement as

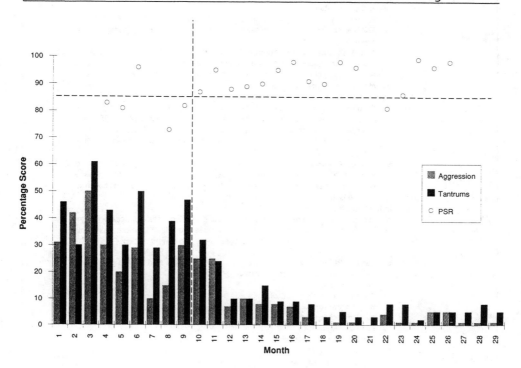

Figure 1.4.   The relationship between PSR scores and an individual's behavior problems in a group home setting.

part of an aggressive effort to strengthen the quality of classroom educational services to the greatest extent possible. In discussions with the district administration and classroom personnel, it was agreed that we would begin by working together to define objectively what the teacher and her staff wanted to accomplish; that is, to define the standards of educational service to which they aspired. Examples of Periodic Service Reviews from other settings and situations were provided to the staff members to give them a set of starting points and some ideas about how to phrase their performance standards; however, they were encouraged to brainstorm together to come up with a set of standards that best fit their particular situation. The resulting PSR was developed, with our guidance as outside consultants, by the classroom team. This team consisted of the resource teacher, who acted as the team leader; the classroom teacher, who was in her first year of teaching; and some classroom aides, who also provided input as to those standards they felt were important.

Figure 1.5 shows some of the classroom standards developed for this situation. The score sheet for this classroom PSR and a full set of operational definitions for each of the standards are provided in Appendix B. In this case, the performance standards are organized into nine separate headings.

1.   General concepts
2.   Administrative
3.   Individual skill programs
4.   Individual behavior programs
5.   Instruction
6.   Staff development
7.   Family involvement
8.   Coordination of program
9.   PSR document

I. **General Concepts**
   A. **Philosophy.** The philosophy of the program is stated in the students' notebooks. The basis of the program is preparation for living, working, and enjoying life in an integrated environment.
   B. **Age-Appropriate and Functional Curriculum.** Spot checks are done monthly to ensure that students are engaging in meaningful activities and that these are engaged in by others of the same age. Checks are also done to see if at least 20% of the curriculum is community based.

II. **Administrative**
   A. **Student Notebooks.** Each student has an up-to-date notebook that includes pertinent forms, schedules, current individualized education program (IEP) and individualized treatment program (ITP), data forms, graphs, lesson plans, progress reports, behavior programs, emergency information, home/school communication, and a table of contents.
   B. **Medical Records.** Available and up-to-date in the school file located in the guidance office. The information must include the name of the medication, dosage, when and where it is to be taken, and the possible side effects. Medication for seizure is also listed in the student's working notebook.

III. **Individual Skill Programs**
   A. **Working Notebooks.** Each student has a working notebook located in the classroom and used by staff daily. It includes the following information: daily schedule, current IEP, lesson plans, datasheets and current behavior plan.

   . . .

   E. **Lesson Plans.** Each objective has an updated lesson plan located in the working notebook. The plan may include:
      1. **Objective**
      2. **Discriminative stimuli**
      3. **Prompt (optional)**
      4. **Correct response**
      5. **Consequence**
         a. **Correct response**
         b. **Incorrect response**
      6. **Intertrial interval**
      7. **Data collection**
      8. **Program change criteria**
         a. **Pass**
         b. **Fail**
      9. **Special criteria (if necessary)**

   . . .

IV. **Individual Behavior Programs**
   A. **Assessment Reports/Intervention Plans.** For any existing program, there is a written assessment report and intervention plan following district protocols. Copies are entered in the student's notebook within 30 days of the start of the school year, the end of the quarter, or upon the student's enrollment. No aversives are to be written into the plan.
   B. **Behavior Protocol and Checklists.** For each written intervention plan, there is a protocol and checklist in the working notebook.
   . . .

V. **Instruction**
   . . .
   D. **Community Instruction.** There are a minimum of five community-based objectives for each student.
   E. **Communication.** The classroom is communication-based, and communication skills are incorporated within each student's lesson plans. The lessons are taught in real-life situations, rather than in isolated settings.

VI. **Staff Development**
   A. **Workshops.** Staff attend workshops and professional meetings pertinent to job duties within school system and out of district, a minimum of two per year.
   . . .
   G. **Mainstream Students.** By the spring, a presentation about people with disabilities is given to the mainstream students. This is documented by presentation notes.

VII. **Family Involvement**
   A. **Parent Participation.** Families attend and are active participants during the development of the IEP. Questionnaires and rating scales are used to gather input from parents.
   B. **Communication.** At least weekly communication between staff and families via phone, notes, and so forth, as documented in the working notebooks.

VIII. **Coordination of Program**
   A. **Roles.** There is a written definition of each team member's role. Copies are located in the central office and the classroom.
   B. **Responsibilities.** Each role has a written list of responsibilities.

Figure 1.5. Sample performance standards from the operational definitions for the PSR in one classroom setting.

Again, it is important to remember that these standards reflect the specifics of this classroom setting. Different classrooms, with students who have different educational needs; classrooms with different levels of resources; and many other variables, would undoubtedly lead to different performance standards in their particular PSR.

Figure 1.6 shows the percentage of standards met (from a total of 44) in each month over the academic year. This figure shows remarkable improvement in the level of performance in the classroom, from 40% to 85%. This is especially remarkable given that this was the teacher's first year of teaching. In addition, the teacher reported that, rather than becoming overwhelmed by the comprehensiveness of what she wanted to accomplish, the PSR system gave her a clear grasp of where she was and where she needed to go.

Supported Employment Application

Our role as consultants to other agencies set the stage for the initial development of the PSR. Since that time, our real payoff has been the application of this system to help us manage our own services. For example, our first opportunity to apply the PSR system internally was in the context of our supported employment service. In 1985, we began the Systematic Training for Employment Program (STEP). From the beginning, we anticipated that this new service would be a management challenge. One reason for this was our plan to make it a facility-free service; that is, there would be no building where staff could gather each day to receive direction from management. The intent and design of STEP was that our direct service staff (i.e., Program Specialists) would be either providing job coaching to individuals at their job sites, supporting individuals in their job searches, or providing instruction in related community skills in a variety of other community settings. We were especially concerned about the difficulty of achieving and maintaining high-quality service where entry-level staff would be on their own with the individuals being served in widely dispersed community locations. In anticipation of this management challenge, we invested considerable resources to develop a comprehensive, competency-based, criterion-referenced staff training program, which we continue to use to this day. It was our belief that this competency-based training program, which is described in more detail in Chapter 5, would result in well-trained staff members with the ability to carry out the programs and services

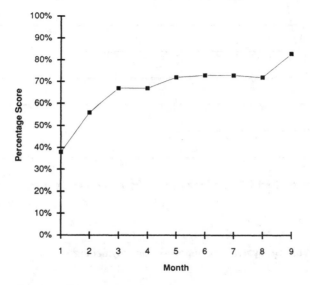

Figure 1.6.   Results of PSR system in a classroom setting.

as designed and agreed upon. More importantly, we expected that they would *do* what had been agreed upon *consistently*.

STEP had been in operation for 6 months when it occurred to us that we should develop a PSR instrument to evaluate and quantify the quality and consistency of our supported employment program. After all, we required that the agencies we consulted with hold themselves accountable using the objective measures generated by the PSR. Wasn't it incumbent upon us to hold ourselves accountable to the same level of standards? We fully expected that, although we might find that some areas needed attention, overall we would be doing fine. We proceeded to develop a set of standards for STEP. The subsequent score sheet and the full operational definitions for these standards are provided in Appendix C. Again, you will notice a related, but different, set of categories for organizing the performance standards. In this case, there are four categories addressing general program activities, individualized service plans, administrative requirements, and staff development for our provision of supported employment services. Some of these standards are similar to those we had developed for the group homes (Appendix A) but others are unique to supported employment and the way we believe such services should be provided.

Figure 1.7 shows the PSR scores for STEP over a 7-year period. When we first evaluated ourselves using this instrument, we discovered that, as an agency, we were operating at a 43% level of consistency. This was a far cry from the 85%–90% standard we expected of ourselves. Only through full application of the PSR management system were we able to increase our scores to 80%, 85%, and 90%. The levels of consistency maintained by STEP are particularly encouraging and support the efficacy of the PSR as a quality assurance management tool. This is particularly true when we consider that STEP is a facility-free service agency that presently provides supported employment services to over 170 adults across a three-county area of southern California.

PSR scores are only one way to measure quality of services. Ultimately, quality must be measured by the outcomes achieved for the individuals being served. The most obvious

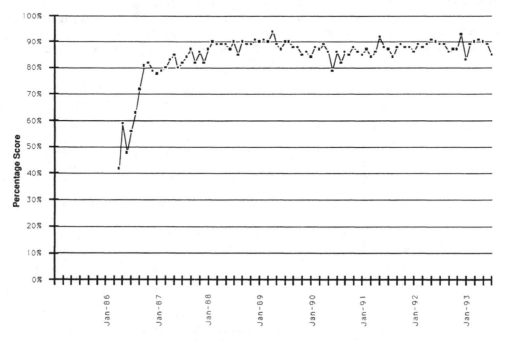

Figure 1.7.   Results of PSR system in a supported employment program.

outcome sought by a supported employment agency is to obtain direct pay positions for its clients—positions valued by society in which the individuals work side-by-side with those who do not have a disability. Another outcome of a supported employment service is to increase the individuals' compensation for work, so that they can have the dignity that comes with contributing to their own support. We believe that, largely because of our PSR system, the individuals we support have successfully earned more than $2 million and that STEP has been acknowledged as one of seven outstanding supported employment service providers in the nation (Dalton, 1992).

SUMMARY

The PSR was developed as an adaptation to enhance the managerial abilities of those of us who operate human service and educational agencies. Such an adaptation is needed because most human service managers have not received significant formal training in management practices. Poor management practices are the primary reason for lack of quality in the provision of human services. The PSR is both an instrument, to help management assess the level of quality in the services they provide, and a system, to help improve that quality.

As an *instrument*, the PSR is easy to understand. It provides a score sheet on which the performance of an interdisciplinary team (e.g., staff, supervisor, and consultant) is scored and given points, depending upon whether or not objectively defined criteria have been met for each of the standards adopted. Scoring may be done in several ways. Some items are scored on a 1-or-0 basis (i.e., an all-or-none basis). For example, the following standard might be scored on a 1-or-0 basis: "For each individual served, there is a current daily schedule in a day planner that lists the day's events by time of day, including when instructional sessions are scheduled to occur." For other items, however, partial credit may be given; for example, the following standard states that "summary graphs for data-based instructional programs must be kept current within one session." An individual's service plan may prescribe that he or she receive data-based instruction for eight different skills, such as setting the table, shopping from a list, using a picture book to ask for a drink, and so forth. In this case, for any given PSR evaluation, there should be eight graphs available that are current and meet the criteria. If only six graphs fulfill the criteria, partial credit would be given; that is, six achieved from a possible eight.

Other items on a PSR do not require review of an individual service plan, because they are not specific to any individual. An example of this is the following standard referring to staff meetings: "Staff attend mandatory monthly staff meetings and quarterly inservice sessions, as evidenced by meeting minutes, printed agenda, and attendance records." In completing the score sheet, performance is evaluated standard-by-standard. The PSR percentage score is calculated by dividing the total score achieved by the total score possible and multiplying the resulting number by 100.

As a *system*, the PSR is more complex. The system is made up of four carefully integrated elements.

1. *Performance standards.* Performance standards are an operationally described delineation of desired processes and outcomes, the sum total of which define the quality to which the agency aspires.
2. *Performance monitoring.* Performance monitoring refers to the methods whereby the agency verifies whether or not it is carrying out the process intended and is achieving its desired outcomes. The results of performance monitoring set the stage for supervisory and management feedback.

3. *Supervisory and management feedback.* Supervisory and management feedback, based on the results of performance monitoring, are provided to improve and maintain performance; that is, the quality of services provided.
4. *Staff training.* Finally, staff training is provided to ensure that staff can carry out the process designed to produce the desired outcomes of the agency competently.

Each element of the PSR is described in the following chapters.

Our experience is that most agencies are familiar with, and in all likelihood, are already carrying out one or more of these functions. It is also our experience that no single component can ensure the levels of quality we describe here. Rather, a total quality assurance system requires the integrated application of all the separate elements.

Research, by its nature, isolates variables and then manipulates them to evaluate their effects on outcomes, which themselves are often equally isolated. This scientific method can make it difficult for the practitioner to apply the research findings in the most useful manner. In this book, we describe the Periodic Service Review as a system that has integrated the findings of empirical research in the field of organizational behavior management. As such, it is a system that can be generalized to any human service or educational setting, and it can give human and educational services a tool for applying the best management practices available toward the accomplishment of their goals and objectives.

NOTE

1. One decade ago, when we began developing the Periodic Service Review at the Institute for Applied Behavior Analysis, we referred to it as the "Program Status Report." Those of you who have attended our management training seminars or who have read our earlier publications (e.g., LaVigna, Willis, Shaull, Abedi, & Sweitzer, in press) on this topic may be familiar with that designation. We, as do others, now appreciate more and more the importance of *individualizing* services for people, to better support them in their pursuit of the best quality of life possible, rather than developing generic and fixed programs based on *our* views of what different *groups* of people need and what *we* think is important for them, and then expecting people to fit into these programs. By changing the designation of the PSR from the *Program Status Report* to the *Periodic Service Review*, we intend to emphasize our focus on the quality of services that are *person centered*, rather than *program centered*.

· 2 ·

PERFORMANCE STANDARDS

In this chapter, we describe the first element of the four that make up our management system. This element involves developing and writing performance standards that apply to the agency's services and/or programs. We emphasize that both process and product standards should be developed for a Periodic Service Review (PSR). Process standards apply to those aspects of the service or program design intended to produce the desired outcomes; and product, or outcome, standards refer to the agency goals and objectives. In this chapter, we also establish some important principles to follow when developing PSR performance standards. These include the needs to emphasize the essential and critical process and product standards of the agency, to avoid a cumbersome system, and to set realistic, achievable standards for the agency. Our discussion of principles also addresses the need to define our performance standards operationally, including the need to specify the procedures that will be used to verify that the standards have been met. First, however, we define what we mean by performance standards and provide a rationale for their inclusion in our management system.

DEFINITION AND RATIONALE

Performance standards are defined as the specifications and the operationalized definitions of staff responsibilities. The rationale for developing operationalized performance standards is that they then provide the basis for performance monitoring, supervisory and managerial actions to improve and maintain performance, and staff training. In fact, the very act of establishing a goal can lead to improved performance and service quality (Locke & Latham, 1984; Locke, Shaw, Saari, & Latham, 1980; Mento, Steel, & Karren, 1987).

Process and Outcome Standards

There are two major kinds of performance standards—product or outcome standards and process standards. Product or outcome standards provide the basis for measuring an agency's success in meeting its goals and objectives. Process standards hold an agency accountable for doing the things it must do in order to reach its goals and objectives (Christian & Romanczyk, 1986). The standard presented below is an example of a *process standard*. It addresses procedural reliability or fidelity checks, whereby an observation is carried out to determine that an instructional program or other agreed-upon service is performed exactly as intended. This is done by comparing staff performance with a formally written protocol that specifies, in concrete terms, exactly what the staff person is to do. If staff performance is consistent with the checklist, it is said to have *procedural reliability* or *fidelity*.

Procedural Reliability. Fidelity checks, carried out by direct observation, once a month for each instructional program for each individual, show that at least 85% of the steps listed in the checklist are carried out by direct service staff when they provide instruction. The responsibility for performing the fidelity checks is the supervisor's. The results of the fidelity checks are to be documented in files maintained in the supervisor's office, by name of the person checked. To receive credit on the weekly PSR, individual files must show that at least 80% of the scheduled fidelity checks were carried out for the last week, and that all scores were at the 85% level or better.

The logic of this process standard is that individuals will be more likely to learn new skills (an outcome objective) if staff carry out instructional programs as designed. In contrast to the process standard above, we present the following example of a product or outcome standard.

Skill Acquisition. Quarterly progress reports show that individuals are meeting the skill acquisition objectives established by them on their annual plans. To receive credit on the weekly PSR, the last quarterly progress report must be in the individual's file and must show that a prorated proportion of the annual objectives have been met.

These examples illustrate how both process and product standards are important. Carrying out a process would be an empty accomplishment if that process did not lead to some meaningful outcomes. At the same time, we cannot expect to reach our outcome goals without designing and carrying out a process. In Table 2.1, both process and outcome standards have been abstracted from a PSR developed for a supported living service. The full score sheet and the operational definitions for all the standards on this PSR are provided in Appendix D, in this case, organized into general service activities, individualized service plan, health and safety, finances and budgeting, positive futures plan, and staff development.

In Table 2.1, a comparison of process standards with outcome standards reveals the relationship between the two: process standards hold support staff members accountable for doing those things designed to ensure that they will meet their outcome standards. In fact, in some cases, it is possible to yoke a process standard together with an outcome standard. This is possible when producing a particular outcome is seen to be dependent primarily on a particular process. Note, for example, Item E in the process column of Table 2.1, which can be yoked together with Item E in the outcome column.

The process standard for developing an individual community integration plan is defined and operationalized further in the protocol provided in Appendix E. This protocol outlines the necessary components of the required social/community integration and participation plan. These seven components include:

- Helping the individual identify an applicable social interest
- Performing an ecological inventory and corresponding discrepancy analysis, transportation analysis, and financial analysis in an effort to identify the skills, adaptations, and resources the individual may need to ensure success
- Planning for the first contact, considering the possible usefulness of such strategies as using potentiating activities (e.g., watching a videotape or reading a book about the activity); personal effectiveness training to the individual to develop some of the social skills that may be necessary for success; imagery, relaxation training, and skill training for the specific activity; obtaining the appropriate materials ahead of time; arranging for a "buddy" for accompaniment; and so forth
- Using similar strategies for troubleshooting and ongoing revision of the plan
- Using such parallel training as tutoring, modeling, practicing, or other strategies to supplement the training directly received during the activity itself

Table 2.1. Comparison of sample process and outcome standards for supported living

Process standards	Outcome standards
A. Personal Effectiveness Training (PET) Consumers attend at least two social skills instructional sessions per week, or as otherwise provided for in their service plans. This is documented.	**A. Bills Paid** Bills are paid by due date on bill, and neither late charges nor service interruptions have been incurred within month. If this is a specific objective for a person, a written plan is in place and implemented.
B. Circle of Support Logistics Groups meet at least once per quarter, unless special circumstances arise. Invitations and coordination are done by focus person or support staff. Minutes of circle of support will be typed and made available to all parties within 1 week after the meeting.	**B. Time Spent in Community** Staff spends the allotted amount of time with the individual in the community. This specific amount of time is decided by each individual, within 30–60 days of receiving services, and it is noted in the individualized service plan (ISP).
C. Circle of Support Content A task grid is generated and at least 75% of tasks are accomplished by the next meeting. One task should always be to seek out a friend.	**C. Objectives Met** Prorated number of ISP objectives met on last report (e.g., ¾).
D. Contact Meetings Staff attend weekly (or otherwise specified) meeting with supervisory contact person and follows through on recommendations (e.g., no past due assignments).	**D. Consumer Evaluations** Staff and services are rated monthly and are scored at least satisfactory by individual and/or staff are working on resolving any difficulties in relationship or dissatisfaction with services.
E. Community Integration Plan Within 60 days of enrollment, every person has active support plan for increasing interactions with people other than staff, and/or for participation in community and socially integrated activities, or as dictated by the person's interests, abilities, and personal goals and objectives, or manager writes a disclaimer.	**E. Social Integration** Individual has been regularly attending activities as addressed on present and past community integration plan (CIP). This is verified by individual report and spot check if necessary. CIP may not be necessary for every consumer, as per manager's disclaimer.

- Fading staff and other adaptations in order to achieve as full reliance as possible on natural supports
- Developing a follow-up plan to ensure ongoing success for as long as the person wants to remain involved with the activity

We believe that the outcome goal of an individual's spending increasingly more time in the community and participating in socially integrated activities will more likely be reached if we develop a detailed plan for each individual, following the protocol shown in Appendix E. Conversely, our experience tells us that without such formally developed social and community integration plans, we will not meet our outcome standard, which holds us accountable for the social integration of the individuals we serve.

On the one hand, a Total Quality Assurance (TQA) system may yoke process and outcome standards together in a one-to-one fashion, as illustrated above. On the other hand, a TQA system may also combine multiple standards to produce desired outcomes. This is a critical feature of the Periodic Service Review. For instance, at one level, it contains such process standards as *carrying out assessments in a timely way, carrying out plans as designed, collecting data,* and so on. Whereas process standards are important, they are only important in that they help us and the people we support to reach desired objectives. It would make absolutely no sense and have little meaning if we were to achieve 100% on a PSR made up on only *process standards,* especially if our objectives were not met. Thus, the PSR also includes *outcome standards.* By including this second level of standards, we can have some confidence that the quality of our services is measured ultimately by the impact it makes on the individuals served.

Selecting Performance Standards

There are three key sources for product and process standards. They may be selected based on: 1) individual needs; 2) administrative requirements; and 3) third-party rules, regulations, and requirements.

Individual-Based Standards   Many outcome standards can be stated in terms of individual change; for example, in terms of skills learned, behavior problems resolved, or other objectives accomplished. Increasingly, however, human services and educational agencies are being held accountable for improving the quality of life for the people they support and to whom they provide services. Setting standards for quality of life outcomes can be difficult because of the subjective nature of "quality." What one person considers to be a good quality of life may not be considered as such by another person. Nevertheless, there are areas where we might obtain general agreement. For example, most people would agree that persons whose relationships and interactions are limited to individuals with disabilities or to individuals who are paid to interact with them, have a poorer quality of life than persons whose relationships and interactions extend beyond these groups to include individuals who are neither disabled nor paid interactants. If we agree on this, then it could become the basis of an outcome standard on a PSR that holds an agency accountable for individuals having such relationships and interactions. Similarly, if we agree that a person who had access to and spent time in settings other than the home, car, job, day-care program, or school had a better quality of life than a person whose settings were limited essentially to home, car, job, day-care program, or school, then this could become the basis of an outcome standard on a PSR that holds the agency accountable for the time, variety, and/or the number of different settings in which individuals spend time.

Administrative Standards   Beyond individual needs, administrative requirements are the second source from which process and outcome standards can be developed for a PSR. Although we might argue that a well-administered agency will be able to serve people better, the immediate benefit to individuals might not be apparent. For example, in a supported employment service, one process standard based on administrative requirements may be to maintain an overall 1:8 staff-to-service recipient ratio. Interestingly, we might even suggest that a richer ratio would be better for the individuals served; however, funding may not support a richer ratio. Accordingly, this standard could be one way to keep within budget. The related product or outcome standard may be that a balanced budget is maintained. Ultimately, of course, an agency must operate within its budget to continue to operate and continue to provide services. In this way, even those standards based on administrative requirements can be viewed as meeting individual needs.

Externally Imposed Standards   External requirements represent the third source of process and outcome standards for a PSR. We would hope, of course, that funding, licensing, and certifying agencies would monitor us against the standards important to provision of quality services. Although we may not always agree, we must meet these externally imposed standards, as well, if we want to stay in business to provide services. This is the rationale for their possible inclusion on a PSR. For example, a process standard may be "to maintain accurate, written records documenting how staff spend their time, with each 15-minute period coded to indicate which of five different possible services were provided to which individuals." The related product or outcome standard might be to pass and maintain a 3-year accreditation review process carried out by a certifying agency, and to maintain certification in good standing. Obviously, certification would be based on the agency's ability to meet a variety of process standards; equally obvious, meeting such process and outcome standards would be necessary for an agency to maintain its funding base and to stay in business. Hence, such standards might be included on a PSR.

In summary, PSRs may include both process and product or outcome standards generated by individual goals and objectives, by administrative requirements, and by the rules, regulations, and requirements of external agencies. Three basic principles should be followed when developing performance standards for inclusion on a PSR. These include the need to emphasize the essential elements of the agency, the need to set realistic standards, and the need to establish standards that have been defined and operationalized in objective terms, including the method whereby you will verify whether or not the standard is being met. To meet the requirement of this third principle, a written standard includes clear descriptions of *what* exactly is to be done, *when* it is to be done, *who* is to do it, and *how* it will be verified. We discuss these principles in the following section.

BASIC PRINCIPLES

The Essentials Should Be Emphasized

The first principle to follow in developing performance standards for a PSR is to emphasize the essential, critical elements of the services provided. A PSR does not and cannot include all the process and outcome standards that an agency attempts to meet. Such inclusion would be overwhelming and impractical. To make the system manageable and feasible, and to make frequent monitoring possible, it is important to identify and develop a set of critical or key standards. The PSR, then, represents a sampling of agency standards, and PSR scores are indicators of, rather than absolute measures of, quality.

A number of strategies can be used to develop an efficient, representative PSR that includes the most critical standards for an agency.

I. *Use the Last Step in a Sequence of Performance.* One strategy is to develop standards around the last link; that is, the last step in a chain (i.e., sequence of performance) in such a way that monitoring the last link in the chain would also measure performance along the earlier links. For example, an agency providing behavioral services may define a sequence of performance relating to behavior support plans. This chain of performance may require that behavior support plans be based on the following "links."

   A. Collection of baseline data
   B. Direct observation of and discussions with the individual
   C. Detailed interviews of staff and parents
   D. Thorough review of records
   E. Preparation of a comprehensive assessment report that summarizes all of the foregoing information

   Given this chain of performance, the agency would not have to include a standard on its PSR for each of the individual elements or links. Rather, it would be necessary to include only a standard that addresses the last link of the chain. Specifically, the agency could hold itself accountable on its PSR with a standard that states:

   > There is a current (within one year) assessment report in the file, accessible to staff, that meets 85% of the criteria in the writing guide for the behavioral specialists responsible for writing the reports.

   If an agency meets this standard, we can assume that the other tasks representing the earlier links in the chain are being met as well, given the way they are organized.

Appendix F is an example of the kind of writing guide referred to in the standard. Therefore, it represents our standard for writing a behavioral assessment report and associated behavior support plan. Review of Appendix F shows that, in addition to the general format of the report, it prescribes inclusion of the reasons for the referral; the sources of the information reported, including baseline data collection, direct observation of the individual, detailed interviews of staff and parents, and a thorough review of records; description of the services provided; and background information, including description of the individual, the individual's living arrangements and day-time services, the individual's health and medical status, and previous or current services the person is receiving to address the behavioral challenges. It also includes a full, functional analysis of the identified behaviors, with the aim of understanding the meaning of the behavior for the person and the function it serves; recommended support plans, including the long-range goals, short-term behavioral objectives, data collection strategies, and intervention procedures to be carried out (including recommended environmental changes, instructional programs, nonaversive behavior support strategies for producing rapid changes, and reactive strategies for situational management); and final comments and recommendations. Appendix F also includes the operational definition for each of these prescribed elements.

II. *Conceptualize Response Classes.*   Another strategy for developing an efficient PSR that emphasizes the critical elements of an agency is to conceptualize services in terms of response classes. This involves groupings of standards that are related in such a way that we can be reasonably confident that, if we do well with some, we shall probably do well with them all. For example, in our supported employment service, we set forth a number of essential tasks for our staff members.

A. They should teach individuals chronological age–appropriate skills
B. They should teach individuals functional skills
C. They should interact with people using a respectful tone and manner
D. They should use strictly nonaversive interactional styles and procedures
E. They should promote the individual's presence in a variety of different community settings (community integration)
F. They should promote the individual's ability and opportunity to interact with others in the community (social integration)
G. They should promote self-advocacy
H. They should promote independence

We believe these standards form a class. That is, we believe that if a staff person behaves in accordance with a representative subset of these standards, he or she is likely to perform well against all of them. For this reason, we include only a subset on our PSR, and we are confident that if we meet a subset of these standards, we probably meet the rest as well.

Conceptualizing the PSR as a set of standards representative of a response class is a powerful view that seems valid. Although a controlled study has yet to be carried out to verify the phenomenon, experience seems to suggest that if an agency performs at the 85%–90% level consistently, it is meeting many standards not explicitly included on the PSR. That is, there seems to be behavioral covariation across a wide range of standards. For example, after 3 years of operating a PSR system that had reached and maintained the 85%–90% level, we sought independent certification of our agency as a qualified provider of supported employment services from the Commission for Accreditation of Rehabilitation Facilities (CARF). CARF is a private, national organization that provides certification to agencies it finds to be in compliance with a host of standards in the areas of service provision, management, record keeping, fiscal control, and so forth (Commission on Accreditation of Rehabilitation Facilities, 1992). Many states will not contract with an agency to provide services unless that agency has CARF certification. Whereas a new service is usually awarded a 1-year provisional certification, we were pleased to be awarded a 3-year certificate at the outset. We attribute this largely to the PSR system. In preparing for the certification process, management staff carefully scrutinized the literally hundreds of standards against which we were going to be evaluated. In most cases, the standards were already being met, although only a small minority of them were being tracked through the formal PSR system. It was a relatively straightforward task to address these remaining standards before the final review.

Understanding the apparent response class phenomenon associated with the PSR system is important. The services and programs provided by many human service organizations are often monitored externally by licensing and funding agencies against what often seems to be a veritable encyclopedic set of standards. Fortunately, capturing a representative sampling of these in a carefully constructed PSR system, and achieving and maintaining an 85%–90% level of performance, seems to ensure a significant level of performance against the universe of standards on which an agency may be evaluated. Conversely, if an agency is not doing well, as measured on a PSR, there may be a host of other standards that are not being met.

There is, however, an important caveat when relying on the response class effect as part of the PSR system. This caveat is: There may be important areas to monitor that, despite our assumptions, do not fall within any of the response classes that have been included on the PSR instrument. There is general agreement that if the management system is not complete, what is not measured may be neglected (Craig & Harris, 1973; Duerr, 1974; Muckler, 1982; Pritchard, Jones, Roth, Stuebing, & Ekeberg, 1989). This phenomenon is at the root of Deming's (1986) cautions concerning management by objective. Therefore, through direct inclusion, through the inclusion of a standard representing the last step in a sequence of performance, or through the inclusion of representative standards from a "class" of standards, every area critical to quality may be included.

III. *Identify Standards for All Job Categories.*   A final strategy for developing a PSR is to select performance standards that are "pivotal" and that cut across different categories of staff (Christian & Hannah, 1983). This strategy reflects the importance of respective contributions from different members of the interdisciplinary team to the overall provision of services. Thus, in addition to including standards for direct service staff, standards should also reflect the performance responsibilities of the professionals who serve on the team, as well as the supervisors, consultants, and even the administration. The responsibility of providing quality services is not the responsibility of the direct service staff alone. The PSR should reflect this multidisciplinary process.

To summarize, there are three strategies to remember when developing a PSR that attempts to capture the essential elements of a service or program; that is, those standards that are thought to be the *most critical* for quality assurance. The first is to organize services into a series of *response chains*, including the last element in the chain as a standard on the PSR—if that standard is being met, those leading up to it are also being met. The second is to conceptualize the service or the program standards as a collection of *response classes*, including only some of the standards in each of the classes on the PSR, with the confidence that if those standards are being met, the others in the class are also being met, and if those standards are not being met, the others in the class are also not being met. The third and final strategy is to include standards that are the responsibilities of each of the job categories thought to contribute to the *interdisciplinary team*, and not to include only the responsibilities of the direct service staff. If these three strategies are followed, they will produce a PSR that is efficient and, at the same time, that incorporates the standards critical for total quality assurance.

Realistic Criteria Should Be Used

It is important that the standards established for a PSR be realistic, that is, obtainable (Christian & Hannah, 1983). Working within the resource capabilities of the agency, that is, given proper consideration of budget, staffing, materials, and so forth, it should be reasonable that the standard can be achieved. The purpose of a PSR is not to establish a set of idealized standards that leave the agency perpetually unable to meet its goals, and bemoaning the lack of resources to ensure a good job. Rather, the purpose of a PSR is to establish a set of standards that will allow an agency to provide the best services possible, *given the available resources*. For example, different sets of standards would be developed for two different classrooms, even when the characteristics of the students were comparable, if the classes had different staff-to-student ratios. That is, the standards for the classroom with the richer ratio would appropriately be more rigorous than would the standards for the classroom with the lower ratio of staff to students.

There are different ways to establish realistic criteria for performance standards.

I. *Use Average Past Performance.* Base the PSR standards on average past performance. For example, support staff may currently take the individuals they serve into the community for shopping once a month; or they might conduct data-based training once a week. The agency could set their criteria at the levels at which they currently operate. If the agency uses this method, and establishes performance criteria at the levels at which they already operate, it would be quite "realistic" that they could and would perform up to the "expected level" in the future. This strategy, however, will produce a status quo performance that will not result in improvement of services. Because the purpose of a PSR system is to improve quality, average past performance is not recommended to establish criteria for service standards.

II. *Use Best Past Performance.* A better approach would be to develop criteria for PSR standards based on best past performance. One way to judge best past performance is to determine how well an agency performed when it prepared for a review by outside monitors or for an annual recertification audit. The notion here is that if an agency could perform at a certain level for "visitors," it should be realistic to expect that level of performance to be maintained on an ongoing basis. Setting the PSR standards based on best past performance would give the agency the opportunity to improve quality.

III. *Establish Objectives.* The most powerful approach to setting the criteria for performance standards looks at neither average past performance nor best past performance. Rather, with the available resources in mind, criteria for performance standards are established as objectives toward which an agency strives (Crosby, 1979). Let us assume, for example, that an agency has always hoped to have its reports submitted to their funding source within 30 days of referral. This goal has not been achieved regularly. Reports usually have arrived 45–60 days after referral. The agency, however, wants to achieve the 30-day criterion; so they set the criterion for their performance standard at 30 days, and then they strive to achieve it. Using this "pursuing the brass ring approach," the PSR system may be used most powerfully to upgrade services and ensure that agencies are performing at the highest possible level of quality. For example, a review of past records in order to set a standard for the number of hours a week each adult in a particular group home spends in community/

socially integrated settings (not counting the day-time program), may reveal that individuals have spent an average of 4 hours per week. This is the agency's *average* past performance. Further review may also reveal that on the week of an annual review by the funding agency, the same individuals spent an average of 10 hours each in integrated settings. This is the agency's *best* past performance. However, agency staff might meet to discuss the use of natural supports, and realize that if a particular approach to scheduling was followed, it would be possible for each individual to spend an average of 15 hours per week in integrated settings. Given this situation, adopting 15 hours a week as the PSR standard for individual time in integrated settings would give this agency the best possibility for improving services.

There is a greater risk in taking this approach. When establishing such objectives, it is possible to overstate the agency's resource capabilities. Later, in Chapter 4, when we discuss the feedback loop, we talk about what to do when the criteria for one or more standards are not met because of lack of resources. In conclusion, agencies should *be realistic* in establishing PSR standards. Standards should be realistically obtainable; should be based on agency resources; and should be set as objectives toward which to strive rather than based on past performance.

Define Standards Operationally

A third principle in developing standards is to base them on explicit criteria (Christian & Hannah, 1983). This requires that each standard be "operationally defined," which should remove subjectivity from the monitoring process. An operational definition is a description of a performance in "reliably observable terms"; in other words, we can agree on it when we see it.

Writing standards with good operational definition involves the specification of at least four performance dimensions (i.e., what, when, who, and how). We elaborate on these dimensions below.

I.   *What Exactly Is the Desired Performance?*   The first part of the operational definition is to establish exactly WHAT is desired; in other words, the topography of the desired performance. This is not a difficult proposition, as the following examples suggest.
     A.   A schedule is maintained by each individual in a day planner and includes:
          1.   Daily activities and appointments
          2.   Reminders about the objectives the person is working on
          3.   Data-based (formal) training opportunities
     B.   A current behavioral assessment is filed in the individual's case file, located at the main office.
     C.   One hundred percent of staff interactions with individuals fall within the categories of positive, instructional, and/or conversational, and all are nonaversive. (*Note:* The operational definitions of positive, instructional, and conversational interactions might be included in a glossary of terms in the agency's training materials.)
     D.   In-service training will be conducted once a week.
     E.   Individual services are provided as designed (i.e., procedural reliability exceeds 85%).

To establish a standard that simply says "every individual maintains a schedule" leaves too much to interpretation. It does not specify with sufficient clarity WHAT is wanted. However, if we operationalized this standard to say that each individual has her or his own day planner, listing planned activities and appointments for each 15-minute period, including when he or she has the opportunity to receive formal training sessions, and so forth, we leave little room for opinion as to whether or not the standard has been met. We may specify even further what is expected by saying that the listed activity cannot be generic (e.g., home-based recreation or leisure), but it must be specific (e.g., shooting baskets, knitting). Because the activity is to be the individual's choice, we may require that the schedule refer to the set of activities from which, and/or the process by which, the choice will be made. We might also expect that this schedule be with the individual or otherwise accessible to her or him, and therefore, available for review.

II.   *When Is the Performance Expected To Occur (What Are the Timeline Requirements)?*   If you have been in a supervisory position for any length of time, you have heard the excuse "It's in the mail," or "I was just getting ready to do it." Moreover, if you have ever requested that a specific activity or document be completed by the end of the day, we feel sure that you have experienced people continuing the activity or working on the document well after what you consider to be the end of the normal work day. Exactly *when* is the "end of the day?" It is important that an operational definition specify exactly WHEN you want a performance carried out; in other words, we need to specify TIMELINES for performances.

It is not enough to say that training data should be summarized on a graph. When this is to be done must also be written into the standard. For example, it might be established that graphing needs to be done within the last training session, or weekly, or daily. Another example might be that behavioral assessment reports on file be current (e.g., dated within the last year). We are not suggesting what the timelines should be, but that it is important for PSR standards to specify in objective, observable terms, *when* something is supposed to be done, as well as to operationalize *what* it is that needs to be done. To take the standard described above regarding an individual's weekly day planner a step further, the timeline might be that support staff should have assisted the person in planning his or her week for the coming week by noon of the preceding Saturday.

III. *Who Is Responsible for Carrying Out the Performance Standard?*   We are frequently amused when we hear a staff person say, "Who, me? I didn't know I was supposed to do that." This may be amusing the first or second time, but a supervisor who hears it day after day frequently throws up his or her hands in exasperation and personally completes the job. The statement "I didn't know . . ." may reflect a problem in the written performance standard. It may not state WHO is responsible. A thoroughly defined Performance Standard should include a specification of the person responsible. For example, "It is the responsibility of the behavioral consultant to write behavioral assessments for residents in group homes"; "It is the responsibility of the Job Coach to assist the individual and ensure that there is a written daily schedule"; "It is the responsibility of the staff member assigned to the individual to provide the services as designed"; "It is the responsibility of the program supervisor to write the ISP"; "It is the responsibility of all staff to interact in a positive manner." Without specifying the WHO in the operational definition, you will be faced with "Who, me?" day after day.

IV.   *How Will Performance Be Verified?*   Finally, each standard should have a clearly defined means to verify that the performance criteria have or have not been met (Christian & Hannah, 1983). This can be done in one of two ways, by a review of *permanent products* or by *direct observation*. Certain performances result in durable changes in the environment, called *permanent products*. A behavioral assessment is an example of a permanent product. A review of the behavioral assessment report in an individual's file can determine (i.e., verify) if the appropriate information is included and whether it is current (e.g., dated within 1 year). Similarly, logs, summary graphs, posted schedules, individual files, professional reports, written plans, checklists, protocols, timesheets, and reinforcement charts are examples of permanent products that can be reviewed to verify whether a variety of standards are being met. When establishing performance standards, you may need to develop new and creative permanent product measures.

For example, about 10 years ago, a situation arose during one of our in-home, intensive interventions (Donnellan, LaVigna, Zambito, & Thvedt, 1985). Our direct service staff were working 6 hours a day with an adult who had sustained a severe brain injury. They followed elaborate schedules and procedures and devoted many hours to data collection. Reliability checks conducted by the supervisor resulted in respectable results. The services were provided in the home of the person's parents. At times, the relationship between the direct service team and the parents was, unfortunately, adversarial. At one point, the person's father claimed that the staff sat around all day, doing nothing. He reported this to the funding agency. Questions were raised about the validity of the data, and whether the staff were simply putting on a show for their supervisor. We did not doubt that the staff were doing what was expected, so we established a permanent product method to verify their performances. They were required to maintain a 15-minute log in which they noted the time, the location, and the predominant activity. Then this could be cross-referenced with the itemized schedule and verified by observing with spot checks by the supervisor.

In a second approach, a whole host of important standards that we might include on a PSR might be verifiable through direct observation only. These, for example, might include reliability checks to determine whether data are accurate (in contrast to scrutinizing a datasheet merely to determine if it has been appropriately completed), fidelity checks to determine whether instructional protocols are properly followed (in contrast to scrutinizing the protocol itself merely to determine if it includes all of the required information and details), observations to verify the quality and/or rate of staff interactions with the people they support, spot checks to determine if a scheduled activity occurred, and so forth.

Doke and Risley (1972) have developed an approach to direct observation that is very useful for verifying certain performances, the *Placheck* (Planned Activity Checklist) method. It involves a simple 4-step process. The first step is to define the target performance, or in PSR terms, to define the performance standard. For example, if an agency were interested in developing a standard that addresses the extent to which residents in a group home were engaged in meaningful activities, it would first define what it meant by "meaningful." This might include: 1) activities of people without disabilities, 2) activities appropriate to the person's chronological age, 3) activities that involve the person interacting either with others in the environment or with chronological age–appropriate materials, and so forth. This definition might also include those activities that would not be considered meaningful, but that might be misperceived as meaningful. For example, if an adult is in the living room where the Oprah Winfrey show is playing on the television, a meaningful activity may not be scored unless there is clear evidence that the individual is watching the show, such as looking at the TV and reacting to the content of the show, and/or if there is acceptable documentation that the person actively chose to watch that show, such as that available in the data generated from a formal "choice program." Similar care might be necessary when music is played in the home. "Is the person rocking? Is the rocking in time with the music?" If the person is rocking, but not in time with the music, it might be best to define our standard so that this individual would not be counted as being involved in a meaningful activity.

Once the first step of the Placheck method is accomplished and the target behavior or performance has been defined, the second step is to record, for a defined interval, the total number of individuals engaged in the target performance. This would involve counting the number of individuals found at home, during the defined interval of time, engaged in a meaningful activity. Then the third step of the Placheck method is to record the total number of individuals present in the area of activity, and the fourth step is to compute the "percentage of persons engaged in meaningful activities," by dividing the total number of individuals in the environment into the number of individuals engaged in the target performance, and multiplying the dividend by 100.

For example, if three individuals were engaged in meaningful activities when a spot check was carried out in the home at 8 P.M. on a Monday night, and a total of five were home at the time, five would be divided into three and the dividend (.60) would be multiplied by 100 to yield a score of 60%. The PSR standard may specify that at least two thirds (66⅔%) of the individuals who are home at any given time are engaged in a meaningful activity, thereby acknowledging that most of the people have some time when they may not be doing something meaningful. In this case, then, a 60% score would represent an occasion when this standard was not being met.

Although some critical standards require that direct observations be carried out for purposes of verification, it is strongly recommended that the results of direct observations be documented on a permanent product record, such as a log or file. In this way, when performing a PSR, each standard can be scored on the basis of permanent product evaluation, including the permanent records of previously performed direct observations. If designed correctly, a weekly PSR should take no more than half an hour. In the following chapter, we recommend you should perform PSR evaluations weekly to produce the most rapid improvement in quality, but no less frequently than monthly to ensure that these monitoring results contribute to a fully active total management system. However, the frequency with which the specific direct observations should be carried out can be more sensitive to resource availability.

For example, suppose in the above example, which involved a PSR standard that addressed the meaningfulness of activity in a group home, the interdisciplinary team decides that, because of limited resources, the Placheck method to verify whether or not this standard is being met can only be performed once a month. At the same time, the team may have decided that they want to perform a formal PSR weekly. During the weekly PSR, when the item for "Meaningful Activities" is reached, the corresponding verification file (i.e., permanent product) will be reviewed. If a Placheck had been performed within the last month, *and* if the percentage score was 66⅔% or better, credit would be given on that week's PSR for meeting that standard. If a Placheck had not been carried out within the last month, *or* if a score of 66⅔% was not achieved, credit would not be given on that week's PSR for that particular standard. In other words, once a Placheck has been carried out and the criteria have been achieved, the same documentation will justify credit for meeting this standard on a PSR for 4 consecutive weeks. The team may also decide that the Placheck would be performed monthly, as long as the standard is met; however, when the standard is not achieved, the Placheck would be carried out weekly until the standard is once again achieved. In this way, the team would have a weekly opportunity to improve or maintain its score, to the extent that it is affected by this particular item.

The point here is that although it is critical that PSR performance standards be developed in a way that *assures verifiability*, the frequency with which verification is carried out can be a function of available resources. This is part of the key to a total quality assurance system—giving oneself permission to establish standards of performance, regardless of resources. For example, an agency that makes data-based decisions regarding individualized services is more likely to provide "quality services" if it establishes a standard for performing interobserver reliability checks, although it may be able to perform these verification checks per quarter only. This is better than failure to establish any standard for reliability whatsoever because of lack of resources.

The following is an example of a written standard that explicitly includes the *what, when, who,* and *how* of an operational definition. It represents one of the standards that our supporting living service would like to meet in assisting individuals to develop a circle of support.

> **Standard:**   Circle of Support—Composition
> **Operational Definition:**
>
> WHAT: The composition of a circle of support includes friends, family, and other people who are not paid staff and who attend circle meetings regularly.
>
> WHEN: The circle of support will meet at least quarterly, or as otherwise scheduled.
>
> WHO: All people on the support team, including the individual being supported, are responsible for identifying and recruiting potential members. The appointed secretary of the circle, however, is responsible for sending out written meeting invitations at least 1 week before a meeting.
>
> HOW: Based on a review of the minutes taken at the last scheduled meeting of the circle, a + is scored if:
> - At least three who attended were not staff; and,
> - At least one who attended was at the immediately previous meeting and is neither a present nor past staff member nor a family member.

SUMMARY

This chapter describes the first element of the four that make up the integrated PSR quality assurance system. This element involves developing performance standards for the agency's services and/or programs. Both process and product standards should be developed for a Periodic Service Review. Process standards are those staff responsibilities believed to be essential to produce the desired outcomes for the people receiving services. Product standards are those minimum individual outcomes for which the agency holds itself accountable. The important principles to remember when developing PSR performance standards are: 1) to emphasize the essential process and product standards of the agency, relying on the response class phenomenon to spread the effect of the quality assurance system to the wider set of standards; 2) to set realistic (achievable) standards for the agency; and 3) to define the performance standards operationally, including a specification of the procedures that will be used to verify that the standards have been met. Standards should be critical for the provision of quality services; they should be realistic; and they should be clearly defined, including what is to be done, by whom, by when, and how performance will be verified. There is further discussion about how to identify and define standards for a PSR system in Chapter 6, on "Getting Started." With the basic understanding of a Periodic Service Review, which includes performance standards with the characteristics described here, we now turn to the second element of the system—performance monitoring.

· 3 ·

PERFORMANCE MONITORING

In this chapter, we define the performance monitoring component of the system and provide the rationale for its inclusion. Then we provide a number of guidelines to follow to ensure that your staff will accept a management system that includes frequent monitoring. These guidelines are important because, if you do not follow them, monitoring may produce significant resistance from staff. The guidelines include using the results of monitoring to provide positive feedback to your staff; involving your staff in developing the standards against which performance will be measured; planning for staff participation in other aspects of the system; keeping the focus of the monitoring process on the entire service team, not only on any one job category or direct service staff; scheduling a period of self-monitoring after the standards have been developed, to allow people an opportunity to prepare for the monitoring process to begin; emphasizing your expectation of professional and competent performance from all staff categories; and providing a forum for staff to comment and provide explanations about the findings of the monitoring process.

Then we discuss the basic principles of monitoring. These include sampling, which allows you to keep the monitoring process practical; regular and frequent scheduling of the monitoring process, to maximize your opportunities for informed action to improve and maintain service quality; and proactive and regular scheduling, rather than the use of monitoring as a reactive strategy for such problems or external threats as responding to deficiencies noted on a licensing or recertification survey. In our discussion of proactive and regular scheduling, we recognize that total quality assurance requires ongoing monitoring. We also discuss the principles of reliability and validity, meaning that different people applying the written standards to the same set of information would agree about whether or not standards were being met and that the standards are relevant and important indicators of quality. Our discussion of monitoring principles concludes with the importance of quantifying, summarizing, and analyzing the results obtained from the monitoring process, and using these results to set the stage for management and supervisory action to improve and maintain quality.

DEFINITION AND RATIONALE

Performance monitoring can be defined as the ongoing verification that staff responsibilities have been carried out. It is the second element of the PSR system that ensures the quality of services and programs, and it is fundamentally important to effective management and supervision. It plays a central role in a total quality management system.

In a study that illustrates the importance of this component in a quality assurance system, Komaki (1986) investigated the differences between two groups of supervisors and managers. One group had been rated independently as effective, and the second group was rated independently as ineffective. The original hypothesis of the study was that there would be differences in the amount of feedback or consequences the two groups provided to their employees; however the findings did not support the hypothesis. No significant differences were found in the amount of feedback or consequences provided by each group. One difference, however, was found. The supervisors and managers rated as effective were found to have carried out performance monitoring with their staff, whereas the ineffective supervisors and managers did not significantly carry out this function. In her discussion, Komaki points out that the lack of differences in the amount of feedback and consequences the two groups provided did not mean that feedback and consequences are unimportant. Rather, the results of her study suggest that the feedback and consequences provided by supervisors and managers to their staff must be *meaningful* (i.e., contingent), and this is possible only if the performance monitoring function has been carried out.

The rationale for including performance monitoring as an element of a total quality assurance system is that it provides the necessary basis for the third element of the system—management and supervisory action to improve and maintain staff performance, which we discuss in Chapter 4. Without observation or monitoring, meaningful feedback cannot be provided. Thus, supervisors and managers who monitor performance are in a position to provide meaningful feedback to their staff; those who do not, are not.

We must emphasize the importance of performance monitoring in effective management and quality assurance because there seems to be a tendency to avoid this function in the field of human services. Why is this? There seems to be a belief that because we are adults (often with professional credentials), and because we have explained performance expectations and they are understood, we should not need to look over our staff's shoulders (monitor). Indeed, supervisors say, "We should be able to rely on our staff's sense of adult responsibility and professionalism." Our experience, however, has shown that, although the staff often are responsible and professional, they may still need ongoing performance monitoring to ensure that they perform responsibly to achieve the expected goals. Even assuming the highest levels of staff professionalism and responsibility, performance monitoring must be carried out if a total quality assurance system is desired, but supervisors and managers often avoid this function. They may justify this in the terms described above. However, other factors may be at play here. In our discussions across the country, management staff from various human service and educational agencies express fear and concern for potential staff resistance to being monitored. These fears and concerns apply to informal resistance as well as the more organized resistance that might be the case in labor union involvement. At the very least, there are fears and concerns that introducing a performance monitoring system might worsen already poor staff—management relations.

Upon reflection, this fear is understandable when we realize that in the past monitoring has been the occasion for punishment for many people. That is, our typical understanding of the purpose of monitoring is that it is used to find out what we are doing wrong, not what we are doing right. Thus, monitoring has, to a large extent, become a conditioned aversive event, and we tend to resist it. It is especially interesting to note, however, that staff being interviewed for employment in agencies that provide frequent monitoring and feedback seem to welcome it when it is explained fully. They often state that in previous jobs they were never told what was expected or how they were doing. A system that announces at the outset its performance expectations and where performance feedback is frequently provided is generally viewed favorably by incoming staff. It seems that our fears of a monitoring system are more applicable to already-existing staff than to new hires.

Although there may be general resistance to monitoring systems from existing staff and management, our experience is that the PSR system, including the performance monitoring component, can be implemented in such a way as to avoid resistance and additional conflicts between staff and management, including those settings with labor union involvement. Moreover, the system may make major contributions toward resolution of such conflicts. Before we discuss the major principles of performance monitoring, the following section presents guidelines we have found helpful in promoting staff acceptance, that is, social validity (Reid & Whitman, 1983) of monitoring.

GUIDELINES FOR INCREASING STAFF ACCEPTANCE

In our more than 10 years of experience in designing and implementing PSR systems for our own agency and in our consulting work with other agencies, we have never met staff resistance to the monitoring features of the system. This lack of experience with resistance ill prepared us for the concerns about the acceptance of monitoring expressed by participants in our management-training seminars. These concerns led us to analyze more closely how we were able to use monitoring as an integral part of the PSR system without generating resistance (Cayer, Dumattia, & Wingrove, 1988). This analysis enabled us to identify certain practices that we had been following implicitly. We now recognize that these practices are important guidelines. We believe that following these guidelines when introducing monitoring into a system can result in avoiding resistance, and this important requirement for effective management and supervision can be fully accepted by staff.

Use Positive Payoffs

The first way that we promote staff acceptance of performance monitoring is by using the results of our PSR monitoring system to provide positive feedback only (Brown, Willis, & Reid, 1981; Christian & Hannah, 1983). Regardless of the outcome score of the PSR review, the results are used to provide three specific kinds of positive feedback.

The first form of positive feedback emphasizes the visibility the monitoring system provides. How many of you actually know how well your services are being provided? What percentage of your objectives and procedures are being met and carried out—20%, 50%? Do you ever become a little anxious because you "really don't know"? We would and we did before we developed the PSR System. Therefore to help people accept monitoring, we emphasize the desirability of the *visibility* it will bring us—"Wouldn't it be nice to know?" We emphasize that we cannot move forward unless we know where we are, and the PSR system can tell us exactly where we are. This form of positive feedback is used quite effectively in the initial stages of implementing the PSR system, when PSR scores might be expected to be very low, perhaps even as low as 20% or so. The point that we make is, ". . . we finally know where we are. This is good!" This requires some preparation and discipline on the part of the manager, of course. The natural tendency might be to become upset and disappointed with a low score. If the manager takes some time to think about it, it becomes obvious that, even if things are bad now, it is good that a management system is in place that will allow clear tracking of where things are and where things are going.

Second, we are able to enhance the palatability of monitoring by focusing on and being positive about those things the PSR reveals we are doing *right*. This means focusing on the standards that are being met and acknowledging the effort and good work this represents. We may focus on standards that have recently come on line, and therefore represent an improvement in the quality of our services and programs, or we may focus on standards that we have been able to maintain over a period of time. We may also focus on some of both.

A third way we provide positive feedback to enhance staff acceptance of monitoring is to focus on the opportunities the PSR reveals for improvement, not on what we have failed to do. Specifically, unmet standards are not characterized as failures, deficiencies, or problems. Rather, they are characterized as opportunities for improvement. Thus, the little circles we enter on a PSR score sheet are not zeros, but are "Os", which stand for Opportunities. We emphasize to staff that we cannot improve as an agency unless we discover our opportunities for improvement. The PSR system allows us to do just that. Discovering these opportunities is, therefore, perceived as a positive process—not a negative one.

We suggest that this is not a mere exercise in rhetoric. A management system that does not, in fact, identify areas for improvement will not be able to make the same contribution to quality assurance. That is, what could be done to improve the quality of services and programs if the quantified results of a monitoring process indicated that the agency was meeting 95% or 98% of its standards? There would be no apparent need for improvement and, therefore, a very low likelihood of improvement. In contrast, however, a monitoring process that helps to discriminate and identify areas for improvement provides the greatest likelihood for that improvement. Given this understanding, it becomes reasonable to react to these identified opportunities positively.

Our experience has been that when we focus on these positive attributes of monitoring, staff are more likely to accept and adopt a monitoring system. However, it has also been our experience that this positive approach to monitoring and to presenting the results is not easy for many managers. There seems to be a strong tendency to respond to monitoring results in negative terms. For this reason, we urge preparation and practice. It is not enough to use positive terminology. The positive words must be expressed without sarcasm and in a positive tone. To say, "We sure have a lot of opportunity here . . ." in a sarcastic tone communicates a much different message than that which would be communicated if we ask, "Isn't it good to see our opportunities so clearly laid out?" in a positive, nonconfrontive, supportive, and accepting tone.

An example of using this positive approach can be found in our experience implementing a PSR system for Systematic Training for Employment Program (STEP), the supported employment services provided by the Institute for Applied Behavior Analysis. As described earlier, we had been providing services for 6 months, with a comprehensive, competency-based training program for staff in place, when we initiated the PSR system. As indicated, our first review resulted in a PSR score of 43%. Rather than upper management expressing disappointment at this performance, however, as might have been expected, great appreciation was expressed for getting the system started and for finally knowing in concrete terms where we were. In fact, having such a firm handle on things was very comforting to us, and our positive expressions were quite sincere. Furthermore, we were able to express our appreciation for all the standards that were being met, because some of them were very demanding and, in our opinion, state-of-the-art in those early days of providing supported employment. This was especially so because we were serving many individuals the extent of whose challenging behaviors made them vulnerable to exclusion by other agencies. Finally, we were excited about the clarity with which we had been able to identify the opportunities we had to improve our services, and we were positive about our confidence in being able to take advantage of those opportunities. This confidence was well founded. We were able to work our way up gradually to the 85%–90% level, and we have maintained that level for more than 5 years. We believe that our positive response to scores below that level enabled the staff to accept the PSR system, which, in turn, enabled us to achieve our eventual level of performance.

To summarize, using the monitoring results of the PSR system to provide positive feedback only is one way to enhance staff acceptance of the monitoring system. The three ways of providing positive feedback of the monitoring results involve characterizing the results as: 1) providing an understanding of how well the agency is doing in its attempts to meet the standards to which it aspires, 2) providing information about those standards that are being met at an acceptable level, and 3) pointing out the opportunities the agency has to improve its services and programs.

Plan for Staff Participation

Another strategy to increase staff acceptance of monitoring is to arrange for active staff participation every step along the way. This includes their participation in setting the standards and developing the Periodic Service Review, participation in the monitoring process, and participation in setting that week's objectives for improvement. In these ways, the PSR system takes on the bottom-up style of management that is characteristic of true total quality assurance systems.

Staff Should Be Involved In Setting Standards   Initially, there may be some management concern that staff may take the easy road if they are asked to set their own standards; that they will set minimal, watered-down standards that will not challenge the agency, and may not lead to any significant improvement in quality. However, contrary to most of our expectations, Christian and Hannah (1983) suggest that, given the opportunity, staff typically set and maintain higher, more relevant, and more feasible standards of performance than their supervisors. Our experience confirms this. For example, at a weekend retreat for parents, board members, management, and staff of an agency to which we provide periodic consultation, one of the most potentially explosive items on the agenda was the issue of "down time." Parents were upset because when they visited their children's group home on the weekends, they frequently found their children sitting around, uninvolved in a meaningful activity. However, it was staff members themselves who raised this issue initially at the retreat, and it was they who proposed a standard that would hold them accountable for assuring that at least two thirds of residents in the home would be involved in a meaningful activity at any given time. The parents stated later that they would have been satisfied with a 50% criterion for meaningful activity, in contrast to the more rigorous standard of 66⅔% set by the staff for themselves. In Chapter 6, where we present a step-by-step plan for developing and implementing a PSR system for an agency, we say more about how to involve staff in the development of standards and how to guide and facilitate this process to develop the strongest possible PSR system.

Staff Should Be Involved In Monitoring   In addition to staff participation in the development of standards, we can involve them in the monitoring process itself (Burg, Reid, & Lattimore, 1979). By operationalizing the performance standards, most subjective judgment can be eliminated from the monitoring process, enabling staff members to participate in the PSR review without compromising the results. Thus, we recommend that when it is time to perform a PSR review, representatives of the team go through the documentation and fill out the PSR score sheet together. For example, in a group home setting, in any given week, the PSR score sheet might be filled out by a team consisting of the QMRP (qualified mental retardation professional), the home manager, and one representative of direct service staff. The next week, it might be filled out by the consulting psychologist, the home manager, and two representatives of direct service staff. This avoids negative staff reactions that might occur if a member of the management or professional team came to the house once a week, gathered up the documentation and filled out the PSR score sheet independently, without staff participation, leaving them to wonder how they were being scored.

We can also involve direct service staff in the actual process of monitoring by having them share in the responsibility of carrying out some of the direct observations necessary for verifying whether or not a specific standard has been met. There is no reason why direct service staff could not (with training) take on the responsibility for carrying out some of the scheduled interobserver reliability checks, procedural reliability checks, and Plachecks themselves. Utilizing direct service staff as an additional resource in this way would have the advantage of allowing the agency to carry out a more ambitious schedule of verification than might otherwise be possible. It would also help to reinforce the point that monitoring and verification are not performed to satisfy management and authority, but rather to provide the highest quality of services and programs possible, a goal shared by all members of the interdisciplinary team. Staff participation in monitoring and verification helps them to accept the PSR system, as does their involvement in developing the actual standards against which performance will be evaluated.

Staff Should Be Involved in Setting Objectives   A third way that staff can participate in the process is to give them an active voice in identifying the opportunities available to them in the coming week. At the end of the weekly PSR session, the person in the role of facilitator can ask, "What opportunities would you like to take advantage of this week?" In fact, the facilitator will, in all likelihood, find it necessary to keep staff ambitions for the coming week realistic, so the objectives can be accomplished. This is more desirable than having staff establish very ambitious goals and then fall short. One way to guide staff selection of an opportunity to tackle in the coming week is to suggest that they take the easiest options. These may not be the most important opportunities available at the time. For example, consider a PSR session that has identified a number of opportunities, two of which are under consideration by the staff as possible objectives for the coming week. One of these may involve helping individuals to develop weekly schedules for themselves, and the other may involve designing and implementing a system of ongoing procedural reliability checks, and achieving and maintaining the procedural reliability indices at an 85% level or better. Staff may argue for tackling the standards relating to the procedural reliability checks. They may, in fact, have a point when they say that procedural reliability is more important for improving quality than is each individual's having a weekly schedule. The reality, however, is that it is much easier to establish and maintain current, weekly schedules, because many activities (job hours, scheduled classes, weekly shopping, etc.) are the same from week to week, than it is to design and implement a system of ongoing procedural reliability checks. For this reason, it would be better to help your staff reach a consensus in selecting the easier option, thus maximizing their chance for success, and keeping the momentum going for the entire PSR system, eventually producing consistent performance against all the identified standards, including those addressing procedural reliability.

To summarize, full staff participation in a monitoring system can reduce their resistance to such systems. Specific strategies suggested for increasing staff participation are including them in the development of the standards against which performance is going to be monitored, involving them directly in the monitoring and verification process and, finally, having them play an active role in deciding which of the unmet standards should receive priority attention. Such staff participation emphasizes the bottom-up, two-way nature of the system, and contributes to staff members' sense of ownership.

Share Responsibility

A third guideline for increasing staff acceptance of a PSR monitoring system is to construct it in such a way that includes standards that reflect different contributions from as many members of the interdisciplinary team as possible (Christian & Hannah, 1983; Ford, 1980; Jones, Morris, & Barnard, 1986; Prue & Fairbank, 1981). If it were used only to monitor the performance of direct service staff, the system would make them particularly visible and vulnerable, thus more resistant to the PSR system. As a shared responsibility, the PSR keeps the focus at team level and does not make any particular job category the subject of scrutiny. For example, if the results of a PSR session in a group home produce a PSR score of 45%, this score does not reflect only the performance of direct service staff, but it also reflects the performance of the entire team. The standards on the PSR would include such responsibilities of direct service staff as carrying out scheduled activities, collecting certain data, maintaining certain records, and performing certain procedures for behavioral support and instructional programs. However, it would also include the responsibilities of the home manager, for example, to perform certain procedural and/or interobserver reliability checks, and to prepare weekly schedules. In addition, it would include some responsibilities of the behavioral consultant, including preparation of annual assessments and quarterly progress reports, and carrying out certain staff training sessions. The PSR might also include standards that list some responsibilities of the QMRP, including developing detailed procedural protocols for each individual's service plan, and ensuring that the necessary training material is present.

This is not to say that the responsibility for meeting any given standard might not be assigned to a single job category or, for that matter, to a single person. Nor are we discussing here what should be done with the performance information gathered through the monitoring process. That is the topic of Chapter 4, "Feedback Loop." The point here is that by including standards on the Periodic Service Review that represent the responsibilities of all of the members of the interdisciplinary team, the monitoring process does not scrutinize any single group. The PSR score generally is not used as a measure of how *you* (direct service staff) are doing; but rather, it is a measure of how *we* (the team) are doing. By keeping the focus on the team and not on the individual or individual job category, there is less likelihood that people will resist the idea of being monitored. Their attitude can be one of "This is a way we can all do a better job," not one of "This is just another way that management is trying to stick it to us." The PSR system's lack of focus on one job category and its focus on the entire team may partly explain why formally organized labor groups, less formally organized groups that represent staff, and individual staff members themselves have tended to accept the PSR monitoring system fully. They see it as balanced and nondiscriminatory. The development of such an inclusive PSR is one of the guidelines we recommend for increasing staff acceptance of a monitoring system.

Schedule Self-Monitoring

A fourth guideline for increasing staff acceptance is to schedule a period for self-monitoring of from 2 to 3 months after the development of a PSR. After the performance standards have been formally developed for the PSR, no formal monitoring should take place for a pre-specified period of time. To begin with, while developing the PSR standards, the staff should be told that once the PSR performance standards have been developed, the team will have an initial period of self-monitoring to get organized and to get their respective responsibilities on line before formal monitoring actually begins. Although some people may not take advantage of this period of self-monitoring, the knowledge that it will be there seems to contribute to a more accepting staff attitude toward the development and implementation of a monitoring system.

As standards are discussed and formulated, it is likely that the staff will become increasingly aware of the number of presently unmet standards they would like to adopt. Rather than this becoming an occasion for not adopting some standards and/or weakening others, it is more helpful if people realize that they "will have time to get ready" before the formal monitoring actually begins. We emphasize the importance of this period of self-monitoring. It is a strategy, however, to increase staff acceptance of the monitoring system; it is not necessarily a strategy to improve staff's consistent service quality. As is typical in fixed interval performance (Ferster & Skinner, 1957), there may be little activity in the initial and interim stages of this self-monitoring period. Staff behavior may only begin to be goal directed toward improved performance as the deadline for beginning formal monitoring approaches. Because improved quality does not begin significantly until formal monitoring and verification begin, why commit to a period of self-monitoring after the formal PSR performance standards have been developed? Because this strategy helps contribute to staff acceptance of the monitoring system. As we have stressed, acceptance is very important.

Emphasize Professionalism

As a fifth means to increase staff acceptance of the monitoring system, we emphasize our expectation of professionalism among the staff, with special emphasis on the expected professionalism of direct service staff. Rather than characterizing the PSR system as necessary because we expect that staff will not perform to expectation without management looking over their shoulders, we suggest communicating the expectation that, when given the necessary information and support, the staff will perform at the highest levels of professionalism. The PSR is portrayed as a system that provides this necessary information and support. Rarely are we disappointed in the response of the staff and in their ability to meet the most rigorous standards.

This recommendation must be emphasized because, unfortunately, management often have low expectations of their direct service staff. Managers may at times characterize their staff as lazy, unmotivated, not very bright, and even dishonest. However, these negatives typically develop within the context of an agency that has not yet reached high-quality services and programs, and whose staff inconsistently perform their responsibilities. Moreover, as we discussed in Chapter 1, such inconsistency and lack of quality are primary reflections of poorly operating management. Our negative views of staff may actually be projections of our feelings of inadequacy as managers and supervisors. The PSR is designed to provide a framework for performing critical management functions, including clearly defining performance expectations for staff; monitoring and verifying the extent to which those performance expectations have been met; providing feedback to staff, based on the results of monitoring, so as to improve and maintain staff performance; and staff development and training to ensure that they have the competencies necessary to do what we ask of them.

When these management and supervisory functions are carried out, staff will perform at the highest levels of professionalism expected of them. Such consistent experiences belie our prior views of staff as lazy, unmotivated, and so forth. In fact, we believe that people are attracted to the field of human services because they want to function as helping professionals. This is true even for those in entry-level positions who could, in many cases, earn more working as waitresses or waiters, or even bussing tables. Placing the responsibility of quality assurance squarely on the shoulders of management may help us to be more tolerant of what we have viewed in the past as staff shortcomings. In this same spirit, it makes little sense to berate ourselves for past "sins" of omission or commission. What we can do is have confidence in the PSR system and its usefulness as a tool to help us improve the quality of our services and programs. We can communicate our firm expectation that all members of the team want to do, and will do, the best job possible with the structure and support of the PSR system. This optimistic set of expectations can not only contribute to staff acceptance of the monitoring system, it can also contribute to a new culture of quality and excellence. People will begin to behave as we expect them to behave.

Provide for Staff Commentary

The final means we recommend to increase staff acceptance of the monitoring system is to provide space in the design of the PSR score sheet for staff comments and explanations that they might want to provide for any of the opportunities identified during a regularly sched-uled PSR session. In this space, staff would be asked to record their comments concerning illnesses, behavior crises, poor weather, staff shortages, unexpected visitors, and lack of funds as explanations for identified opportunities. An opportunity is an opportunity, but the staff will feel better when their explanations are acknowledged (Christian & Hannah, 1983); therefore, we take care to do so. Furthermore, these comments can help us to analyze our PSR results and to decide what managerial and supervisory action may need to be taken. This analysis and the subsequent actions are discussed in the following chapter.

To summarize, utilizing the results of monitoring and verification as a basis for provid-ing only positive feedback is an important guideline to follow in order to increase staff acceptance of a monitoring system. Using monitoring results positively is described in three specific and different ways. A second guideline is to arrange for staff participation—first, in the development of an agency's performance standards; second, in the monitoring and verification processes themselves; and third, in deciding which standards require pri-ority attention. Including standards from different job categories on a single PSR, so that no single job category is made visible or vulnerable, is a third important guideline. Additional guidelines include scheduling a period for self-monitoring, giving the staff a chance (if they choose to take it) to prepare for the formal monitoring before it begins; emphasizing the expectations management has of professional staff performance; and treating staff explana-tions with respect by providing a space to record them on the PSR score sheet. In our experi-ence, these are all very useful means to increase staff acceptance of a monitoring system. With these in mind, we now discuss the basic principles to follow in the actual monitoring process.

BASIC PRINCIPLES

Sampling

An agency is likely to develop standards that address, among other things, individualized service plans and objectives. These might include standards for having certain assessments on file and current, or standards for having a minimum number of measurable objectives, both in total and in certain specified domains (e.g., community, vocational, domestic, and recreational). These might also include standards for having the strategies and procedures designed for reaching each objective described in detailed protocols; standards for carrying out scheduled activities, procedures, and strategies; standards for collecting data and carry-ing out certain procedural and interobserver reliability checks; and so forth.

Given so many standards, it would not be practical to review every possible individu-alized service plan each time there is a PSR session, whether weekly or monthly. This would require a "team" of reviewers. A sampling procedure should be used to simplify the review process. For example, in a group home with four to six housemates, we would not recom-mend that each individual's records be examined each time a PSR is performed. Rather, at each review, an individual's name should be selected randomly. This individual's records would then be scrutinized, and the standards would be judged as met or not met against that individual's records. The subsequent PSR "score" would, then, reflect the team's perfor-mance around these specific standards, as they were met for the ISP selected for review.

Furthermore, the individual's name should be placed back in the hopper and be avail-able for drawing at the next PSR session. This makes it possible that the individual's service plan could be selected for 2 (or more) weeks in a row, just by chance, and conversely, that another individual's service plan might not be selected for several weeks in a row. This sampling approach can protect us from any tendency we may have to neglect a person's service plan because we think there is little likelihood that it might be reviewed that week. If the team wants to maximize the PSR score it will be obliged to pay equal attention to every individual's service plan, because there is no way of knowing whose will be scrutinized at the next PSR session to verify the team's performance against those standards that are specific to service plans. Such random sampling makes monitoring efficient and practical and produces the widest possible effect on staff performance and on the improvement of service and service quality.

Regular and Frequent Scheduling

Many agencies have monitoring systems, but monitoring traditionally is done annually, or even quarterly. Our experience is that monitoring should be done frequently and regularly if it is to be an active part of a system to increase staff follow-through. Ideally, perform your PSR review weekly to be most effective, especially at the beginning of the process. This should be continued until PSR scores have reached the 85%–90% level and have remained stable at that level over a period of time. If this is not possible because of limited resources, a formal PSR review should be carried out at least monthly, keeping in mind that verification of individual standards could take place even less frequently, as resource limitations may dictate. Monthly PSR reviews may also be sufficient to maintain a service or program at an 85%–90% level, once that level of quality has been reached.

In the preceding chapter we discussed how a different schedule of verification for individual standards, through direct observation, might vary and relate to the weekly or monthly schedule for carrying out the inclusive PSR. The PSR is based on two different sets of permanent products. The first of these are the permanent products that represent primary sources of information, such as assessment reports, datasheets, instructional protocols, and so forth. The second set of permanent products are those that represent secondary sources of information, such as the recording of the direct observations that have been carried out at other times to verify satisfaction of certain performance standards; for example, files of results of procedural and interobserver reliability checks, the nature of interpersonal interactions, follow-through and performance of scheduled activities, and so forth.

PSR evaluation of permanent records should be done regularly and frequently. The principles of regularity and frequency of monitoring are basic to ensuring the primary purposes of monitoring staff performance, which are to provide the basis for management and supervisory action, to improve and maintain staff performance, and to improve the quality of an agency's services and programs. More frequent monitoring ensures more frequent management action, which results in accelerated quality improvement.

If monitoring were used only to assess the status of a service or program, it might be sufficient to carry out the monitoring process quarterly, semiannually, or annually. However, the active use of monitoring and its results prod us forward to take responsible and timely actions. Regular and frequent monitoring, therefore, represents the second element of the PSR total quality assurance system.

Proactive Scheduling

A third principle of monitoring is to schedule it proactively, not reactively. Traditionally, monitoring is performed in reaction to possible decertification, termination of funding, loss of licensure, or in reaction to a list of deficiencies levied by an external oversight agency. If monitoring is used only to bring performance up to a given level and then is discontinued, performance will deteriorate. For a quality assurance system to maintain high levels of performance, monitoring must be *continuous*.

This point is important because it is common for a system of monitoring to be put in place in reaction to such external threats. Ironically, these reactive monitoring systems typically are a critical component of an agency's corrective plan of action. However, over and over again, once deficiencies have been corrected, and the agency is no longer at risk or faced with an external threat, the monitoring system is discontinued. The agency may have made real progress toward improving its services and programs as part of this corrective plan of action, but with cessation of monitoring, comes cessation of momentum, and all too soon the agency is back to business as usual . . . until the next crisis, when the cycle begins again. An external threat occurs, a plan of corrective action is put into place that includes frequent monitoring to assure that deadlines are met, the inspection is passed, the crisis is averted, things go back to usual, and so on, and so on, and so on.

If we needed evidence of the contribution monitoring could make to a quality assurance system, we would not have to rely on formal research, although such formal research has been reported (e.g., Komaki, 1986). We all have the common experience of repeatedly improving quality through the use of monitoring, only to have performance decrease with the discontinuation of this critical management function. In developing observational categories within which to record supervisory and management behavior, Komaki, Zlotnick, and Jensen (1986) delineated performance monitoring (i.e., collecting performance information) as one of the three primary supervisory functions, and as likely to be necessary for effective supervision and management. Because of both our experience and the research, we integrated proactive monitoring as a central element of the PSR system, along with the principles of regularity and frequency.

Reliability

The fourth important principle of monitoring is that it should produce consistent results, regardless of who does the monitoring. In other words, the results should be reliable. Given that a Periodic Service Review has operationally defined standards, we would expect that different sets of trained people, looking at the same set of documentation, would agree on which standards were being satisfied and which were not. For example, suppose there were two service offices as part of an agency, both of which provided supported employment services to individuals in their respective counties. Suppose further, that based on the most current reviews, service office #1 achieved a PSR score of 87%, and service office #2 achieved a PSR score of 64%. It would be important to know that the team that achieved the 87% score was meeting more standards than the team that achieved the 64% score. We would hope that the team that rated service office #1 higher did not score the performance standards loosely or subjectively. We would also hope that the team that rated service office #2 did not score the performance standards more rigorously. A higher score should indicate better performance and higher quality, not more lenient evaluation.

There are several ways to ensure the reliability of the PSR monitoring tool. The first is to base the monitoring on operationally defined performance standards that follow the formula described in the preceding chapter. The second way is through *consensus monitoring*. That is, at the time of a PSR review, the monitor enlists the help of a supervisor or key staff member to judge whether the criteria for a standard have been met. For example, when it is time to review whether the standard for *graphing* has been met, the group home consultant might say to the supervisor, "Take a look at Fred's graphs. He has asked that we help him keep track of five target behaviors. The graphs for these three were completed yesterday, but it looks as if someone hasn't quite gotten to graphing *silly* behaviors. What do you think? Were the criteria for this one met?" In other words, the monitor and the supervisor should agree that the performance criteria were either met or not met.

A third way to ensure the reliability of our results is through *independent* reliability checks. We have found several ways to conduct these checks. For example, in some group homes, we ask the program supervisor to do weekly or monthly PSR checks themselves. Then we compare the results with those of the consultant. Another strategy is to have the staff or supervisors from one of our other departments (e.g., a visiting team) perform a PSR review for another department. The scoring pattern of the "home team" is compared with the scoring pattern of the "visiting team." A discrepancy analysis would identify which standard(s) might need to be revised to improve overall reliability. We have also found it useful to ask "visitors" and "trainees" to our programs to conduct independent reliability checks. This is a true test of the clarity and explicitness of our performance standards.

If the monitoring system is reliable, we would expect that different people, different teams, and visitors using the same instrument would have similar results. That is, their scores should be in the same "ball park." Differences in ratings from different sources (i.e., lack of reliability), typically indicate a problem with the performance standard itself; that is, the explicitness and clarity of the operational definition. We may need to go back to the drawing board and design more explicit scoring criteria. Differences in ratings may also suggest "drift" on the part of the monitor. That is, the monitor may have changed the criteria for scoring, which are not reflected in the "operational definition." We may need to "retrain" the monitor on the use of existing standards, or modify the standards to bring them in line with new information.

The process of conducting checks to maintain the reliability of the monitoring tool is absolutely necessary if the integrity of the PSR system is to be maintained. We suggest that monthly reliability checks be conducted in the early stages, when the performance standards are first being developed and field tested. Once reliability is of the desired level, checks may be thinned to once a quarter. It may be necessary to conduct more frequent checks when new persons take on the role of monitor.

Validity

A fifth principle of monitoring deals with the validity of the system. For a system to have validity, it must address important, meaningful, and relevant service standards. We can ensure, therefore, the validity of the monitoring system by including both process and product standards that measure the degree to which individual needs are met and desired individual outcomes achieved, and by including standards that address critical administrative and third-party requirements. We can increase the validity of the PSR further by encouraging direct service staff to participate in the development of the performance standards, as well as in other components of the PSR system.

Validity is specific to the services being provided. Standards that are valid and relevant for one service area may or may not be valid and relevant for another. As we discussed in the preceding chapter, the standards that might be adopted by an agency, a program, or service of an agency are likely to reflect the particular individuals being served, resources, philosophy, service design, and other factors specific to that particular program or service.

To the extent that a PSR satisfies the principle of validity, we have some assurance that improvement in the PSR score is a reflection of improvement in the quality of an agency's services and programs. In Chapter 2, we recommend that outcome and process standards be developed from three categories—individual needs and objectives, administrative requirements, and external, third-party requirements. Although administrative and third-party requirements may contribute to the validity of a monitoring system, if they are the primary emphasis of a monitoring system, staff members will see the monitoring system as largely irrelevant and invalid. This may partially explain why monitoring systems developed to meet externally imposed standards rarely endure. In contrast, if staff members participate in developing the standards for the monitoring system, if they are provided guidance and leadership in selecting meaningful outcome and process standards for the individuals being served, and if the standards relating to individualized services are given emphasis in and are the focus of a monitoring system, the key administrative and third-party standards can be accommodated more easily.

Although administrative and third-party standards may increase the validity of a monitoring system, to focus on them might have a negative effect on the perception of validity; that is, staff acceptability of the monitoring system. For this reason, we make an additional recommendation. When developing performance standards for a Periodic Service Review, individual outcome and process standards should be given primary attention. When these person-centered standards are fully developed, attention can be given to the key administrative and externally required standards. This rank order of attention makes particularly good sense when we consider that many administrative and externally imposed requirements have their basis in individual needs.

As an example, let us look at data collection. Many standards around data collection could be included under the rationale of any of the three categories. Data collection, for example, is often required by the management and administration of an agency, and it is almost universally required by external oversight and funding agencies. However, our experience has been that if the interdisciplinary team identifies critical data collection standards that measure important person-centered outcomes (e.g., whether or not certain skills were mastered, behavior problems were resolved, friendships were formed, time was spent in the community, money was earned), and if they identify standards that show that the processes designed to produce those outcomes have been fully carried out (e.g., that daily schedules have been developed and followed, that certain assessments have been performed, that training and behavior support plans have been detailed in protocols for staff training and procedural reliability checks, that procedural and interobserver reliability checks have been carried out), then many, if not most, of the administrative and external requirements concerning data collection will already have been met. In fact, if the team is aggressive in developing good person-centered process and outcome standards, administrative and external requirements typically are exceeded. Accordingly, by first addressing performance standards that are related to individual needs and outcomes, we may preclude the need to include many standards justified exclusively on the basis of administrative or external requirements. As a result, the monitoring system is likely to be viewed as being driven by individual outcomes, leading to its actual validity, as well as to its perceived validity by staff.

The validity of the PSR monitoring system is enhanced each time it is used, because each time it is used it only measures performance against the operationally defined, pre-specified, agreed-upon standards. When we go through the process of developing performance standards with staff, and when we develop and organize the details of the monitoring system, in a sense we make a tacit agreement with the staff to measure our performance *only* against these standards. If we hold to this policy, the staff members are much more likely to view the system as consistent and objective. If, however, at the time of the PSR review, the monitoring team adds new standards because of what is found at the time of the session, or changes the scoring criteria, the system will be viewed as whimsical and subjective. Consequently, validity will be jeopardized. If new standards and criteria are to be added, they should be developed with participation of the staff and with their agreement— as we described above.

Quantification, Summary, and Analysis

The PSR monitoring tool yields results that can be quantified, summarized, and analyzed. These are important and especially useful to management and consultants. At the first level, the PSR system allows each standard to be scored numerically, either in binary fashion (yes/no), or with the number achieved from a total number of possibilities. This method of quantification subsequently lends itself to summarization through a percentage score that is summarized further by placing it on a summary graph. This percentage indicates to management how the agency is doing across a wide range of standards. By placing the score on a summary graph, management also has a clear picture of whether the status or performance level of the agency fits within a pattern of improving or stable quality, or within a pattern of declining or unstable quality. Finally, the PSR can be analyzed to determine which specific standards are being met, as well as those that represent *opportunities* for improvement because they remain unmet. This analysis can include a review of the staff commentary to provide additional insights into why an opportunity may exist.

Sets Occasion for Action

Perhaps one of the most important principles of monitoring is that it should set the occasion and form the basis for management, supervisory, and consultative action. This point was well made by Komaki et al. (1986). In their development of a framework within which to categorize management behaviors, they established three major areas: providing antecedents to staff performance, performance monitoring, and performance feedback. In another study (Komaki, 1986) in which these categories were used, an effort was made to discriminate between effective and ineffective supervisors. The authors concluded that effective supervisors carried out more monitoring than ineffective supervisors, and that such monitoring provided the basis for the performance feedback they provided to their staff. In contrast, ineffective supervisors were found to provide a comparable amount of feedback, but they did not have the information that objective monitoring typically provides in order to make that feedback meaningful; that is, contingent. We must remember that the primary purpose of a monitoring system is not to know about performance for the sake of knowing about performance, but to use this performance information as a basis for management and supervisory action to improve and maintain performance.

SUMMARY

In this chapter we discussed monitoring as the second major element of the Periodic Service Review system. Recognizing the resistance that many people have to monitoring, we first discussed guidelines that, if followed, could increase staff acceptance of the monitoring system. These guidelines include using the results of monitoring to provide positive feedback to staff, involving staff in developing standards and in the monitoring process, addressing all participants of the interdisciplinary team with the monitoring instrument, allowing for a period of self-monitoring, emphasizing the professionalism of direct service staff, and providing for staff comments and explanations as part of the monitoring process.

Having established those guidelines, we then discussed some of the important principles that apply to monitoring systems themselves. These principles included:

1. *Sampling*, which allows the monitoring system to be used frequently and practically and takes advantage of standards that have been selected and organized as representative of response chains and response classes.
2. *Regular and frequent scheduling* of the monitoring process, to maximize the opportunities for informed management and supervisory action.
3. *Proactive scheduling* of monitoring, rather than using monitoring as a reactive strategy to address problems or external threats. The principle of proactive scheduling recog-

nizes that to achieve and maintain high quality, monitoring must be part of an ongoing total quality assurance system.

4. *Reliability*—the monitoring system must be able to produce comparable scores when carried out by different people using the same documentation.
5. *Validity*—the monitoring system monitors the agency against performance standards that are meaningful to its goals and objectives.
6. The monitoring system must lend itself to *quantification, summary, and analysis.*
7. Monitoring *sets the occasion for management and supervisory action.*

· 4 ·

FEEDBACK LOOP

In this chapter, we describe the third major component of our management system—the feedback loop. Initially, we state that feedback should be based on the results of formal monitoring. The principles we discuss include the primary use of visual feedback, and the importance of using positive verbal feedback. We also discuss the importance of taking advantage of the feedback session to provide further clarification and training and to set reasonable and realistic objectives for the immediate future. Following our discussion of these basic principles, we also address corrective actions for those situations where the basic feedback strategies cannot improve performance and quality sufficiently. These corrective actions include continued focus on the system, not on the individual. Although we address focus on the individual performer, such focus is considered to be a special case within the Periodic Service Review (PSR) system. Finally, we discuss the possibility of failure and the necessary administrative actions in the event that a match cannot be produced between what the job requires and what the staff person is able and/or willing to do.

DEFINITION AND RATIONALE

The feedback loop is defined as managerial, supervisory, and consultative action based on performance monitoring. It represents the third element of the PSR system for total quality assurance, following the development of performance standards for the PSR instrument and the use of the instrument as a monitoring tool. The purpose of such management and supervisory action is to improve and maintain staff performance and to maximize the quality of an agency's services and programs. A large body of research literature, as summarized in a number of review articles (Illgen, Fisher, & Taylor, 1979; Kopelman, 1982; Nadler, 1979; Prue & Fairbank, 1981), shows that feedback, that is, information return related to performance (Murrell, 1973), can be used to improve and maintain that performance.

Providing feedback to staff, as monitoring, is another important management function that we avoid because of its past association with punishment. When our supervisor asks, "Could you come into my office at 4:30 this afternoon? There is some feedback I want to give you," few of us would not think that the feedback will be negative. In fact, because we have been taught to precede criticism with a compliment, compliments themselves frequently are conditioned aversive stimuli. When our supervisor begins a conversation with a compliment, we may cringe in anticipation of the scolding we feel is sure to follow. Punitive feedback generally is characteristic in human service and educational settings, as well as in business and industrial settings (Komaki, 1983). This contributes to such ongoing problems as hostility, resistance, absenteeism, high turnover, low morale, and other staff problems.

That punitive feedback results in a range of staff problems is no longer debatable. We need only read the newspaper or review our rates for workers' compensation insurance.

47

Indeed, some of the problems generated by punitive feedback can be horrific, including aggression in the workplace. In our management training seminars, we frequently ask the audience, "How many of you have ever feared physical attack from an employee?" We continue to be surprised by the number of people who respond in the affirmative. Upon reflection, we should not be so surprised. The media bombard us with reports of disgruntled employees who physically attack their supervisors, or fly into a rage and gun down the front office staff, or go on a rampage of mayhem and destruction. In recent years, such incidents have been reported in post offices, public schools, business offices, airplanes, and other settings. For example, statistics reveal that deaths in the workplace due to attacks by disgruntled employees rose steadily from 8 to 25 annually in the years 1978 through 1987, with 32 deaths having occurred within the postal service since 1986 (*USA Today,* May 15, 1993). These tragedies have increased to the point where "750 were slain on the job" in various work settings in the United States in 1992 (Fields, 1993, p. 3A). Most physical attacks by angry employees do not result in death, of course, and it is probably safe to say that most aggression is verbal, not physical. But whether verbal or physical, minor or severe, we believe that the punitive feedback style of most managers is partly responsible for abusive retaliation.

Somewhat less frightening, in contrast, the typical punitive style of management feedback may cause the "passive resistance" we sometimes encounter. There is no question that passive resistance can be a source of great frustration for a supervisor or manager. On the face of things, an employee may seem cooperative and understanding, expressing agreement with what should be done, and perhaps even seeming to share our concerns about a particular situation. However, even given assurances that the task will get done, excuses may continue and the task will remain undone.

Generally, punitive work environments may also explain frequently observed escapist behaviors, including high absenteeism and high turnover. Physical escape may be the least troubling behavior. Often, staff members who come to the job physically may be off to Hawaii or to some other vacation spot mentally. Our punitive feedback may account for low morale in our staffs. The supervisor may feel at a loss here—if monitoring is to set the occasion for action, what should that action be if unmet standards have been identified and if improved performance and quality are the aims? The PSR system incorporates an approach to providing feedback that is designed to avoid the problems that can result from styles and patterns of feedback typically found in the workplace. Accordingly, PSR feedback is designed to minimize aversive control to the greatest extent possible. We discuss a number of important principles in this regard in the following section.

BASIC PRINCIPLES

Visual Feedback

The primary feedback principle incorporated into the PSR system to motivate staff change is to provide that feedback graphically. This is done by presenting and posting the PSR graphs. These become the focus of attention during regular contact meetings between supervisors and their staff. We discuss some of the research on visual feedback as well as some considerations that should be remembered when integrating visual feedback into a total quality assurance system in the following paragraphs.

The effectiveness of visual feedback in changing staff behavior is well documented in the organizational behavior management literature. In one study, Quilitch (1975) investigated strategies for increasing the number of activities provided by staff to residents with developmental disabilities. The first effort to solve this problem was a memo from the executive director restating the policy that, during regular work hours, staff members should not congregate in the staff lounge. To the contrary, they should provide activities to the people they were committed to support. The effect of this memo on staff behavior was nil. The second strategy was to provide additional staff training so that they might have a better appreciation of the positive effects of a rich schedule of activities and how to go about providing this. As in the case of the previous memo, this training produced no observable change in staff behavior. The third strategy was to provide visual feedback on the number of individuals who were observed while engaged in activities daily. The graph of the number of activities observed showed a sharp upward slope. Visual feedback, therefore, was found to be an effective tool for changing staff behavior.

Similarly, Kreitner, Reif, and Morris (1977) found that when visual feedback was provided in a community mental health setting, group therapy sessions more than doubled, individual therapy sessions more than tripled, and daily routine performance more than doubled. Hutchison, Jarman, and Bailey (1980) found that visual feedback increased the number of staff members attending team meetings by 20%, and increased the number of agenda items completed by 30%. Finally, Welsh, Ludwig, Radiken, and Krapfl (1973) concluded that visual feedback of staff's completion of daily behavior modification projects is a simple, convenient, and efficient means to promote training activities in cases where individual improvement is so gradual that such improvement cannot function as a reinforcer.

Many of us work in situations where our efforts may produce very small increments of improvement in the overall skill level of the people we support. With such small incremental improvement, it may be difficult to find reinforcement for our work performance—reinforcement that could encourage work at the highest levels of quality possible. It seems that visual feedback may be the source of reinforcement we need.

In reviewing the above and other research literature on visual feedback, it is clear that research has focused primarily on visual feedback of staff performance in important, but isolated, areas of concern; for example, provision of age-appropriate and functional activities, attending meetings, and the number of therapy sessions. In integrating this research into the PSR system, we have made a critical adaptation. The visual feedback is not provided for staff performance against individual standards; rather, it is provided as a summary indicator, that is, as a percentage score reflecting staff performance across the entire range of standards included on the PSR instrument.

This makes the PSR system very efficient and powerful. If we are interested in improving quality in 50 different areas, for each of which there are operationalized performance standards, we have found it unnecessary to provide a feedback graph for each of the 50 individual standards. A summary indicator—a PSR graph of staff performance across all 50 standards—has effectively improved staff performance on all 50 standards. Moreover, when a new standard is introduced, it has not been necessary to provide visual feedback of staff performance for this new area. It seems to be sufficient simply to add the new standard to the PSR instrument, and to incorporate performance measurement into the summary indicator portrayed in the overall PSR feedback graph. Although we have had success in producing improved performance against a specific standard by incorporating it into the PSR instrument and providing performance feedback as part of the summary indicator, this efficient and powerful use of visual feedback has not yet been demonstrated or verified in a controlled study. Such a study would be worthwhile and would represent a meaningful contribution to the research literature on visual feedback.

Updating and posting PSR graphs for each group home, classroom, or other service unit is a key strategy for motivating staff to follow through with their responsibilities and to perform at the highest levels. Visual feedback quite literally is a graphic arrangement that allows "performance to be seen." To say to staff, "We are performing at a 75% level" does not provide visual feedback. However, to post a graph publicly, where staff can *see* it, and to show on that graph where that 75% performance fits relative to past performance and how it contributes to the quality trend of the agency, does provide visual feedback. Plotting the data point on a graph and putting that graph in a desk drawer, or even posting it on a wall in an administrator's office where staff will never see it, does not provide visual feedback. However, posting such a graph in the classroom or in the group home, where service staff can see it, does provide visual feedback. To be effective as a management strategy to improve staff performance, visual feedback must be posted where staff members can see it.

When providing such weekly, bimonthly, or monthly feedback to the staff, some considerations should be remembered. In a system with more than one service unit, such as a school with several classrooms or a system with several group homes, competition between units should not be encouraged. Our experience has shown us that such competition quickly becomes aversive, by holding the "poor performers" up to public exposure and ridicule. For example, at one point we were contracted as behavioral consultants for an agency operating 10 group homes under its umbrella. As a matter of course, we performed regular PSR evaluations, along with the staff and home manager of each of the homes, and posted the summary PSR graph for each home in that home. However, at a monthly, agency-wide meeting attended by agency management and representatives of each of the group homes, not only did we present a summary graph illustrating the average PSR performance for the entire agency, we also presented summary graphs for each of the individual group homes. Because of the nature of this process, 5 of the 10 group homes were publicly exposed as performing below average, and it follows that each month one home would be exposed as performing below the others in the system.

The staff reacted with justified anger and alarm. In these group homes, we were advocating nonaversive strategies for behavior support plans. However, our own strategies with the group home staff were perceived as unpleasant; that is, aversive. In response, we continued to produce graphs at the group home level and to post them there. At monthly agency-wide meetings, however, we presented only the agency-wide, average, PSR graph. This allowed each group home to compare itself to the mean, but their performances relative to the mean and to the performances of other individual homes were not public. This *noncompetitive,* more *anonymous* approach proved effective in improving staff performance and quality, but with more social validity. The staff felt that this approach was not aversive; therefore, it was more acceptable to them. Interestingly, we discovered that staff from the different group homes often shared their PSR scores with each other, anyway. What seemed to make the difference was who controlled the information and who decided when, with whom, and how to share it.

For these reasons, posting a PSR graph should be limited to the setting or service unit for which the performance was measured (e.g., classroom or group home) with copies submitted to upper management only. Individual service units should be informed of agency performance as a whole, but not of the performance of other units. In large agencies, results of individual service units should be submitted to the agency management. These results could be combined to produce a graph of the average performance for all service units. In this way, an individual service unit can compare its individual performance against the average for the agency, and the system is kept as noncompetitive and anonymous as possible. This is fully in keeping with the characterization of the PSR system as an internal, nonaversive, accountability system. *This is something we are doing for ourselves because we want to do a good job and because we want to provide the highest quality of services to the people we are trying to support.*

While keeping the system noncompetitive and anonymous, a system of interlocking graphs can, at the same time, provide upper management with tremendous access to hard information concerning daily operations at the service delivery level. Such graphs can be summarized by service category, by region, or by other organizational unit. The basic PSR feedback graph should be designed at the *unit of service* level that is as close to service delivery as possible. The individual classroom or group home would represent such a unit of service, as might a single apartment shared by three roommates receiving supported living services, a group of individuals receiving service from a specific job coach in a supported employment agency, or a work crew in a employment enclave. Having produced PSR feedback graphs at this basic level of service provision, management can then summarize performance at a higher level of organizational unit, such as at the school level for classrooms, at the county level for a supported living or supported employment services, and so forth. Summary could then proceed to the next level of organization. For example, in a large agency that provides educational services, supported living services, and supported employment services, a graph could be prepared to summarize the agency's performance for each of its services and then summarized into an agency-wide graph to illustrate its performance across all its services. Figure 4.1 illustrates such an interlocking system of feedback graphs.

In addition to providing staff with visual feedback at these various levels of organization, such a system gives management virtually unparalleled access to performance information. This is of particular importance with the trend toward community-based services. Increasingly, services are not being provided on site, but are being provided in the real world. Center- or facility-based services allow management physical proximity and frequent opportunities to observe and evaluate performance. Staff now increasingly provide services in the field, often without on-site supervision. An interlocking system of PSR graphs can give management very specific and detailed information about performance in each of the agency's services, at every level of the organization, thus allowing for even more focused and productive management action in order to improve performance and quality. It would be easy, for example, to identify which service, county, or primary service unit is performing below 80%, and to give management attention to support this unit in an effort to boost performance.

In conclusion, visual and graphic presentation of performance is the primary principle for providing feedback in the PSR system. Research has demonstrated the effectiveness of

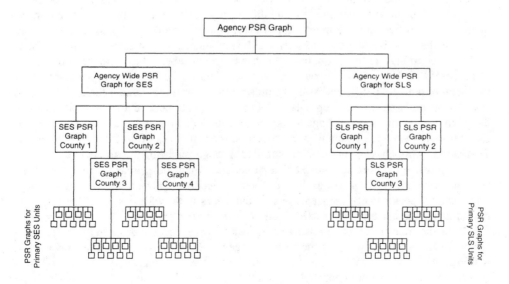

Figure 4.1   Interlocking system of feedback graphs. (PSR = Periodic Service Review, SES = Supported Employment Service, SLS = Supported Living Service.)

visual feedback in improving staff performance across a wide range of performance areas (e.g., Hutchison et al., 1980; Kreitner et al., 1977; Quilitch, 1975; Welsh et al., 1973). In the PSR system, visual feedback is provided in the form of a summary indicator, giving management an efficient tool for producing widespread improvement in the quality of an agency's services and programs. An interlocking system of PSR graphs also gives management detailed information about the day-to-day provision of services and gives it the opportunity to take appropriate action, when necessary, at every level of the organization. It is important that the visual system be managed in an anonymous and noncompetitive way. This will contribute to the positiveness of the system, which is the second principle employed in the feedback loop of the PSR system.

Positive Reinforcement

In addition to providing visual feedback, supervisors and managers should provide verbal feedback. It is imperative that the verbal feedback is positive (Brown et al., 1981; Komaki, 1983). This can be done in several ways. In the preceding chapter, we suggested the exclusive use of positive feedback as one of the guidelines to ensure that staff would not resist the monitoring system. We suggest three ways in which positive feedback can be provided. First, management can emphasize and focus on the visibility the system provides (i.e., the team can *see* where it is on the feedback graph). After the discussion about visual feedback, it is clear that the term "visibility" is used literally. Second, management can make positive statements about the score the team has already achieved and the high standards of performance this score represents. Third, management can be positive by characterizing unmet standards as opportunities for improvement and by portraying the discovery of those opportunities as a good thing. The previous chapter provides a further discussion of these strategies. We suggest that management make a point of using these three forms of verbal feedback during the monitoring and feedback session, and if necessary, training should be provided to the agency's management staff related to the use of the positive feedback strategies.

There are other reasons for being as positive as possible when providing performance feedback to staff besides wanting to avoid the negative side effects associated with punishment. First, positive reinforcement is a powerful motivator in itself. There is every reason to believe that positive feedback to staff will be sufficient, in most cases, to improve staff performance to high levels of quality. This has been our repeated experience with the application of PSR systems in a variety of agencies. Those who believe that punishment, or the threat of punishment, is necessary to motivate change might ponder the fact that there does not seem to be any conceptual or empirical reason to believe a behavior that can be modified through punitive contingency management would not and could not also be modified through contingency management based on the principles of positive reinforcement. That is to say, a behavior that can be modified through punishment can also be modified through positive reinforcement. Extreme situations when the primary principles of the feedback loop, including use of exclusively positive feedback, have not proven sufficient to improve staff performance are treated as special cases in the PSR system. These are discussed under the heading "Corrective Action," later in this chapter.

A further reason for using positive feedback is that it sets an example for staff, and it establishes an atmosphere and a theme for an agency. Over the years, we have been faced with agencies aggressively trying to establish a system of nonaversive behavioral procedures for their behavior support plans, but trying to impose these new standards through punitive management styles with its staff. It simply does not make sense to punish staff for using punishment strategies. There is a very encouraging trend toward the use of nonaversive procedures with those individuals with severe and/or challenging behaviors in addition to having those challenges associated with a developmental disability, mental health problem, or other disorder (e.g., Durand, 1990; Evans & Meyer, 1985; LaVigna & Donnellan, 1986). It is proper and fitting that management treat staff with the same dignity and positive approach that it expects staff to treat the people for whom they provide services. The feedback loop element of the PSR system, accordingly, calls for the fullest application of the principles of positive reinforcement.

Clarification and Training

In addition to the use of visual feedback and positive reinforcement, the PSR system uses the feedback session as an occasion for further clarification and training. There may be many reasons for not meeting certain standards. At one level, staff may not be aware of or understand what it takes to achieve one or several performance standards. Thus, during the feedback session, we take the opportunity to "clarify the criteria." At another level, staff may not have been trained to do what is expected. Thus, staff may be provided with the needed training in a feedback session. Through this additional approach to feedback, we assert that management is willing to claim some ownership for performance problems.

For example, suppose a PSR evaluation discloses that one of the unmet standards has to do with carrying out at least 80% of the scheduled activities as part of the service design for a group home. Suppose further that staff comments indicate they feel constrained by predetermined schedules. They may stress the importance of giving the people they support choices as to what they might want to do. They might feel it is important to be able to take advantage of such an unexpected opportunity as the occasion of a circus coming to town to cancel one night's scheduled activities so that everyone could attend the circus. The group home manager could take this opportunity to clarify and recall for staff that the 80% criterion was selected by the team to allow for exactly this kind of spontaneity. The manager may also provide a review of the choice protocol and describe how individual choices can be documented so as to not be reflected as compromises of, or as taking precedence over, scheduled activities. In fact, scheduled activities can be viewed as default activities, to be engaged in only when no better options exist. The tone the manager should strike here is "Perhaps I have not done as good a job as I could have explaining this. Let me try again." The message to staff should be that the unmet standard was not so much a reflection of their own poor efforts; rather, it was at least partially a function of the manager's failure to provide sufficient information.

Mutual and Realistic Goals

The final principle of the feedback loop during the PSR and feedback session is to set mutual and realistic goals for the coming week, or for whatever period of time precedes the next PSR session. The question to pose is "What opportunities do we want to take advantage of during this coming week?" The facilitator's role here is to help the staff to be realistic about what they can accomplish. It is better for them to establish a modest goal and to succeed than it is for them to be too ambitious and to fail. Small goals accumulate and the feedback graph helps keep the team on track toward the ultimate goal of 85%–90%, or higher, performance.

Examples of standards that might be modest and relatively easy to achieve might be for staff to maintain certain schedules in written form; for staff to enter certain comments into an individual's record, once a shift; or for staff to suggest at least three different community activities to the person each day in an effort to increase the person's time in and enjoyment of the community. In contrast, examples of standards that might be more ambitious and relatively difficult to achieve would be to have every individual's circle of support include at least one person who was neither a relative nor a present or past staff person and to have that person regularly attend circle meetings; to have each individual spend a specified period of time in a socially integrated community activity without staff presence or participation; or, as suggested in the preceding chapter, to design and implement a comprehensive system of ongoing procedural reliability checks.

Involving staff in setting mutual and realistic goals was mentioned in the preceding chapter as a strategy for increasing staff acceptance of the monitoring system. It is typical when selecting an opportunity for improvement, for the team to focus on what they might consider to be the more important opportunities. It is easy for the facilitator to be seduced into this trend. The danger here is that these "important" and more ambitious opportunities may also represent those opportunities that will be the hardest to meet. As a result, the system could begin to bog down, and the PSR graph could begin to plateau. This would be counterproductive. Momentum is one of the keys to the effectiveness of the PSR system. This is more readily accomplished by tackling the easier opportunities on a week-to-week basis. Eventually, all the performance standards will be addressed, in their turn.

If a particular standard is critical because of the effect it might have on health or safety, or if there is another legitimate reason for giving priority attention to a standard that is difficult to achieve, that standard can be treated as a special case. This would involve a variation of the PSR system, in which performance against the "focus" standard is portrayed on a separate graph. Accordingly, this would provide visual feedback to staff regarding their performance against this standard, even as they are receiving feedback against the entire range of standards included on the PSR. As we describe earlier in this chapter, this represents a more direct application of the research on visual feedback that has typically involved narrow areas of staff responsibility. This is opposed to the primary use of visual feedback in the PSR system in which a single indicator is used to provide feedback across a wide range of staff responsibilities.

To summarize, the preceding paragraphs describe the basic principles of the feedback loop; that is, those supervisory and management actions, based on the results of monitoring using the PSR instrument, designed to improve and maintain staff performance and to improve the quality of an agency's services and programs. Specifically, these principles include emphasis on visual feedback, use of exclusively positive verbal feedback, further clarification and training, and setting mutual and realistic goals. A PSR feedback session is designed and structured around these features. We believe that emphasis of the feedback loop on visual feedback, which gives visibility to staff performance and reflects that performance back to the staff, and the motivating effect this has on staff members, works as well as it does because it taps into the most powerful motivator of all—the intrinsic motivator of doing a job well. Positive verbal feedback is designed more to motivate staff to continue to participate in the system, than to motivate change. We think of visual feedback as an intrinsic motivator because it is a reflection of job performance itself; it is inherent to the actual job performance by staff. It simply enhances the motivating potential of that performance by giving it visibility and feeding it back, thereby maximizing the most critical rewards available within an organization (Buhler, 1989). However, extrinsic reinforcers, reinforcers not inherent in merely doing the job, could be incorporated into the PSR system as well. It is to these that we now turn.

EXTRINSIC CONSEQUENCES

It is reasonable to expect that employees will perform at the level at which the organization reinforces them. We believe that the PSR system is a system in which the operative reinforcer is knowledge of a job well done. The *intrinsic* reinforcer of *seeing* how well we are doing seems to be a powerful motivator. How else can the effectiveness of visual feedback to improve staff performance be explained? We emphasize this because, as human service agencies, we often have neither the resources nor the flexibility under our various accountabilities to boards of directors and governmental funding and monitoring agencies, to consider aggressive pay scales related to levels of performance or other extrinsic motivational systems, particularly when there is a significant cost attached. Fortunately, the intrinsic motivators built into the PSR system seem effective in producing improved performance. Should we lament having these constraints? Would the PSR system be strengthened further were it enhanced by extrinsic consequences beyond the positive verbal feedback that has been discussed?

Debate has raged in the field of organizational behavior management over the advantages and disadvantages of pay for performance (Hopkins & Mawhinney, 1992). On the one hand, it has often been taken as an article of operant faith that increased reinforcement for desired performance would produce increased worker productivity and quality. Such confidence in the laws of behavior has been supported by many studies that have demonstrated that pay for performance does increase productivity (Anderson, Crowell, Sucec, Gilligan, & Wikoff, 1983; Dierks, & McNally, 1987; K.M. Evans, Kienast, & Mitchell, 1988; Feeney, Staelin, O'Brien, & Dickinson, 1982; Gaetani, Hoxeng, & Austin, 1985; George & Hopkins, 1989; Johnson & Masotti, 1990; Komaki, Waddell, & Pierce, 1977; Luthans et al., 1986; Nebeker & Neuberger, 1985; Potter, 1989; Snyder & Rourk, 1989; Wilk & Redmon, 1990).

On the other hand, pay for performance has also been criticized for a number of reasons (Rollins, 1988). These criticisms include the charges that tying extrinsic reinforcers to a task diminishes the value and attractiveness, that is, the intrinsic reinforcement value, of that task (Deci & Ryan, 1985; Slater, 1980). Extrinsic reinforcement has also been found to decrease quality and creativity in job performance (Amabile, 1983; Condry, 1977; Deci & Ryan; Koestner, Ryan, Bernieri, & Holt, 1984; Kohn, 1988; McGraw & Cullers, 1979; Slater).

Skaggs, Dickinson, and O'Connor (1992) evaluated the effects of extrinsic rewards on intrinsic motivation. As in the study they were replicating (Mawhinney, Dickinson, & Taylor, 1989), they found that extrinsic rewards did not reduce intrinsic motivation to do a task, *once the extrinsic payoffs were discontinued.* That is, those participating in the study were as intrinsically motivated to perform the experimental tasks after receiving extrinsic rewards as they had been to perform those tasks before receiving extrinsic rewards. Unlike the Mawhinney et al. (1989) study, however, Skaggs et al. found that extrinsic rewards *did decrease the intrinsic motivation to perform a task, as long as the extrinsic payoffs were being provided.* One implication that they discussed for this finding was the importance of carefully defining the standards that would have to be met if extrinsic reinforcers were to be used. For example, if, before receiving extrinsic rewards for doing a task, a person was intrinsically motivated to perform at a certain level of productivity in terms of both rate of production and quality of production, and if an extrinsic reinforcer was provided to motivate a higher rate, that higher rate would be produced, but perhaps at the price of quality, because the intrinsic motivator to produce at a level of quality would have been decreased by the extrinsic motivator being provided for a higher rate of production. This reminds us of the operant rule: What you reinforce is what you get.

This is one reason we urge that the standards developed for a PSR system operationalize not only what, how many, and when things need to be done, but also that the performance standards operationalize the level of quality that must be achieved. For example, one PSR standard might be that a formal behavior assessment report should be done for each person referred to an agency for behavioral services. To meet the rate of productivity requirement, the standard may specify that the report should be completed and in the individual's file within 30 days of referral. To address the quality of the report, the standard may specify further that the report should be reviewed and evaluated by a peer (or supervisor), and that it must score at a level of 85% or better to be acceptable. (See Appendix F for a sample evaluation instrument for scoring a behavior assessment report.) Similarly, it might not be sufficient simply to specify that data must be taken; interobserver reliability checks must be carried out according to a schedule, and reliability indices of 85% or better must be maintained. A final example might be that it is not sufficient for a standard to specify that there must be plans for increasing social and community integration; in addition, those plans must follow certain protocols (see Appendix E). Definitions of standards must incorporate the criteria for quality desired, not only the level of productivity desired.

This concern for incorporating criteria for quality in performance standards applies to outcome measures, as well as to process measures. For example, one performance standard might establish that residents in a group home should spend a certain number of hours per week in the community, as an outcome of its protocols; that is, as an outcome of its process for increasing the social and community integration of its residents. If care is not taken in defining, for example, the kinds, numbers, and variety of settings, the staff might sacrifice the *quality* of community integration for the sake of meeting performance requirements that address the *number* of hours the residents spend in the community.

This concern increases in relation to the extent that the quality assurance system relies on direct pay for performance and other extrinsic motivation. Direct pay for performance may decrease intrinsic motivation and misdirect staff to concentrate only on those areas that have been specified explicitly as criteria for receiving the extrinsic reinforcement. Furthermore, even if areas of quality concern could be incorporated adequately in performance standards, the system would still need to have social validity; that is, it would have to be acceptable to the staff (Reid, Parsons, & Green, 1989b). Our own limited experience with extrinsic payoffs is that, although they may marginally increase performance beyond the levels achievable through such intrinsic reinforcement as visual feedback systems, and although care in operational definitions can prevent the sacrifice of quality for the sake of productivity, staff do not like extrinsic motivators.

For example, at one point in developing the PSR system for our supported employment service, performance bonuses based on a lottery system were provided. Based on performance as measured by the PSR standards, staff received internal lottery tickets. The better their performance, the more lottery tickets they earned. Once every 3 months, the lottery tickets were placed in a big box and a ticket was drawn. The first name drawn earned a $1,000 bonus; the second, a $500 bonus; and then drawings were made for a $100 bonus and several $50 bonuses. The system cost $8,000 a year, which was within the agency's budget. Obviously, the staff were motivated to earn as many lottery tickets as possible. However, the PSR system had already been in place for more than a year, and PSR performance was already at a high level. As a result, the net effect of the extrinsic feedback system seemed to be marginal, as illustrated in Figure 4.2.

The agency might have continued with this bonus/lottery system but for one thing. The staff were very vocal about their dissatisfaction with the system. Consistently and repeatedly they communicated to management that they did not want the bonus system. Some of their concerns could have been addressed by converting the lottery approach to a direct pay for performance approach. However, spreading $8,000 over the eligible number of employees would have given the agency a $25/month bonus budget per employee, per month. It was questionable whether this would have provided sufficient extrinsic motivation to improve performance beyond the levels that had already been achieved. More important, the staff seemed to be saying that the bonus system was demeaning. It suggested to them that the job itself was not important, and they were not considered professional enough to want to do a good job without an extrinsic incentive. Given this lack of social validity, the bonus/

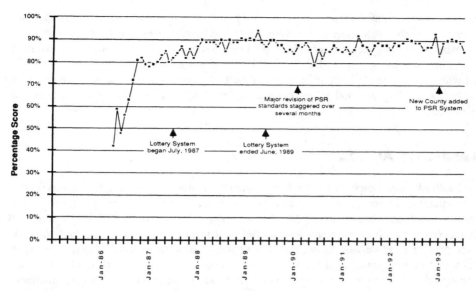

Figure 4.2   Effects of an employee lottery system on PSR performance.

lottery system was terminated. Figure 4.2 suggests that, although there may have been some decrement to performance as a result of terminating these extrinsic motivators, this conclusion is not totally justified because the change coincided with an expansion and revision of PSR standards. When standards are strengthened and expanded, a decrease in PSR scores may occur until performance catches up to the new requirements. This might be the more likely explanation for the slight decrease in observed performance. In any event, performance since then has increased and is now comparable to what it was under the bonus/lottery system. Since the change, annual staff morale surveys disclose high satisfaction with the PSR system. No one has asked for a return to the bonus system.

The power of visual feedback and the other principles of the feedback loop suggest that major expenditures for an extrinsic motivational system are not necessary to get the full effects of the PSR system. Furthermore, the intricacies of pay for performance are fraught with subtleties and nuances that suggest caution for agencies that want to include pay for performance as part of their system. This is an area where future research can provide more direction. If an agency wants to use extrinsic consequences, there are some low-cost strategies that could easily be implemented by management and that may not have some of the drawbacks of the more expensive pay for performance. For example, we might suggest that the director of an agency send a personal letter to individuals on a service team that has performed at the 90% level or better in the PSR system for 3 months in a row, acknowledging and complimenting them for that accomplishment. Additional examples of low-cost reinforcers might include a picture and article in the agency newsletter and award certificates. Although formal research must be carried out, such low-cost reinforcers, as part of a formal PSR system, neither seem to have a potential for decreasing intrinsic motivation, nor causing staff dissatisfaction, as do pay for performance or more expensive extrinsic motivational systems.

Traditionally, we believe that job satisfaction will lead to improved staff performance. As managers, we continually strive to create nurturing, supportive work environments, in order to give staff the greatest job satisfaction possible. We often fall short in both areas. Staff members frequently are dissatisfied with their jobs and their performances fall short of our hopes and expectations. Even when we manage to create job satisfaction, performance may fall below our aspirations. However, contrary to traditional thinking, the data suggest that the converse may be true, that *improved performance leads to good job satisfaction* (Porter & Lawler, 1968). The PSR system described here focuses directly on performance. The experience of agencies that have adopted this system is that the resulting improvement in performance has given staff their high levels of job satisfaction, their staff are satisfied with and take pride in their jobs and in their accomplishments. Rather than good job satisfaction leading to good job performance, good job performance leads to good job satisfaction.

CORRECTIVE ACTION

The feedback loop component of the PSR system is capable of producing high levels of staff performance and improvement in the quality of an agency's services and programs. Occasionally, however, while following the strategies described above, a PSR graph may level off and reach a plateau, or begin to drop before it rises to the 85%–90% level. In these cases, corrective action may be necessary. This section describes examples of the corrective action that may be taken in those special circumstances when the feedback loop has not been effective. These corrective steps use one of two possible strategies. The first involves a continuing focus on the system, whereas the second involves a focus on the individual performer.

Focus on the System

When corrective action is needed to break out of a plateau or a dip in the PSR graph, the strategy of continuing to focus on the system or team level may produce a number of constructive changes that can have a wider effect on service quality than might be accomplished if the corrective action focused only on the individual performer. All too often, we assume that the staff fail to do what has been asked because they are lazy or oppositional. In contrast, it is possible that they lack the structure or resources necessary to do what has been asked. The solution may, therefore, be to change some aspect of the job structure in order to improve performance. For example, in one setting where we were providing consulting services, 12 individuals were being served by 6 staff (a 1:2 ratio of staff to service recipients). When staff were asked for whom they were responsible, each staff member explained that he or she was responsible for "all 12." In other words, they had a cognitive set of a 1:12 ratio. It is not surprising that little was being accomplished and few services were actually being provided. Our suggestion was to "change the structure." Each staff member was assigned two individuals for whom he or she was accountable. This was conveyed in a new "staff assignment schedule," and a change in the job structure. Not only did this change in structure improve performance, the staff also reported relief and greater job satisfaction.

Other examples of increasing structure as a form of "corrective action" include providing more detailed schedules of activities and providing more detailed descriptions or checklists (Bacon, Fulton, & Malott, 1982) of the jobs to be performed (job task analyses). Sneed and Bible (1979), for example, found that giving each staff a "duty card" increased their consistency in carrying out certain responsibilities. If our analysis of PSR results indicated that a plateau or dip was caused by a particular person's not performing certain specific responsibilities, we might solve this specific problem by having that person carry a duty card that provides a reminder of the key responsibilities. However, we might produce even greater improvement if we establish duty cards as standard operating procedure for all staff. As a permanent change in the job structure, every staff member would have a duty card prompting the performance of certain tasks, and the tasks listed on the duty card would be individualized to the staff member as those most likely to be overlooked or skipped over in the press of everyday concerns.

The experience of one agency's use of the PSR system provides another example of changing job structure as an approach to corrective action. This agency, which provides supported employment services, went through a period of expansion during which new people were enrolled and new job coaches were hired. In one of these new groups, beginning PSR scores were at slightly over 50%, and performance gradually began to improve, as expected. However, PSR scores began to level off when the team reached a level of performance slightly over 70%. Analysis of this performance indicated that, among other reasons, one factor contributing to this was that the new job coach was not getting his monthly and quarterly progress reports in on a timely and accurate basis. However, rather than focusing on this person, the decision was made to keep the focus at the systems level. This was done because, although filing accurate reports on a timely basis was a continuing and consistent opportunity for this particular job coach, it was not unusual for others to have this as an opportunity for improvement from time to time.

The agency took advantage of this opportunity by changing the job structure. This was accomplished in a number of ways. First, a new practice was announced whereby "report writing meetings" were scheduled on the first Monday afternoon of each month. At these meetings, management was available to provide technical assistance to the staff. For example, staff members might need help writing up a particularly sensitive mediator issue, or assistance coming up with a new teaching strategy for a skill area in which one of the individuals they served was not showing improvement. Before implementation of these meetings, job coaches had always had access to management when they needed such assistance; however, the time and place were not prescribed. Staff were expected to seek such help whenever they needed it.

Second, the PSR standard was expanded. Where previously, it simply required that monthly and quarterly progress reports include certain information and that they be submitted by the first Monday of the scheduled month, now a new clause was added—". . . or staff will attend that month's report-writing meeting." That is, the PSR standard for report writing required that either the completed report be turned in on time, or that staff attend the report-writing meeting. Previous to these changes, job coaches were paid for a 37½-hour week (i.e., a 7½-hour day). During this time, they only had direct service responsibilities for the people they were supporting for 6 hours each day. That left 1½ hours each day for them to perform their indirect responsibilities (e.g., report writing, job development, training). (In this case, failure to get reports in on time did not seem to be a resource problem. Staff had enough time to meet this responsibility.) However, given that the supported employment services were facility-free and community-based (i.e., there was not a building where staff and their service recipients gathered or were expected to be each day), no requirements had been placed on job coaches as to where they should spend their indirect time. At their option, they could have written their progress reports at home, at the job site, at another community location, or at the agency's administrative offices. This flexibility continued under the new job structure, except that, if the report was not completed and submitted on time, staff members were required to attend a report-writing meeting at the administrative offices.

Staff reaction to this new job structure was interesting. Some management expected staff members to view the new arrangement as aversive. To the contrary, the staff saw the new arrangement as one in which management was finally giving them the support they needed to write their reports. The fact that such assistance had always been available notwithstanding, making it available at a specified time and place made it more visible and ensured that it would be used when needed. Staff behavior fell into one of three patterns. Some job coaches consistently got their completed progress reports in on time, as they always had, and never attended report-writing meetings. Others attended the report-writing meetings from time to time, when they needed technical assistance on one or more parts of the report, and otherwise submitted their progress reports on time. The third group came to the report-writing meeting every month, on a regular basis. It was not that they needed technical assistance so much as they needed this external control that told them when and where they were going to write their reports. The job coach whose performance prompted this change in job structure for everyone fell into this last category. With this change in job structure and other corrective action, PSR performance began once again to rise, eventually reaching 90%–95%. The overall performance of this job coach was such that he was promoted eventually within the agency. There might have been quite a different outcome if his tardiness in submitting progress reports had been dealt with individually and in a traditional manner. In this case, not only was his performance improved, but the performance of other job coaches in meeting this important process standard was also improved.

Beyond changing the job structure, another example of a constructive change would be to revise the staff-training program. This would be the obvious action, if the PSR analysis disclosed that the same standard represented a consistent opportunity for improvement because staff did not actually know how to perform the associated tasks. For example, it may be that a PSR performance standard requires staff to run two social skills instructional sessions each week for the individuals who are supposed to receive this service. The team may discover that, after a period of time, this standard is still not being met and that this continuing opportunity to do better is contributing to a leveling off in PSR performance below the 85% mark. Moreover, this may occur despite the fact that the introductory staff-training program incorporates a number of competency-based instructional objectives in the area of social skills training.

However, examination of the training program and interviews with staff may disclose a number of other things. These discoveries may include findings that staff have difficulty helping the individuals they serve to select the specific social skills they want to learn; difficulty developing role-play scenes that can be used to assess, train, and evaluate their existing skills in an identified area; and difficulty in the actual mechanics of running a formal social skills instructional session. These abilities may not have been specifically taught to the staff. Given these findings, corrective action taken to improve staff performance in this area may include a revised training program that provides a script outline for staff to follow in teaching commonly lacking social skills, including such standardized role-play scenes for each of the skill areas as "saying no" and "complimenting others," and a fidelity checklist for staff to follow that lists and describes the actual mechanics of running a formal social skills training session. These training materials could be used in a training process that includes:

1. Giving staff time to read and review the training material.
2. Giving staff an opportunity to evaluate another staff member carrying out a social skills training session using a fidelity checklist. (See Appendix G for an example of a fidelity checklist that could be used to assess the quality of a social skills training session. It addresses both teaching style, methods and content. Appendix G also provides an example of the curriculum that might be used to teach two skills: how to say "no" and how to ask for help. The fidelity checklist also assesses adherence to this specific content.)
3. Repeated practice using the fidelity checklist to evaluate another staff member, until the evaluation was reliably the same as an experienced rater. This could involve either live or previously taped and evaluated sessions.
4. Giving staff an opportunity to run a social skills training session with feedback from an experienced rater using the fidelity checklist.

5. Repeated practice running a social skills instructional session, with feedback from an experienced rater, until the staff person is able to score 90% or better using the fidelity checklist for three sessions in row.

Such a revision in staff training in the area of social skills instruction would be very likely to have an impact on the standard that calls for such training sessions twice a week. In fact, the PSR system can be used very effectively as a needs assessment instrument to help an agency identify those areas in which it needs to do a better job of training. Those standards that keep turning up as opportunities for improvement may be those areas most in need of additional staff training. Staff training is discussed in more detail in Chapter 5.

In addition to changing the job structure and/or revising or providing additional training, a final example of a constructive change to get out of a PSR slump might follow from the conclusion that a standard cannot be met because insufficient resources exist. This could occur if, in their ambition to deliver the highest quality services possible, staff established a standard beyond the resource capability of the agency. In such an event, two courses of action would be appropriate and in keeping with the spirit of the PSR system. The first would be for the staff to organize a barriers resolution meeting to address the identified resource limitations. The question the team would pose to itself is how additional resources might be obtained so that the performance standard could be retained as a realistic objective. In such a meeting, the ground rule should be that all suggestions for a solution would be welcomed, and no criticism of any of the suggestions allowed. This approach can establish an atmosphere that produces creative brainstorming by staff. Once all the proposed solutions are listed, they can be discussed (but not criticized), and the team can select those ideas it wants to implement. Once again, management may be surprised at how creative and motivated staff can be, and how relieved they may be to know that the responsibility for and the burden of coming up with solutions can be shared.

Alternatively, when the reason for not meeting one or more standards can be attributed to insufficient resources, it would be equally appropriate to revise the standard so that it becomes achievable. For example, there may not be sufficient staff resources to carry out formal procedural reliability checks weekly. Accordingly, the standard may be revised to require such checks on a monthly basis. It is a fundamental principle that a program's performance standards be realistic. In the interest of producing the highest level of quality possible, it is preferable that a standard be calibrated to fall within the realm of the possible, as opposed to eliminating a standard altogether. All other things being equal, an agency that carries out even quarterly procedural reliability checks has a greater chance of producing better individual outcomes than one that does not hold itself accountable for carrying out any procedural reliability checks.

Focus on the Individual

The preceding paragraphs have provided three constructive changes that could be employed to break out of a PSR slump. Constructive changes refer to corrective action at the systems level. Attention is not focused on an individual staff person. Alternatively, instead of taking corrective action at the systems level, management may decide to focus on the individual. This course of action may be based on the analysis and conclusion that the PSR plateau is caused by the performance (or lack thereof) of a particular staff person, and the opportunity to improve is hers or his alone. In such cases, a productive approach, consistent with the principles of the PSR system, would begin with the supervisor developing *individual* performance standards for that person's job. This would be done with participation of that employee and others employed in that position within the agency. An example of such individual performance standards for a behavioral specialist is provided in Appendix H. It provides a checklist allowing behavior specialists and their supervisor to quantify performance against individual performance standards that have been operationally defined. The operational definitions are also provided in Appendix H, and they address performance responsibilities in the areas of administration, clinical practice, consumer and outcome evaluations, specialist training and supervision, and reporting special incidents.

There are similarities in the standards of an overall Periodic Service Review and those of individual performance standards on a job description. The primary difference is that the former include standards for which the team as a whole is responsible, whereas the latter are the responsibility of the individual. The relationship between individual performance standards and service standards as they would appear on a PSR are seen in Appendix I, which illustrates both for a behavior services unit. The first section of Appendix I provides the *PSR score sheet* and operational definitions for the standards of service aspired to by the agency providing this service. Subsequent sections of Appendix I provide the *individual performance standards* and operational definitions for all staff positions in this unit. These include individual performance standards for the *unit manager*; the *unit supervisor*; the *behavior specialist*, who acts as a consultant to other agencies and who is responsible for performing behavioral assessments and developing behavior support plans; and the *intervention specialist*, who is responsible for providing direct services to individuals needing support.

If the individuals who make up a team all carry out their responsibilities, that is, meet their individual performance standards, team performance as measured on the PSR should be high. This raises the question as to why the PSR system is not based on such a series of job descriptions made up of individual performance standards for each member of the interdisciplinary team. In other words, why do we begin by developing a PSR system with service-level performance standards? Why not begin with individual performance standards for staff?

Although the establishment of individual performance standards might seem to be a logical first step, the PSR system is deliberately designed at the service level for two primary reasons. The first is one of practicality. Because the PSR system focuses on the organizational unit, it consumes less time and fewer resources than it would were it to focus on each individual staff member. For example, a small group home may have 15 people assigned to the interdisciplinary team. The recommended minimum frequency for carrying out a PSR review in such a setting is once per month. However, if the PSR system focused on the individual, 15 separate PSR reviews would be required per month. Such a requirement would be impossible to fulfill. The individual approach simply is not practical, regardless of its attractive logic.

The second reason the PSR system is designed at the service level is that this promotes team spirit and the bottom-up quality toward which the PSR system strives. Phrases such as "This is what *we* want to accomplish," "How are *we* doing?", and "What opportunities do *we* want to take advantage of?" would not fit comfortably in a system that focused on the individual. Results obtained with the PSR demonstrate that by focusing on the *team's* performance, individuals are motivated to perform at their highest levels. As we have stated, only rarely in the PSR system does an individual fail to make a satisfactory contribution to the team. Cases when attention needs to be focused on an individual are treated as special, with the first step in the corrective action being development of individual performance standards.

Of course, once individual performance standards have been developed for a position, these can then become the heart of the formal job description for that position, as we illustrated in Appendix I with the individual performance standards for manager, supervisor, behavior specialist, and intervention specialist, which are the staff of a behavior services unit. These can then be used to provide further orientation, training, and guidance for all people serving in that role. As a matter of course, as the need arises, most job descriptions could eventually be converted to the individual performance standard format. Such whole-sale conversions, however, are not necessary to develop and implement the basic PSR system. Once a set of individual performance standards has been developed or is otherwise available because of previous development, the supervisor can proceed with corrective action focused on the individual.

These additional steps of corrective action involve all the recommendations for monitoring and feedback that have been discussed for the program, but now as they would apply to an individual. These steps would include frequent monitoring using the individual performance standards, visual feedback as the primary form of feedback during the monitoring/feedback session, emphasis on positive verbal feedback, and so forth. Following this individual approach, we are attempting to improve that individual's contribution to the whole, just as we have when previously focused on the team.

For example, the PSR scores of a supported living service that provides support for individuals with behavior challenges may level off. Analysis may reveal that one reason for the leveling off is that many of the standards of the behavioral services component (e.g., comprehensive and timely behavior assessment reports, support plans, and quarterly progress reports) are not being met. Further analysis may reveal that the primary responsibility for this may be the performance of one behavior specialist. Consequently, efforts should focus on the identified specialist. The supervisor should sit down with the specialist regularly (ideally weekly, but no less frequently than monthly). They would go through the documentation jointly, judging whether each standard was or was not met. They would calculate the score achieved for that review session, would plot that score on the specialist's individual performance graph, and the supervisor would provide constructive verbal feedback. Feedback should be positive in three deliberate ways: 1) "Isn't it good to see where we are with this?" (being positive about the visibility that the system provides); 2) "There are some high standards here that you are meeting very well." (being positive about those standards that are being met); and 3) "Isn't it nice to see the opportunities for improvement laid out so clearly?" (being positive by characterizing unmet standards as opportunities for improvement and not as deficits, problems, or deficiencies). Further verbal feedback should be provided in the form of additional clarification and training. Finally, the feedback session should end with a question: "Which of these opportunities do you want to take advantage of this coming week?"

The staff member coming into the first meeting probably is aware that his or her performance has not been up to the mark. There may even be some fear that notice is going to be given or that he or she is going to be fired. Given the design of the monitoring and feedback session, however, the usual reaction is one of relief. Frequently, the spontaneous reaction is to offer to fix everything immediately. At this individual level, as at the systems level, the supervisor may have to guide the staff member to keep short-term objectives reasonable. The system works best if improvement is allowed to proceed in small increments, which add up over time to the desired level of high performance. In addition, encouraging an individual to set easily achievable, short-term objectives contributes further to the credibility of the system.

Treating individual staff performance situations as special cases will lead to improvement in individual performance, in most cases. For a surprisingly small number of staff, both the systems-level PSR strategies and the individual performance strategies may not produce the desired outcomes. In the PSR system, this result is conveyed as a continued failure to match the agency's requirements with the individual's interests and abilities. In such cases, administrative action may be necessary. This action may include the reassignment of the individual to a position more within the person's interests and abilities, as documented by the PSR system.

In some instances, administrative action may be necessary to terminate the individual's employment with the agency. At this point, there should be documentation sufficient to support such a step. For example, there should be ample documentation of the lack of match between the job's requirements and the person's performance, and ample documentation of multiple plans of corrective action that the staff person had established as objectives, but which the person had failed to achieve. With this decision made, we suggest that the person be informed in the most supportive way possible. First, the person would probably be well aware that the match simply was not there. By characterizing the reasons for job separation as a failure in match, not as a failure of the person, we can reduce the sense of devastation and of personal failure that many people feel at a time like this.

The fact that a match did not occur is simply that. It is not evidence that the person is a bad person or a failure. This should be conveyed to the person in the most supportive terms possible. In fact, given the detailed PSR documentation that management should have about what the person is able and willing to do on a regular basis, considerable outplacement advice and support might be provided. The reasons for recommending this supportive approach to termination of a staff person's employment is not simply a reflection of a generally positive and humanistic approach to management. It is also good business practice (Solomon, 1983). To the extent that management terminates a person's employment with unnecessary personal attack, it increases the likelihood that that person might retaliate against management in some way. This might be with a wrongful discharge suit or a worker's compensation claim for stress. When such actions are justified, they should be pursued. However, it is possible that such actions, on occasion, are taken in retaliation against an agency and management team whose actions the aggrieved person believes to have been unfair and hurtful. Such actions might be avoided by using a softer approach.

SUMMARY

This chapter describes the feedback loop integrated into the PSR system as a major element. Feedback should be based on the results of formal monitoring. Reliance on the principles of visual feedback and positive verbal feedback is emphasized, as are strategies of taking advantage of the feedback session to provide further clarification and training, and to set reasonable and realistic objectives for the immediate future. Corrective action is also recommended for those situations where the basic strategies of feedback are insufficient to improve performance and to bring the quality of services and programs up to the desired level. These corrective actions include a continued focus on the system or organizational unit level, such as through changing the job structure, by providing different training for staff, or by addressing the adequacy of resources. It is only as a special case that focus on an individual performer is recommended, through application of the principles of the PSR system to the individual. Finally, the possibility of failure to produce a match between what the job requires and what the staff person can or is willing to do is discussed, and the necessary administrative actions, in such an event, are described.

· 5 ·

STAFF TRAINING

Staff training, unlike performance standards, monitoring, and feedback, is recognized as essential to provision of quality services. In this chapter, we discuss systematic training to develop staff competencies at two different levels. First are the general skills the staff need to perform their job responsibilities, and second are the specific skills they need to provide the services agreed to in an individualized service plan. In the "General Skills" section, we discuss the objectives and content of training, how training is conducted, how the results of training are evaluated, training techniques, and procedures for promoting attendance and participation. In the "Specific Skills" section, we introduce you to a simple, but powerful, three-tiered approach that establishes staff competence first at the spoken level, then at the role-playing level, and finally at the in vivo level; that is, where staff can provide the actual service to the individual in the proper manner. At the conclusion of the chapter, we discuss the limitations of training when trying to improve the quality of provided services. We make the point that training is necessary, but not sufficient, to achieve such improvement.

DEFINITION AND RATIONALE

In previous chapters, we have discussed performance standards, performance monitoring, and performance feedback. The fourth and final element of the Periodic Service Review (PSR) system is staff training. Staff training is a necessary element of any human service quality assurance system, which works to maximize staff performance and the agency's quality of services and programs. Training is a necessary component of the PSR system, because entry-level staff often do not have the skills and experience necessary to perform many assigned tasks. We define staff training as instruction to ensure a level of competence among staff that will enable them to perform their responsibilities.

Given this definition, a 1-day workshop, or even a 2-week, preservice training program, organized around a comprehensive list of topics, does not qualify as *training* (Harris, 1980). Such approaches might be characterized better as *awareness* training, wherein staff are exposed to new information, increasing their awareness in these areas. In this form of training, no provision is made to determine or document mastery of a defined set of skills. With our definition, however, in order to qualify as training, the training objectives must be stated in terms of operationalized competencies that are evaluated against a set of specific and objective criteria. This approach to staff training is an element of our PSR system, and it occurs at two different levels. The first involves competency-based, criterion-referenced training designed to give staff those general skills and competencies they need to perform their jobs. The second involves competency-based training designed to teach the specific skills staff members need to carry out a particular individual's service plan. The two different approaches are described in the sections that follow. Human service agencies tend to view training as the solution to the challenge of quality assurance. By including training as a major component of the PSR system, we acknowledge that staff training is necessary to achieve high-quality services and programs. While it is true that it is necessary, it is not sufficient. In the final section of this chapter, some of the limitations of training to contribute to the quality of an agency's services and programs are discussed.

COMPETENCY-BASED, CRITERION-REFERENCED TRAINING: GENERAL SKILLS

The following discussion of general skills training as an element of the PSR system uses as an illustration the competency-based training program developed at the Institute for Applied Behavior Analysis (IABA). Other agencies may choose to approach training in different ways. What is important is that training must play a major role in the total quality assurance system. In our description of the training program that follows, we do not intend to highlight the content as much as the structure and design of general skills training, because these may have greater utility to other agencies. The content will vary as a reflection of an agency's mission, clientele, philosophy, methods, and so forth. Accordingly, the content is described simply as a way to illustrate the overall system of general skills training. This general skills training program is described under five subheadings: objectives of training, how training is conducted, evaluation procedures, training techniques, and procedures for promoting attendance and participation.

Objectives of Training

Our training program is organized around a comprehensive list of topics, as shown in Table 5.1. Undoubtedly these topics are familiar to most professionals in human services, particularly those supporting individuals with a developmental disability. However, the specification of the skills and competencies under each topic area that staff are expected to have as a result of completing the training program may vary from agency to agency. The entire training program encompasses the 16 topic areas in Table 5.1, and it includes 69 skills and competencies. A complete list of these competencies and the 119 separate criteria by which they are evaluated is provided in Appendix J.

Establishing these competencies for staff is the objective of the general skills training program. For example, one competency under the topic *ethical issues* states that staff "*understands that the client has the right to be informed, and should be, of all aspects of treatment, including goals, methods, procedures, and possible benefits and drawbacks associated with the program.*" A second example, under the topic *basic principles of behavior*, says that staff "*is able to describe the three-part contingency of antecedent-behavior-consequence and label each element.*" These and the other competencies listed in Appen-

Table 5.1.   Training topics

1. Orientation	9. Positive reinforcement
2. Administrative requirements	10. Data recording
3. Full inclusion and social role valorization	11. Behavior assessment report and support plan
4. Ethical issues	12. Positive programming
5. Public relations	13. Reducing behavior problems
6. Managing client records	14. Evaluation and troubleshooting
7. Basic principles of behavior	15. Generalization and maintenance
8. Instructional strategies	16. Supported employment

dix J are the instructional objectives of the training program. In other words, the objectives of the training program are that staff will understand that the people being supported have rights, that staff should be able to describe the contingencies of behavior, and so forth.

How Training Is Conducted

We conduct general skills training as a self-instruction program. This avoids the logistical problems that can develop so rapidly in trainer-dependent training programs. Assume, for example, that a training series begins with a new group of staff. What happens if new staff are hired while the original training series is still in progress? Do the new staff join the series midway through the training? If so, would they be able to keep up with the others? If not, what do they do while they wait? Do they get assigned to work with individuals needing support, although they have not been trained? Do they stay off the payroll until another training series begins? Would they be willing to do that? If the training program is competency based and criterion referenced, can trainees with different rates of learning be accommodated? How? These complications multiply each week, as more and more new staff begin—one, two, three, or more at a time.

A self-instruction training system can avoid many of these problems. We have developed a self-instruction training packet for each set of competencies. During training, the trainee works through each packet in turn, in the sequence indicated in the outline of training that each trainee receives. In addition, instead of having a training officer or staff development personnel per se, a proctor, who is either a senior staff person or supervisor, is assigned to each trainee. The proctor orients newly hired staff members to the training program and is available to the trainees to answer any questions and to clarify any points of confusion. Staff members may go to the proctor with either a process or a content question. A process question might be as simple as where to locate the videotape described in the self-instruction packet. A content question might be a request for further clarification of how to apply the principle of "chronological age appropriateness" to scheduling activities for an adult with significant cognitive challenges. The proctor is also responsible for evaluating the trainee against the criteria, and for placing documentation in the trainee's file as each competency is mastered.

Evaluation Procedures

Procedures to evaluate the competency-based training program have been designed on a number of levels. First, each trainee is evaluated to determine whether each of the individual competencies has been mastered. For this purpose, mastery criteria have been developed for each of the competencies, which require that the trainee clearly and objectively demonstrate the applicable skills and/or knowledge. The 119 mastery criteria for each of the competencies are shown in Appendix J. Depending upon the competency being evaluated, these criteria can include passing objective tests at a specified minimum level; identifying or naming certain items or materials; describing certain procedures; filling out certain forms and documents correctly; or responding in certain prespecified ways to pictorial, taped, or written material or vignettes. They also include discriminating those items in a set that exemplify certain principles or concepts; role-playing certain procedures and situations in a way that corresponds to the acceptable protocol; successfully carrying out certain field assignments; given certain material, filing that material in the appropriate place; maintaining accurate records for a specified period of time; and so forth. A competency is considered to have been mastered by the trainee only after all the applicable criteria have been satisfied.

Once the criteria for mastering a competency have been satisfied, the proctor documents progress in the trainee's training record. If a criterion is not mastered, the proctor reviews the material with the trainee. The trainee may also be directed to review parts or all the training material developed for that competency. Finally, on occasion, the proctor may provide some remedial experiences for the trainee, to facilitate acquisition of mastery. These remedial experiences can include additional readings, videotape viewings, field exercises, and activities and tutorial dialogs with the proctor. When the trainee feels ready, the mastery criteria are then reapplied. This process continues until all the criteria are met. When all topics are mastered, the training record, which serves as documentation, is placed in the staff member's personnel file.

In addition to this trainee-by-trainee, competency-by-competency evaluation procedure, the PSR system itself is considered to be an evaluation of the adequacy of training. If the agency demonstrates the ability to achieve and maintain an 85%–90% level of quality, this can be taken as prima facie evidence that, at a molar level, the training program is adequately preparing the staff to perform their responsibilities. At a molecular level, as mentioned in an earlier chapter, individual PSR items can be analyzed and patterns identified that may indicate that the staff may not be adequately prepared in one or more areas. This ongoing evaluation serves as a training needs assessment, and indicates those areas of the training program that may require a revision.

Finally, the evaluation of training includes feedback from trainees about their training. Each trainee is asked to complete a specific evaluation for each topic. In addition, staff members anonymously complete an annual survey in which they are asked how they feel about the quantity and quality of training they received and whether they feel they have learned new skills and methods to help them perform their jobs. Staff members are also asked to suggest areas for improvement. The information gleaned from these surveys is considered, along with the other evaluation data, and these form the basis for revisions of the competency-based, criterion-referenced training program.

Training Techniques

As indicated above, each topic has an associated training packet developed by the IABA staff (Shaull, LaVigna, & Willis, 1992). Each training packet consists of some combination of independent readings, videotapes, and self-directed field exercises and activities. The combination of these experiences is intended to give staff members the skills that are targeted objectives for each instructional module. The independent readings consist of selected sections from such published sources as Cautela and Groden's (1978) book on relaxation training, Donnellan, LaVigna, Negri-Schoultz, and Fassbender's (1988) book on teaching people with challenging behaviors, and Liberman, DeRisi, and Mueser's (1989) book on social skills training. Independent readings also include original material written by agency staff especially for the training program, such as that for the topic on evaluation and trouble-shooting.

Similarly, the videotapes consist of material available from other sources, and material the IABA has produced specifically for use with the training program. Videotapes from other sources, for example, include *Supported Employment: The Right Match*, produced by Holden Lewin Productions for the California State Department of Rehabilitation (1987), and *Regular Lives*, produced by State of the Art, Inc. (1987). These two tapes are among the instructional materials we use in the topic on social role valorization and full inclusion. An example of the videotapes that have been produced by the IABA specifically for the training program is one that demonstrates a number of reactive strategies for safe situational management when dealing with escalating problem behavior. This tape is used in the topic on reducing behavior problems.

Finally, one field activity that may be provided as an instructional experience involves a process in which trainees are directed to spend one half day in the field with a senior staff member. This field activity is designed as part of the topic on managing case records. It is intended to give trainees concrete orientation to a specific job site and the specific individuals receiving services, and to orient them to the case file so that it will make more sense later. By doing this, trainees will be able to relate what they see in the case file to something concrete that they have seen in the field. This is designed to make it more likely that trainees will master the instructional objectives; that is, the competencies that have been established for the topic on managing agency records.

Procedures for Promoting Attendance and Participation

We use a number of procedures to promote attendance and participation. The first of these involves a process standard on the PSR, which defines the time-frame within which a new employee should complete the training program. Staff members are expected to master 7 of the 16 topics in the first week of preservice training; during which time, no other responsibilities are assigned. One additional topic is expected to be mastered for each subsequent 2-week period of employment. Thirteen of the 16 are expected to be mastered within the first 3 months of employment, and all 16 should be mastered within the first 6 months. Progress is tracked as a formal PSR standard, as shown in Appendix C. If staff are on schedule at the time that a PSR is performed, a + is given; if not, an opportunity for improvement is identified. In the same way that the PSR system motivates good staff performance generally, this specific standard contributes to staff motivation to complete the training program. PSR scores cannot be maximized unless staff are trained in a timely manner; therefore, management and staff are motivated to work together to meet this standard.

A second procedure for promoting attendance and participation is to specify the time and place for training to occur. Training should occur during two primary time slots. The first is during the first week of employment, when staff members are not assigned any significant responsibilities beyond participation in the training program. This instruction occurs in the administrative offices, where all the training materials are housed. It is also where the trainee will have predictable access to the assigned proctor. After the first week of employment, when the new staff member has completed training for at least seven topic areas, direct service responsibilities are assigned for 6 hours daily. During the remaining 1.5 hours of their 7.5 hours of paid time per day, trainees are expected to attend to and to participate in the training program to completion. During these indirect hours, such other duties and responsibilities as data summary, preparation of client progress reports, and attending supervisory contact meetings may be assigned. Timely completion of the training program, however, is taken as the priority, as we emphasize by including it as a standard on the Periodic Service Review. As salaried employees, staff members may also choose to work on an instructional unit at home, which is accomplished by simply checking out the unit for home use. Independent study away from work, however, is the employee's option—it is not required by the agency.

A different procedure has been established for part-time and substitute staff members, who are not salaried, but are paid per hour. We have determined the average number of hours to complete an instructional unit based on history. Part-time, hourly staff members are paid for completing an instructional unit, based on the number of hours that have been predetermined for that unit. Completion is confirmed by their ability to demonstrate mastery, based on the criteria established for the instructional unit. These staff members are not paid on the basis of the number of hours they may have actually put in to complete that unit, which could be more or less for any given unit. Their responsibility to complete the training program on this basis is explained at the outset as a condition of employment.

We use a major procedure for full-time employees to motivate attendance and participation in the training program. This requires completion and demonstration of the competencies as a condition for achieving full employment status with the agency. That is, rather than requiring the traditional 3-month probationary period, full employment status— including the employee benefit package—and an initial raise are contingent upon, among other criteria, completion of the competency-based training program. This usually takes from 3 to 6 months. If the process extends much beyond the standard 6-month period, however, it is treated as a special case, and extra management support and guidance are provided.

Ultimately, the most powerful motivator for staff attendance and participation in the training program may be the natural incentives inherent in the situation. Staff members know that within a very brief period of time, they are going to be on their own in the community with individuals who may require significant support, perhaps as soon as 8 days after they begin employment. Given the behavioral and developmental challenges that many of these individuals must face, and given the lack of training and experience that many entry-level staff bring to the job, the thought of being on their own can be quite intimidating. They are naturally motivated to learn all they can in the training program; after all, it was designed specifically to give them the competencies they need to carry out their jobs. A naturally occurring process of negative reinforcement seems to act as a powerful motivator for staff participation. The more they learn, the less anxious they become. This seems to provide further impetus to complete the training program.

The competency-based, criterion-referenced training program, which has been in place at the IABA since 1985, has recently undergone a major revision based on our ongoing evaluation of the system. Moreover, computer technology has allowed us to adapt and individualize the training program for other agencies with ease. This has made it possible for many agencies to start with a stronger training program as an integrated component of their PSR system than they might otherwise have done. However, for those agencies with training programs already in place that may differ in the extent to which the training program is competency-based and criterion-referenced, it probably would not be advisable to invest a lot of time developing a comprehensive training program as an initial step in developing a PSR system.

We suggest this for a number of reasons. First, the PSR system itself serves as a training function, by clearly describing expectations, by supporting procedural protocols and checklists, and by the frequent monitoring and feedback it provides. Second, as we suggested earlier, the PSR system can serve as a needs-assessment tool for further training, identifying through a continuing pattern of opportunities, those areas where more or different training might be beneficial. Third, to delay the implementation of the PSR system while waiting for the completion of a comprehensive training program will delay the initiation of a quality assurance system that can begin to have a positive impact on the services and programs of an agency almost immediately. When the PSR is in place, the training component can always be revised and improved, as, indeed, we expect it would be.

In any event, a training program designed to give staff members the general skills they need to perform their responsibilities is only one of two levels of ongoing training that may be required for a fully realized PSR system. Human service agencies and schools often develop individualized service plans and individualized education programs. Accordingly, each individualized plan dictates a unique set of goals, objectives, methods, and evaluation procedures. The individualized nature of these consumer-based service plans makes it unlikely that the specific staff skills needed for implementation can be taught as part of a general competency-based training program. At best, the general skills-training program prepares staff to learn, among other things, how to provide the specific services in an individualized plan. A system is needed to teach the specific skills that staff members need to provide the specific services to the individual. The PSR process for doing so is described in the following section.

COMPETENCY-BASED, CRITERION-REFERENCED TRAINING: SPECIFIC SKILLS

Once the staff have mastered the key general skills taught through the competency-based training program, our attention is turned to helping them master the skills required to provide specific individual services. The first step in this process is to specify each component of the specific service to be provided in a detailed procedural protocol. With such detailed protocols available, we can then proceed to training in a three-tiered process that establishes competence at three different levels—oral competence (can the trainee describe each step in the protocol?), analog or role-playing competence (can the trainee demonstrate each step in the protocol?) (Adams, Tallon, & Rimell, 1980; Hultman, 1986), and in vivo competence (can the trainee carry out each step in the protocol when actually working with the individual?) (Billingsley, White, & Munson, 1980; Gresham, Gansle, & Noell, 1993). As simple as this three-tiered method of training is, it is surprisingly powerful as a training strategy. After staff have been trained to the in vivo level of competence, ongoing fidelity can be monitored through a regular schedule of procedural reliability checks, to ensure against procedural drift.

To illustrate this system for specific skill training, the following example shows how the process might be applied in a group home or supported employment agency working with people who have challenging behaviors. Both instructional programs and behavior support plans would be operationalized and task analyzed on detailed protocols. An example of such a detailed protocol is shown in Table 5.2. This table is an example of a protocol that describes in detail the differential reinforcement of low rates of behavior (DRL) schedule (Dietz & Repp, 1973). The schedule was designed and offered to "Jim" as part of his service plan to help him control his teasing of housemates. As the protocol indicates, this is one of four strategies that make up Jim's behavior support plan for this particular behavior.

With this protocol as a focus point, training proceeds with the objective of giving the staff oral, analog, and in vivo competence. The first step toward giving the staff oral competence is to give them time to read and review the protocol. After this, the protocol is explained and discussed orally by the consultant or supervisor. This part of the process is important for a number of reasons. First, oral explanations are important for those staff members who may not be as proficient as others with written instruction. Although we use simple language to write protocols, use of some technical language may be unavoidable. Some procedures are sophisticated and subtle, with mere nuances of difference from other procedures that staff may use at other times. Although explicit written protocols are indispensable for documenting the specific details of a procedure, oral explanations and discussions can be invaluable for the staff training process.

Second, the protocol is not developed unilaterally by a supervisor or behavioral consultant. Support plans are based on a thorough assessment process in which the consumer and his or her circle of support, including the staff, are involved fully. During this process, different ideas for support come up and are discussed fully. At the point when the protocol is written, if the process has gone the way it should have, there will already have been an agreement in principle as to which support services to include in the plan. This development process for the service plan is engineered, in part, to give staff ownership over the services they provide. The oral explanation and description of the protocol are encouraged partially to continue to foster staff ownership. The spirit is one of "This is what I think we talked about. Did I get it right?" Of course, it is also important during this phase of training for the author to provide the necessary tutorial, so that staff members gain an appreciation for the technical requirements of the procedure, which might have dictated such elements as, in the DRL example, the criterion for reinforcement, the amount of reinforcement, and so forth.

Table 5.2.   Example of detailed procedural protocol

Behavioral Support Protocol and Checklist #2 (of 4)

Name: Jim
Support Plan Name: DRL (Reduction of Teasing)
Locator: IABA #1A

Target Behavior and Definition:

Teasing: This is defined as mimicking others' behavior, snapping his fingers, clapping his hands behind others, getting into others' belongings, getting too close to peers' or staff members' faces, or annoying others in other ways. Each episode is separated by a 5-minute interval without the behavior.

Data Collection Methods:

1. Record incidents of teasing according to the operational definition above.
    a. Use prepared data frequency sheet on person's clipboard.
    b. Record all incidents that occur throughout the program day.
    c. Record immediately (or as soon as possible) after the behavior occurs.

Data Summary Methods:

1. On a daily basis, transfer to "Data Summary Sheet" incidents of teasing. This will be done by the service staff or supervisor.
2. Tally weekly and monthly, and include average daily rates. This will be done by the house supervisor.
3. Graphing of incidents of teasing will be done by house supervisor.
4. Graphing will be cumulative, abscissa limits are 6 months by days, ordinate limits are 0%–100%.

Procedure:

DRL (Differential Reinforcement of Low Rates of Responding) for teasing.
1. *Intervals.*   This procedure will be performed throughout one daily interval (wake-up to bed).

Changes: _____   Dates: _____

2. *Self-Employed Tangible Monitoring System.*   Set two cups on the counter with three sticks in one cup. Moving a stick from cup 1 to cup 2 will symbolize an incident of teasing to help Jim visualize his behavior.
3. *Reinforcers.*   At the end of each successful interval, Jim will celebrate by relaxing with a soda.
    a. The schedule recycles to the beginning of each day.
    b. Jim has agreed that he will not drink soda at other times.

Changes: _____   Dates: _____

4. *Criterion for Decreasing Number of Responses Required for Reinforcement:*   After 10 out of 13 consecutive days of meeting criterion, the number will be reduced by one until Jim reaches his goal of not teasing others.
5. *Criterion Levels:*   Initial Criterion = 2 per day

Changes: _____   Dates: _____

6. *Target Behavior Occurrences*
    a. Contingent upon teasing, Jim will be reminded to move a stick from cup 1 to cup 2.
    b. This is not a punishment procedure, with an implication of losing rewards. Rather, it should be approached by staff in a neutral manner, "Jim, you have _____ sticks left. Remember that you are trying not to tease other people."

7. *Prompting and Social Reinforcement*
    a. Jim should be reminded often of his program. He should be reminded what his program is for and of what he is trying to do.
    b. Praise Jim throughout the day for his appropriate social interactions with staff and peers.

After the protocol has been fully explained and discussed by the author, the staff supervisor, or other trainer, staff members are invited to ask any questions that they may have about it. At this point, these should be few, because most questions, in all likelihood, would have been asked and answered during the discussion. Nevertheless, this is the time when any remaining questions can be posed. When all the questions have been asked and answered, evaluation of staff members' oral competence can be carried out. This can be done on a private, individual basis, or within the context of a staff meeting; although the evaluation of such competence should be performed for each individual staff person who is going to be responsible for implementing the procedure.

The advantage of evaluating individual oral competence in the context of a large group is that further learning can take place as staff members have the opportunity to observe each other go through the evaluation process. This may be difficult for some initially, because many may feel vulnerable in such a public process. It may be easier to accept such a process after a culture has been fully established that recognizes that the use of protocols and the evaluation of competence is the team's way of holding itself accountable for doing what it wants to do, and what it has committed to provide to the individual. One approach that might facilitate the development and nurturance of this culture and spirit of self-accountability would be to have the staff take turns "testing" each other. In this way, the staff supervisor could act as a backup, to ensure that the protocol is being interpreted correctly and that procedural drift does not occur during this stage of the training process.

The training steps for establishing oral competence described above are summarized in Table 5.3. Although it would be possible, and in some cases even necessary, to develop an individualized evaluation instrument for each procedure, Table 5.4 shows a generic evaluation form that might be sufficient to assess oral competence for the DRL schedule under discussion, and for similar schedules of reinforcement. Development and use of such generic forms can contribute to the ease of a system that might otherwise become burdensome. (Other suggestions for keeping the training system practical and feasible are discussed later in this chapter.)

Once oral competence has been achieved, the individual staff member moves on to establish analog and role-playing competence. As described earlier, in this stage in the training, competence is demonstrated by the staff person's ability to demonstrate the different aspects of the procedure. The straightforward steps followed in this second tier of training are listed in Table 5.5. The staff person is asked to demonstrate, in a role-playing situation, each of the different components of the procedure. Again, performance can be documented on a generic evaluation form. See Table 5.6 for an example. Role-playing practice can continue until the desired level of accuracy is achieved. At that point, the staff person can move on to the next tier of training. Alternatively, if criteria are not achieved within the specified number of trials, corrective action may be taken. This may include more active prompting from the trainer, the opportunity to view a videotape of someone carrying out the procedure, or any other corrective plan that might assist the staff person to achieve analog competence for the procedure.

Table 5.3. Process steps for oral competence

1. Staff read and review each item on the protocol.
2. Entire protocol is explained by the supervisor.
3. Questions answered.
4. Competency test is given.
   a. Staff able to describe each step in the protocol.
   b. Staff must exceed 90% accuracy.
   c. If less than 90%, return to step 1.
   d. If fail _____ times, corrective action taken.

Table 5.4.   Generic evaluation form (checklist) for oral competence

Evaluation Form for Oral Competence

Activity/Skill	Possible Score	Score Obtained
Clearly defines target behavior(s)		
Identifies onset/offset criteria		
Identifies *what* to record		
Identifies *where* to record		
Identifies *types of antecedents* written on ABC recording sheet		
Identifies when to reinforce (intervals)		
Identifies reinforcer to be given		
Identifies how to deliver the reinforcer		
Describes what is to be said at time of reinforcement delivery		
Describes reinforcer exclusivity rule		
Etc.		

Achieving oral and analog competence are the objectives of the first two tiers of specific skill training, respectively. The third and final tier has as its objective in vivo competence. This requires the staff trainee to carry out the actual procedure with the individual receiving support, in a real-life setting. Table 5.7 shows that the training steps for establishing in vivo competence are similar to those for establishing analog competence. Again, performance could be documented on a generic form, as shown in Table 5.6; however, Table 5.8 shows a checklist of key procedural components for the DRL protocol that could be used to document a staff person's competence in carrying out this procedure.

Once the acceptable level of accuracy has been achieved in vivo, training now makes a transition to a system of ongoing procedural reliability checks. Procedural reliability checks would involve periodic observations of staff carrying out the procedure by a peer, supervisor, consultant, or other designated person. During this observation, staff performance should be compared to the requirements listed in such procedural fidelity checklists as that illustrated in Table 5.8. We should emphasize that an ongoing system of procedural reliability checks is not a challenge to staff integrity or intelligence. Rather, in keeping with the spirit and culture that we want to establish and nurture, these checks should give staff members a regular opportunity to recalibrate their work against the procedural standards

Table 5.5.   Process steps for role-playing competence

1. Can demonstrate each step on the protocol when directed to "Show me _____."
2. Must exceed 90% accuracy.
3. If less than 90%, return to practice.
4. If fail _____ times, corrective action taken.

Table 5.6.   Generic evaluation form (checklist) for role-playing competence

Evaluation Form for Role-Playing Competence

Activity/Skill	Possible Score	Score Obtained
Points out or demonstrates target behavior(s)		
Points out or demonstrates onset/offset criteria		
Points out *what* to record when demonstrated		
Shows *where* to record		
Points out and labels *types of antecedents* when they are demonstrated		
Shows when to reinforce (intervals)		
Points out reinforcer to be given		
Demonstrates how to deliver the reinforcer		
Describes what is to be said at time of reinforcement delivery		
Describes reinforcer exclusivity rule		
Etc.		

that they have established, and to protect themselves against procedural drift. Procedural drift is an unavoidable problem that can be protected against only by such a quality assurance mechanism as an ongoing system of reliability checks (Billingsley et al., 1980; Gresham et al., 1993).

The three-tiered method of specific skills training described above is fairly straightforward—it might even be described as simple. It is, nevertheless, a very powerful approach to training staff who are often asked to perform sophisticated and complicated procedures. The procedures we teach staff to implement might involve strategies for teaching people with a wide range of cognitive abilities and disabilities, a variety of domestic, adaptive (self-care), community, recreational, vocational, social, and communication skills. The procedures we teach staff to implement might also involve the use of various sophisticated procedures for behavioral support, including different schedules of reinforcement, antecedent control strategies, active listening, and other reactive strategies.

For example, Appendix K provides a detailed protocol developed to assist and train staff in active listening (Gordon, 1970) to the individuals they serve. Active listening pro-

Table 5.7.   Process steps for in vivo competence

1. Real life
2. Can demonstrate each step in protocol in actual daily performance of activity
3. Must exceed 90% accuracy on procedural reliability
4. If less than 90%, return to practice.
5. After practice, return to step 2 above.
6. If fail _____ times, corrective action taken.

Table 5.8.   Checklist of key procedural components for DRL protocol

Procedural Fidelity Checklist

Name: Jim   Program: DRL   Target Behavior: Teasing

Staff Observed _____   Date _____

1. Staff record teasing behavior immediately.	Yes	No
2. Staff record teasing behavior on correct form.	Yes	No
3. The behavior staff record falls within the correct definition of teasing.	Yes	No
4. Staff record correct number of episodes of teasing according to movement cycle.	Yes	No
5. Staff prompt Jim to the monitoring counter.	Yes	No
6. Contingent upon occurrence of teasing, staff label the behavior for Jim.	Yes	No
7. Staff remind Jim to move one stick from cup 1 to cup 2.	Yes	No
8. Staff remind Jim he has "X" sticks left and that he needs one left to celebrate with a soda.	Yes	No
9. Staff reinforce Jim periodically throughout the day for having appropriate peer relations.	Yes	No
10. At the end of the interval (bedtime), staff prompt Jim to the counter again.	Yes	No
11. Staff show Jim that he has at least one stick left in the cup, and he can celebrate for working to control his teasing.	Yes	No
12. Staff enthusiastically reinforce Jim with praise and enjoy a soda with him.	Yes	No
13. Staff remind Jim of his contract tomorrow.	Yes	No
14. If Jim does not have any sticks left in cup 1, staff show him the empty cup. Staff also encourage him to work harder on not teasing tomorrow.	Yes	No
15. Staff recycle the teasing sticks at the end of the interval.	Yes	No

vides a specific strategy for interacting with a person who is upset, or who may become upset, in such a way that the person calms down or does not escalate and become increasingly upset. The protocol we have developed is an attempt to operationalize Gordon's method. It addresses when to listen actively; how to listen (including general guidelines with ample examples); how to set the stage for active listening (whether at home or in the community); how to avoid what Gordon calls roadblocks to active listening; how to monitor what is happening, in order to determine if the person is calming down or is becoming more upset; the timing for making a transition to another stage of the interaction; when to return to active listening after having made a transition to another stage; the need to set criteria for deciding that active listening is not working to de-escalate the situation (i.e., the need to establish fail criteria); and what to do if fail criteria are met.

If the professional staff did not take the time to task analyze these procedures in the form of detailed protocols and to provide training using the three-tiered approach just described, or in some comparable way, it is unlikely that the agency would be able to meet the quality standards that address procedural fidelity and consistency. Complicated procedures require detailed recipes for "how to do it."

Although this training approach may seem straightforward, many agencies may not feel they have the resources to carry out the training described here. However, there are a number of ways in which this level of training can be made practical and feasible for most agencies. First, we described training in small groups. This process would reduce the resources needed for training large numbers of staff efficiently on an individual basis. Second, although it may take some time initially to write a detailed protocol, such as that illustrated in Table 5.2, it can serve as a template for preparing subsequent detailed protocols. This template might be used to develop other DRL schedules to support other individuals, or it might be used as a shortcut when revising "Jim's" DRL strategy should his teasing begin to abate. In procedural templates, many key elements of the strategy are likely to remain the same. These common elements would need to be written into the protocol only once. As additional applications of the strategy are planned, only those elements that are individualized or that must be added to or removed from the protocol would need to be changed. The protocol for active listening illustrates how much of a protocol for a fairly sophisticated procedure may be generic, and how much may need to be individualized for the service recipient.

It would place an unrealistic burden on resources to develop such detailed protocols from scratch for each procedure in an individualized service plan. However, once they have been developed for a few, the demands on resources lessen because the basic formats can be used as templates for development, revision, addition, and customization of protocols for new individuals. This process becomes simplified through the use of generic procedures that may require no significant revisions to be incorporated into a service plan. An example of this may be found in Appendix G, which provides standardized training modules and a fidelity (i.e., a procedural reliability) checklist for providing social skills training to adults receiving supported living services. If a consumer chooses to learn any of these skills, an instructional approach has already been worked out as a suggested way to begin.

Therefore, although an up-front investment of resources may be needed, an agency's development of detailed procedural protocols need not represent an unrealistic demand on available resources. Furthermore, even the up-front investment that it might take to develop a core set of protocols initially can be spread over a scheduled time period, as available resources might allow. If having protocols for every procedure in a service plan is established as a PSR standard, and if an agency establishes a process whereby it can meet this standard eventually, quality of services to the individual is likely to improve, even as the process unfolds and the standard is pursued. *From the very beginning of the process, as protocols are developed, procedures will have more definition, fidelity, and consistency.*

A second way that the three-tiered approach can be made practical and feasible for agencies is to recognize that it may take some time for the staff to learn the specific elements and nuances of a strategy the first time. However, as they use the same strategy in the context of another, or revised, service plan, it will not take them nearly as long to learn how to do it. For example, it may take some time for a staff person to get to the point of in vivo competence in active listening, as may be called for in service plan #1. It will take less time for that same staff person to achieve that level of competence in active listening, as it may be called for, in service plan #3, and then even less time for plan #4, #5, and so on. This approach to training creates a staff who are increasingly fluent in using those strategies that may be common to different service plans. This reduces the amount of time needed to maintain a three-tiered training system for specific skills.

A final way that the three-tiered system can be made practical and feasible for an agency is to simplify the paperwork system used to track and document staff competence. The documentation system could be daunting, considering the necessity to document each staff person's competence for each procedure for which he or she is responsible for each individual served. Table 5.9 shows a possible control sheet for documenting staff achievements in procedural competence efficiently. Such forms could be devised either by service recipient or by staff, allowing the team to see at a glance those staff people who are trained and available at any given time to be assigned the responsibility for providing certain services to an individual.

LIMITATIONS OF TRAINING

In previous sections of this chapter, a self-instructional, competency-based, criterion-referenced approach to general skills training and a three-tiered approach to specific skills

Table 5.9. Control sheet for documenting staff training

Behavior Support Plan Competency Checklist

Key:
V = Staff correctly verbalize program components
S = Staff correctly role-play program in simulated situations
R = Procedural reliability on program implementation (90% or above)
O = Interobserver reliability on data collection (90% or above)
+ = Meet competency criteria
− = Do not meet competency criteria

		Staff: Date:																		
		V	S	R	O	V	S	R	O	V	S	R	O	V	S	R	O	V	S	R	O
1	Nm																				
	SP																				
2	Nm																				
	SP																				
3	Nm																				
	SP																				
4	Nm																				
	SP																				
5	Nm																				
	SP																				
6	Nm																				
	SP																				
7	Nm																				
	SP																				
8	Nm																				
	SP																				
9	Nm																				
	SP																				
10	Nm																				
	SP																				
11	Nm																				
	SP																				
12	Nm																				
	SP																				
13	Nm																				
	SP																				
14	Nm																				
	SP																				
15	Nm																				
	SP																				
16	Nm																				
	SP																				

Nm, consumer name; SP, support plan.

training are described. Training comparable to these approaches is a basic component of a comprehensive PSR system, and it is the last of the four components of the system. To summarize, the four basic components of a PSR system designed for total quality assurance include performance standards, monitoring, feedback, and training. Often, training may be overemphasized as the solution to quality assurance. All too often, the field of human services focuses on lack of training to explain poor staff performance and on provision of staff training as the solution. Training is necessary, but it is not sufficient to ensure the quality of an agency's services and programs.

For example, it is relevant to note that the approach to training described above was in place for a full 6 months before the PSR system was adapted and implemented for the IABA's supported employment program. Reference back to Figure 1.4 reveals that, after 6 months of operation, the supported employment service was performing at a PSR level of only 43%, despite having had the training program in place. It was not until the entire PSR management system was put in place, including training, that the scores increased up to an 85%–90% level, where they remained.

The general finding in the field is that inservice training, even when used in a comprehensive approach, is extremely ineffective in improving quality (Klaber, 1969). Ayllon and Azrin (1968) had an early insight as to why this limitation may exist. They point out that training could be considered as unconsequated instructions to staff and, as such, would not be expected to exert a significant effect on staff performance. They point out further that such training, if carefully consequated, could be effective in improving staff performance. The PSR system described in this book, among other things, is designed to be such a system of careful consequation. Consider the PSR system in the explicit language of applied behavior analysis. The first component, involving operational definitions, means nothing more than clearly defining our desired target behaviors. Monitoring refers to behavior observation. Feedback refers to consequences designed to increase desirable behavior. Finally, training refers to systematic instruction; that is, positive programming (LaVigna et al., 1989), designed to teach and increase desirable behaviors.

Defining target behaviors, observing behavior, and explicitly designing behavior support plans to affect target behaviors are parts of classical applied behavior analysis. So much so that if the reader has not already posed the question, we might anticipate that at some point a staff member may catch on and ask, "Hey! Wait a minute. Aren't we being treated just like 'clients' here?" In anticipation of this question, it is best to have an answer ready. For example, "You bet! And we shouldn't be doing anything with the individuals we support that we wouldn't be willing to have done with ourselves. Furthermore, it is about time that we had an opportunity to benefit from these powerful strategies. Why should the individuals we serve be the only ones to have this advantage?" Anticipating the question and responding in this way make it possible not only to provide a model for staff as to how the individuals we support do not differ from us, and they should be given the same consideration and respect that we would demand for ourselves, but also to reaffirm the PSR system as a system of self-accountability.

SUMMARY

In this chapter, we address staff training at two different levels. The first involves the general skills that staff need to perform their job responsibilities, and the second involves the specific skills they will need to provide the services agreed to in an individual's service plan. In the general skills section, we discuss the objectives and content of training, how training is conducted, how the results of training are evaluated, the techniques of training, and procedures for promoting attendance and participation. In our discussion of specific training to enable staff members to provide the services described in an individual's service plan, we describe a three-tiered approach that establishes staff competence at the oral level, the role-playing level, and the in vivo level. Finally, we discuss the limitations of training when trying to improve the quality of services provided; that is, we indicate that training is necessary, but insufficient to improve the quality of services an agency provides.

Training is the fourth component of the PSR total quality assurance management system. The four components are performance standards, performance monitoring, the feedback loop, and staff training. In all likelihood, you may have recognized one or more of these elements as part of the management practices you already follow. If so, good, because this means you are ahead of the game. Our experience, however, is that it takes all four components, integrated into a cohesive management system, such as the one we describe, to produce improvement in quality of provided services.

· 6 ·

GETTING STARTED

In this book, we describe a system of total quality assurance for human and educational service settings that consists of four key elements: performance standards, performance monitoring, performance feedback, and staff training. Our experience is that many agencies have one or more of these features in place, incorporating to a greater or lesser extent, the basic principles and procedures we describe. Our experience is, equally, that it is the whole that makes the system work and that use of isolated parts cannot create a productive context for ensuring quality in an agency's services and programs. To the extent that one or more of the components are already in place, the task of developing the full system may involve a simple evolutionary process, with the current element(s) acting as a set of starting points from which to launch further systems development.

For agencies starting from scratch and for those for which the concepts and strategies we describe might represent a revolutionary change in their approach toward quality assurance, the following suggestions provide guidance about getting started. Although you need not consider these to be requirements, they may provide a useful set of guidelines in what otherwise might seem to be an overwhelming task. In this spirit, we suggest the following steps for developing and implementing a Periodic Service Review (PSR) system.

IDENTIFY AND DEFINE SERVICE UNIT

Define the unit of service for which the PSR will be developed. This could be a classroom, a group home, an apartment setting as part of a supported living service, a group of individuals served by a supported employment agency, or any other unit of service that makes sense to your agency's organizational structure and mission.

Develop Draft Standards

Develop a draft of the performance standards you feel represent a major step in the right direction for your agency or the agency to which you provide consultation. It is not necessary to develop an interlocking PSR system throughout the agency as the first step. The point is to get a system established that will continue to evolve and grow, and provide continuing momentum for ongoing improvement in quality. For the same reason, it is also unnecessary to develop an initial Periodic Service Review of a unit of service that includes every possible standard you can imagine. The important thing is to get the system started. Also, to the extent that they may be helpful, do not hesitate to use any of the sample standards provided in the appendices to this book. You need not reinvent the wheel, and to the extent that there may be matches in philosophy, design, and resources, the sample performance standards in the appendices could provide a useful beginning, either as they are written or as they might be revised to match your agency's specific situation more closely. In addition, when developing the draft PSR, ensure that it includes the following features.

Performance Standards for Multiple Job Categories

The PSR should include performance standards that address contributions from more than one job category. The PSR is not a system for focusing on direct service staff; rather, it is a system that recognizes that quality assurance is a team responsibility. This must be reflected by a range of performance standards in the PSR. If any group feels it is singled out for monitoring, there is likely to be resistance to the system. In the spirit of team play and "what's good for the goose is good for the gander," a good strategy is for the person who will act as the facilitator of the PSR to include performance standards that will be his or her personal responsibilities.

Include Process and Outcome Standards

Be certain that both process and outcome standards are included on the PSR. Inclusion of outcome standards keeps the team focused on why your agency is in business, whereas process standards remind everyone that it is the process that will produce desired outcomes. If the process is followed, but the desired outcomes are not being produced, the process must be changed.

MEET WITH STAFF

Plan your staff meeting with an agenda that covers the following items. (Having key staff members read this book might be suggested as an activity to prepare them for the meeting.)

Introduce the Spirit and Framework of PSR

Emphasize the bottom-up qualities of the PSR, its positive nature, its essence as a system of internal and self-accountability, and its organizing qualities. Many people, upon hearing a description of the PSR, may regard it as a lot of additional work. However, when it is understood and used appropriately, it can make everyone's job easier. Rather than being regarded as an additional set of tasks to complete, it should be understood as a system of *organizing* what has to be done. It is a system that can give the staff a sense of control over what needs to be done, in contrast to business as usual, which often leaves staff overwhelmed when faced with all that needs to be done and anxious about what they might overlook in their haste to complete their tasks.

Present the Draft PSR

At the meeting, present the draft PSR as a set of starting points for staff discussion. Be open to the staff's suggestions for changes and revisions—their sense of ownership is important. However, your role as facilitator is essential; this is not a totally laissez faire process. Guidance and leadership are important. Ultimately, the responsibility for developing the PSR quality assurance system and the responsibility for designing a process that is capable of producing the desired outcomes is management's. One approach to providing guidance is to pose the right questions to the staff. For example, if you ask whether the team should take responsibility for providing the services that have been incorporated into an individualized service plan, or whether team members should have the flexibility to provide whatever strikes their fancies, it is likely that the staff will agree that the service plan serves as a contract with the individual who is receiving services, and that the team should regard meeting the terms of that agreement as a serious responsibility. This commitment by staff would then open the way to establishing standards for developing protocols, training, procedural reliability checks, and so forth. The point is if staff members do not consistently provide agreed-upon services to individuals, the failure is not their's, but the failure of the system; hence, it is necessary to change the system.

Similar questions can be posed regarding decision making based on objective information. For example, should the team make decisions that affect individuals based on objective data or based on subjective opinion? The obvious answer to this and similar questions will lead to developing performance standards that contribute to the PSR and over which the staff feels a sense of ownership. The draft PSR itself provides the context for such useful questions as "Which of these standards do you think can contribute to the quality of our services and programs?", "Are there any performance standards here that you think will detract from our quality assurance efforts?", "Which standards do you see here that you think we can improve upon, or which need improvement to be most helpful to us?"

Emphasize the Self-Monitoring Period

Remember to remind the staff that there will be a period of self-monitoring. This will make it easier for the team to develop and stick to a rigorous set of standards. The staff will feel comfortable knowing that they will have an opportunity to improve their performances before the formal monitoring process begins, whether or not they ultimately take advantage of that opportunity.

Stress the Concept of the Team

The PSR must focus on the team, not on the individual or on direct service job categories only. Moreover, both process and outcome performance standards should be included.

Encourage Staff to Review Chapter 2

Reviewing Chapter 2 will ensure that all the principles for developing performance standards are understood and respected.

REVISE THE PSR

Revise the PSR based on staff input, continuing to ensure adherence to all the principles for developing performance standards. It is critical that the staff see that they have influenced the performance standards on the PSR instrument. The bottom-up quality of the system and emphasis on the system as one of self-accountability must be highlighted at every step of the way.

For example, suppose there is a disagreement about the time-frame within which behavioral data should be entered on a data-recording sheet. Professional staff maintain that the standard should be to record data within 5 minutes of resolving an episode, whereas direct service staff maintain that the standard should be to record behavioral data by the end of a shift. Assuming that agreement can be reached for having a standard that requires interobserver reliability checks and that reliability indices be maintained at a level of 85% or better, it may be strategically important for promoting the acceptance of the system and for affirming the bottom-up quality of the system to adopt the end-of-shift standard initially.

This, of course, would be done with the understanding that, for example, if reliability indices of 85% or better could not be maintained, the more rigorous data-recording standard would be adopted as a revision to the process, in an effort to improve the accuracy of data that form the basis of the client-related decisions made. When revising the PSR on the basis of staff input, remember that no one standard is likely to be critical. It is the entire system that must be emphasized and strengthened. The process of improving the system is a continuous one. Improvements can always and should always be made.

DEVELOP PSR MATERIALS

As the first formal PSR is being written, organize a work group with representatives from different job categories, to develop the major forms, logs, journals, datasheets, and other permanent products to be used for documenting and verifying the processes and outcomes of your agency's services and programs. Assign as a chairperson to this committee an individual who is in full support, and is knowledgeable about the PSR system, both in terms of its spirit and its technical requirements.

The development of forms and formats should not be an open-ended task. A period of about 1 month should be sufficient. That is not to say that at the end of that time, all the required permanent product and documentation forms will be developed; rather, that within that time-frame, a critical mass should be developed that will allow for reasonably strong initial implementation of the PSR system. Once again, it is important to remember that you are installing a proactive system. The level of performance initially documented by the system is almost incidental. The important thing is that, with the implementation of the PSR, a system will be in place that will increase the quality of your agency's services and programs. If some documentation forms are not immediately available, they can be developed as the process unfolds.

SCHEDULE SELF-MONITORING

Schedule the self-monitoring period you have described at the orientation meeting. This is everyone's opportunity to prepare for the formal monitoring process. A period of from 1 to 2 months should suffice. At the very least, this period could be used by the facilitator and the forms and documentation committee for further development of the documentation and verification forms that will be the permanent products for regularly scheduled PSR sessions. However, except for specific committee assignments, there may not be much activity. People, being people, will wait for the last minute. This period of self-monitoring is not a primary strategy to produce changes in quality; rather, it is a strategy that contributes to staff acceptance of the system. Again, the system is the focus.

INITIATE MONITORING AND FEEDBACK

Begin formal monitoring and feedback weekly, if possible, but no less frequently than monthly, using all the principles described in this book. The night before the first formal PSR session, it may be a good idea to practice positive oral responses, should the PSR percentage score seem disappointingly low. First, practice being positive about finally having the system in place and about the visibility that it provides to the team about where they are. Second, practice being positive about the standards that are being met, regardless of how many or how few these may be. Finally, practice being positive in characterizing unmet standards as identified opportunities for improving quality, rather than as problems or deficiencies. Remember, your agency cannot improve its quality of services and programs without a system in place that is capable of identifying opportunities for improvement. It is good news when a system does its job, not bad news. Practice the night before may be necessary because of our strong tendency to be negative when faced with evidence of an area needing improvement. Reviewing the chapters on monitoring and feedback may also be helpful last-minute preparations for the first formal PSR session.

REVIEW AND EVALUATE THE PSR

At a minimum, schedule a review of the PSR system after the first month of implementation, after every quarter in the first year of implementation, and at least every year thereafter. These reviews should be based, in part, on formal feedback from staff about what they think works in the system and what they think needs improvement. This is the opportunity to add, revise, or otherwise strengthen the PSR performance standards; to add, revise, or otherwise strengthen documentation and verification materials; to add, revise, or otherwise strengthen staff training; or to make other process or systems changes in order to continue quality improvement.

This is not to say that implementing changes must wait for a formal review. Because monitoring and analysis occur virtually continuously in the PSR system, changes in an effort to improve quality could and might be made at any time. One reason for scheduling formal reviews of the system is to give new staff a clearly defined opportunity to make an impact, so that staff ownership of the system can extend beyond the first generation of staff that participated in its creation.

When significant changes are made, however, it is a good idea to mark these on the PSR graph, because such changes can produce an increase or decrease in PSR scores. For example, the addition of new or more rigorous standards may produce a transitory reduction in PSR scores, until the system raises itself to the 85% or better level. Conversely, a change in process, such as establishing regularly scheduled monthly report-writing meetings, as described in Chapter 4, could produce a permanent increase in PSR scores.

EXPANSION OF PSR SYSTEM

Once established, the system is so powerful and so effective, it should start supporting itself with ongoing expansion and revisions. Be on guard against the danger that upper management might expand this as a top-down system. It will work best if everyone keeps a focus on its bottom-up qualities. Should barriers to the development and implementation of the PSR system arise, organize a barrier-resolution meeting, as discussed in an earlier chapter, and guide the staff in their problem solving and generation of solutions for surmounting such barriers. This system empowers staff and gives them even greater ownership of the system.

This chapter provides some steps to follow in developing a PSR system in a human service or educational setting. There is no magic in the suggested steps, and your agency might very well and very successfully choose to follow a different path. For example, with enough support from staff, it might be possible to develop a wider interlocking system of Periodic Service Reviews throughout your agency at the outset, defining a unit of service in each service category of your agency, and then proceeding accordingly. Whatever the approach, keep your eye on the system; keep it positive; and keep staff involved.

· 7 ·

CONCLUSION

In the preceding chapters, we have presented a management system for human service and educational settings—the Periodic Service Review (PSR). The four major components that make up the system are an organized and integrated set of operationally defined performance standards, performance monitoring, performance feedback, and staff training and development. These components and the rationale for including each of them in a management system were addressed in separate chapters, and they originate from and were explicitly discussed within the framework of organizational behavior management. The PSR system is, however, characterized and continuously referred to as a management system for total quality assurance (TQA). This phrase is used deliberately to highlight the congruence of the system with the Total Quality Management (TQM) movement inspired by Deming (1986).

TQM seems to be generally accepted as—at least a part of—the solution to the recovery of excellence and quality in U.S. products and services. Any agency that has begun the process of change with the goal of improving quality almost certainly has come in contact with the ubiquitous TQM literature and the many management consultants available to assist agencies in their efforts to install a TQM system. In fact, consultant services are probably necessary, because many managers find the principles of TQM difficult to translate into concrete managerial action and operational procedures, especially as they might be extended to human service and educational settings. Our major motivation for writing this book is to share a concrete, easily adaptable management system that could help human services and educational agencies in their efforts to achieve excellence in the quality of the services and programs that they provide. We believe that those who have started this effort within the framework of TQM will find that the PSR system represents the operational application of many of Deming's (1986) 14 points. As such, the PSR system contributes to the momentum toward excellence that an agency has already established; it is not a departure in a different direction. For those agencies not as far along, the PSR–TQA system may offer the opportunity of a strong beginning. In any event, the following provide an analysis of how the PSR system relates to Deming's 14 points, organized around a restatement of each of the points, in turn (Deming, 1986, pp. 23–24).

1. *Create and publish to all employees a statement of the aims and purposes of the company or other organization. The management must demonstrate constantly their commitment to this statement.* The PSR system was developed explicitly to create "constancy of purpose" toward the improvement of an agency's services and programs. This is emphasized in Chapter 3, which covers monitoring. We point out that monitoring, and other components of the system, must be used *proactively*, as an ongoing system for total quality assurance. Furthermore, as described, rather than using the system *reactively*, its proactive give-and-take between the monitoring and feedback functions must be carried out on regular and frequent bases. We point out that, whatever the levels of quality achieved with the

PSR system, if the system is discontinued, there will, in all likelihood, be a corresponding degradation in quality.

In Chapter 2, where we discuss the development of standards for a PSR, we make two suggestions that serve to demonstrate our constant commitment to the aims and purposes of the agency. These involve including outcome standards on the PSR and emphasizing developing PSR standards based on our aims and purposes in providing services to the individuals we support. At the Institute for Applied Behavior Analysis (IABA), these outcome and person-focused service standards act as ever-present reminders of our philosophy, which is written and made available to all of our staff.

> It is the philosophy of IABA that the person who lives with the challenge of a developmental disability is entitled to live his or her life with the full dignity of a developing human being, as a self-reliant and productive member of society. In order to actualize this philosophy, we have as our primary purpose the provision of programs and services that allow people to live or work in environments and with a life-style that is as normal as possible. Specifically, our philosophy is that individuals who receive our services should:
>
> A.   Have life-styles and living situations like individuals without developmental disabilities.
> B.   Have control over their homes. (This control is what distinguishes a home from a facility.)
> C.   Receive support services consistent with the desires and changing needs of the individual. People should not need to change living situations to receive necessary services.
> D.   Make informed choices about where they live and the services they receive.
> E.   Receive appropriate services in natural settings.
> F.   Benefit from supported living services, regardless of the nature or significance of their developmental disability.
>
> Our objectives in actualizing this philosophy are to provide opportunities for consumers to make their own choices and decisions regarding their everyday life; provide opportunities for the consumer to participate in, and contribute to, community life through work, volunteer activities, and community associations; integrate the consumer into community recreational, social, and cultural events and activities; assist the consumer to build natural, informal support networks; plan services *with* rather than *for* the consumer; and design service delivery from the consumer's perspective and emphasize person-centered services.

As we state in preceding chapters, the specific standards included on a PSR should, first and foremost, reflect the philosophy of your agency. By creating and publishing this to all employees, everyone will be able to understand the fundamental principles that underlie the standards included on the PSR, and the PSR will provide a concrete system for expressing management's constant commitment to these aims and purposes.

2.   *Learn the new philosophy, top management and everybody.*   By the new philosophy, Deming (1986) refers to the philosophy of Total Quality Management, with the emphasis on the consumer and the continuing improvement of products and services. He maintains that this new philosophy is needed because we are in a new economic age, requiring Western management to wake up to the challenge, to learn their responsibilities, and to take on the role of leadership for change. As with the aims and purposes of the agency, the PSR can be a vehicle for facilitating top management and everyone learning this new philosophy, as it can be expressed by both outcome and process standards.

We *are* in a new economic age. The dollars available for human services and education seem to shrink daily. The responsibilities of management in human service and educational settings are no less challenging than for those providing services for a profit. Planning must be done for tomorrow, not only for today. There are many examples to illustrate the relevance of this point in the field. One, as mentioned above, is the need to give good value for dollars spent. Although our agencies may not be providing services strictly to make a profit, they do need to operate in the black (i.e., make a profit) in order to continue to provide services. Ultimately, this means meeting the needs of the consumers of our services and producing long-term "customer satisfaction" with the services we provide.

A second example is that management must take responsibility for the continuing improvement of services through recognition and encouragement of new service models and paradigms. An example of these changing models and paradigms is the movement toward the community and the increasing provision of community-integrated services. This movement is being driven by consumer orientation. It reflects the growing awareness that people who are challenged by a developmental disability deserve a good quality of life. They have the best chance to achieve this if they live, work, and play alongside people who are without disabilities and who are not being paid to be with those who have disabilities. This movement has produced some interesting changes. No more than 10 or 15 years ago, for instance, small group homes were seen as the major alternative for people who had previously lived in state institutions. Today, however, group homes are considered passé. The supported living service model now is seen as more capable of meeting consumer needs and having the potential of providing a better quality of life. In the meantime, some agencies are still wedded to the institutional model, and some are *just getting into* the group home model, not realizing that the train has already left that station. Management must assume the responsibility and leadership roles in recognizing that new opportunities for improving services must be sought and embraced actively. What is state-of-the-art today may seem primitive tomorrow. Primitive services will not survive in the new economic age, except as relics of the past.

Much the same can be said for educational systems. What was accepted as a good curriculum 10 years ago no longer has educational validity (Falvey, 1989). The relevance of the PSR system to Point 2 is both direct and indirect. Its direct relevance is its use as a tool for change. The implementation of a new service or program for an agency can be facilitated through the PSR system. This can keep the agency nimble and capable of redefining its service standards, not only in terms of the process—which is the main thrust of Point 2— but also through a continuing evolution of its outcome standards.

The standards incorporated into a Periodic Service Review can also represent an indirect application of the PSR system to Point 2, in the sense that this book does not make specific recommendations as to which standards should be included on an agency's Periodic Service Review. In fact, the point has been made that PSR standards should reflect, among other things, the agency's own design, philosophy and mission, clientele, and resources. We hope and expect that an agency would include standards that support Point 2, such as standards that would call for regular surveys of consumer satisfaction (both direct consumers, i.e., those individuals receiving support services; and indirect consumers, e.g., parents, case managers, employers, and neighbors), and standards that would call for maintaining certain levels of satisfaction. It is conceivable, however, that an agency would include standards that conflict with Point 2, such as a standard calling for the maintenance of the current number of residents in a large congregate living arrangement. Such a standard may be in conflict, for example, with the responsibility of management to assume the leadership toward change.

The PSR–TQA system has both direct and indirect congruence with Point 2. However, full realization of Point 2 would go well beyond the system. It would have an impact on the very philosophy and mission of the agency and *all* its related policies and procedures.

3. *Understand the purpose of inspection, for improvement of processes and reduction of cost.* This is exactly the purpose of monitoring in the PSR–TQA system, to improve processes and the ability of those processes to produce a quality service in the most cost-effective way. Furthermore, with the PSR, there is a heavy emphasis on process standards, which are an outright attempt to build quality into the service in the first place. If outcomes are not being achieved, consumers are not satisfied, and their quality of life is not improved, this would be seen not as the fault of staff, but rather as an identified need— specifically, a need to improve the process. Also, rather than being based on mass inspec-

tion, the system requires monitoring on a sampling basis, explicitly using inspection as a basis to determine whether processes are being carried out as designed and whether they are producing the quality of service intended. By very carefully specifying process, the PSR allows an examination of cost-effectiveness and the testing of alternative processes that may produce the same or improved quality in a more cost-effective manner.

4.   *End the practice of awarding business on the basis of price tag.*   In other words, if we decide between service providers strictly on the basis of which is least costly at the moment, in the long run it may prove to be a more expensive way of doing business with many needs going unmet and problems remaining unresolved. For example, an agency may need to purchase services from a behavioral consultant to carry out an assessment on behalf of a person and to make recommendations on how the agency might better support that person. In our experience, it is almost certain that a consultant who can carry out an assessment and recommend a support plan that satisfies the criteria in Appendix F will be more expensive than a consultant who takes a less thorough approach. However, it is also our experience that the more thorough approach is more likely to lead to more rapid and better outcomes.

There are a number of ways that these "better outcomes" may result in lower total costs:

a.   With quality services, it may be possible to reduce reliance of the person on paid supports and to foster greater reliance on natural supports, for example, support provided by a coworker instead of a paid job coach in a supported employment agency, or support provided by a neighbor instead of a "community training specialist" in a supported living agency.

b.   With quality services, the necessity to physically manage people because of their behavior is nearly eliminated, thus producing a dramatic decrease in staff injuries and associated worker's compensation claims. At IABA in 1993, for example, our work has supported approximately 300 individuals, many if not all of whom have histories of behavior that have made themselves and others vulnerable, and only one worker's compensation claim was made due to an injury resulting from a behavioral incident involving one of the people for whom we provide support services. This exceptional record has led to a decrease in our agency's worker's compensation insurance premiums.

c.   The PSR is a proven total quality system for increasing an agency's ability to carry out its processes. In previous chapters, we have shown that this improvement has increased from initial PSR scores of 30%–40% up to 85%–90% and better. This means that productivity and quality have both been increased without an increase in costs, that is, the total cost per service outcome unit has been decreased.

In fact, while we may invest a lot at IABA in our provision of high-quality support services, we find that our total costs are less than other agencies supporting people who share some similar characteristics. Hence, we find ourselves fortunate in having long-term relationships with many of our funding agencies. We put a high premium on the loyalty and trust that exists between us.

5.   *Improve constantly and forever the system of production and service.*   The PSR system is meant to be a permanent, proactive system, leading to constant improvement of services and programs through an active process of systems change and corrective action, based on both the ongoing analysis of monitoring results and a periodic, reflective critique of the system by all staff, on at least an annual basis. Rather than reliance on a static set of standards, both ongoing analysis and periodic reviews/evaluations are designed to create a dynamic and evolving set of standards that will continually improve the services and programs of the agency.

6. *Institute training*.   A major component of the PSR system is the provision of training to staff on the job. This gives them both the general skills they need to perform their jobs and the skills they need to provide agreed-upon services to specific individuals. (This component is discussed in detail in Chapter 5.)

7. *Teach and institute leadership*.   We suggest that the design and implementation of a PSR system networked throughout an agency represents a major step in the overhaul of management and supervision, in the spirit intended under this point. According to Deming (1986), the aim of supervision should be to help people do a better job. The PSR is designed as a tool to help supervisors and managers do just this.

Summary and interlocking Periodic Service Reviews, as described in Chapter 4, and management-level Periodic Service Reviews represent an overhaul of the supervision of management, as well as of the supervision of direct service staff, when used in a fully implemented PSR–TQA system. We believe that a hierarchy of interlocking PSRs and management-level PSRs give upper management an unprecedented level of awareness about what is happening (or not happening) throughout the agency, even one that provides its services in widely dispersed community locations.

Appendix L is an example of a management-level Periodic Service Review for the management team of our supported employment service. Through this PSR, the management staff are held accountable for certain well-defined responsibilities in the areas of staff training and supervision; the management of employment sites; oversight of the services provided to our clients; public relations; troubleshooting; data management and reporting; and process, outcome, and third-party evaluations. These at least begin to define the leadership role that we want our supervisors and managers to learn and to institute, as does their implementation of the PSR–TQA system generally, as we describe in this book.

8. *Drive out fear. Create trust. Create a climate for innovation*.   Deming believes that this is important for everyone to work most effectively for the agency. There are a number of ways that the PSR system is engineered to drive out fear. These are explicitly discussed in Chapter 3 as guidelines for increasing staff acceptance, that is, decreasing staff fear, of the monitoring system. These guidelines include, among other things, reliance on positive feedback only; actively involving staff in developing performance standards, in the monitoring process itself, and in deciding which opportunities for improving quality they wanted to address; and keeping the PSR focused on team performance, rather than individual performance or the performance of any one job category. Finally, the emphasis, characterization, and utilization of the PSR as one of self-accountability, rather than as one of oversight by the powers that be, also helps avoid fear and resistance. As an agency, we strive to develop all our services, staff systems, and procedures to be as free of aversive control as possible. This is the best way we know to "drive out fear, create trust, and create a climate for innovation."

9. *Optimize toward the aims and purposes of the company the efforts of teams, groups, staff areas*.   Deming (1986) believes that it is critical to remove the barriers that exist between different departments or staff groups, such as the barriers that may exist between supported living staff and supported employment staff, between "professional" staff and direct service staff, between management staff and support staff. As we describe, the emphasis of the PSR system is the team. Little emphasis is placed on the individual performer. When we identify performance or quality improvement opportunities, we approach them as a systems challenge. Accordingly, we then attempt to improve the system. We place a focus on the individual performer only as a special case. The construction of the PSR as an instrument that focuses on the team and the team feedback that is provided through the PSR summary graph help break down the barriers that may exist between departments and/or between different groups of staff.

10.   *Eliminate exhortations for the work force.*   The premise underlying the PSR system is that poor performance, either in productivity or service quality, is a function of the system in place and is not a function of the individual staff performer or any particular category of staff. Hence, we are in agreement with Deming in thinking it would be counterproductive to admonish staff to improve something that is largely outside their control. Unfortunately, we have observed that such negative management styles are characteristic of many human services and educational agencies, thus contributing to the adversarial relationships between staff. The PSR–TQA approach is designed as a primary strategy for the purpose of producing an improvement in services and programs. Again, it is relevant to note that individual performance is a focus as a special case only. When using the PSR approach, we rely on the system and changes to the system as the most direct and effective way to improve quality. Exhortations to staff have no proper role in the PSR system.

11a.   *Eliminate numerical quotas for production. Instead, learn and institute methods of improvement.*   We have written this book because our experience has told us that the PSR–TQA system represents, in and of itself, a very powerful method of improvement for both productivity and quality, and one that can be learned and instituted by managers in both human services and education. In designing and implementing the PSR–TQA system, leadership provided by management and supervision should include facilitation and guidance. This is accomplished through modeling a positive attitude and by reacting to unmet standards as opportunities to examine and improve the system and not as a reflection of the lack of integrity, intelligence, or intent of the individual performer, nor as an occasion to punish staff. Productivity is not improved through the setting of work quotas for service staff but rather through an ongoing examination and improvement of process, with leadership by management and supervision.

Setting standards for process and outcomes, in terms of productivity and quality, is not the same as setting quotas. Setting quotas would involve top down production goals imposed by upper management on staff, with implied threats or actual aversive consequences if the goals are not met. In contrast, in the PSR system, productivity and quality goals (process and outcome standards) are developed and agreed upon by staff, in a process facilitated by management; inspection (i.e., monitoring) is carried out and made visible (through feedback) to determine whether the agreed-upon standards are being met, and training is provided to staff to give them the competencies they need to carry out the process. That is, setting standards, monitoring, providing (visible and positive) feedback, and training are the primary methods integrated into the PSR system for improving productivity and quality. In addition, the process standards included on the PSR are continuously evaluated for how they may be changed to improve productivity and quality.

11b.   *Eliminate M.B.O. Instead, learn the capabilities of processes, and how to improve them.*   Management by Objective (MBO) is to management and supervision what numerical quotas are to production and service staff. As such, the discussion under 11a above applies here as well. Deming's (1986) suggestions to eliminate management by numerical goals only appear to be in conflict with the quantified standards that form the starting point of the PSR system on the surface, since a more thorough understanding of TQM leads to an appreciation of the emphasis Deming places on Statistical Process Control (Deming, 1975; Deming, 1986). Deming is not opposed to quantification, monitoring, and feedback per se; in fact, his approach to managing for quality requires it. Deming calls for leadership from managers and supervisors and challenges us to take on the responsibility for examining process and changing the system to improve outcomes, as opposed to setting quotas and objectives and exhorting staff to meet these goals.

Deming also appears to be opposing the emphasis on productivity (i.e., quantity) in most management by objective systems, at the cost of quality. The issue of integrating both quantity elements and quality elements into the operational definitions of both process and outcome standards was recognized as an important issue for a PSR–TQA system as discussed in Chapter 4. In taking on their leadership responsibilities, management needs to assure that the standards incorporated on a Periodic Service Review reflect process and outcome—and quantity and quality.

Upper management can also take a leadership role by participating in the PSR system directly, not only by sharing responsibility for some of the process and outcome standards on the PSR but, when appropriate, by developing a management-level PSR. By sharing with their staff the content and the feedback produced from a management PSR, the management can communicate very clearly to staff that it is aware of its personal responsibilities for the quality of the agency's services and programs. This can contribute positively to the team spirit of the agency and to good staff morale.

12. *Remove barriers that rob people of pride of workmanship.* As described above, the responsibility of all staff should be changed from sheer numbers to quality. The comments immediately above also apply here. In addition, a PSR–TQA system is designed and implemented in such a way as to cultivate the ownership of staff over what they do. The emphasis is on the bottom-up qualities of the system, full staff participation, and expectations of staff professionalism. (See Chapter 3, in particular, for suggestions to ensure staff acceptance and ownership of the system.)

In addition to the comments made under Points 11a and 11b, the PSR is sensitive to this issue of intrinsic reinforcement, as we discuss in Chapter 4. The intricacies of direct pay for performance were discussed in the spirit of Point 12. Our experience is that the visibility provided by the PSR system gives both staff and management a tremendous feeling of pride in the quality of services they provide. These feelings are enhanced ultimately by the impact that the agency's services and programs have on individuals and on their quality of life. It is also reinforcing to receive the occasional external compliment (e.g., Dalton, 1992).

13. *Encourage education and self-improvement for everyone.* The PSR emphasizes training, as we discuss under Point 6. What we mean here is an emphasis on ongoing training and education. This has not been addressed explicitly as a part of the PSR system, but there is no inconsistency between the PSR system and this point. In fact, the PSR system could easily be used to promote this by incorporating a standard that states that the agency maintains vigorous programs of education and self-improvement. These programs might have a number of features. For example, they might, among other things, provide tuition reimbursement as an employee benefit; they might maintain a policy of flexible work hours to enable staff members to continue formal education while working full time; they might provide special recognition to employees who contribute new ideas that are implemented by the agency to improve the quality of its services and programs; they might invite each employee to establish a self-improvement goal, and provide special recognition for accomplishing that goal; they might organize a Journal Club, wherein members of a study group research topics of their own choosing, in order to help solve certain challenges that have been identified by the group; and so forth.

As we suggest, any of these ideas, and others like them, could be supported and promoted by way of a standard on the Periodic Service Review. Certainly, there is nothing about the PSR that is inconsistent with a vigorous program of education and self-improvement. In fact, the suggestion that unmet standards be characterized as opportunities further enhances the spirit of learning that pervades the PSR system.

14. *Take action to accomplish the transformation.* In Chapter 6 we recommend a specific set of action steps with which you can accomplish the transformation and adopt the PSR–TQA system. You may want to consider a different approach, but the PSR system

lends itself to concrete action steps to improve the quality of the services your agency provides.

Based on the above analysis, the Periodic Service Review–Total Quality Assurance system seems to be congruent with Deming's (1986) 14 points and the Total Quality Management movement inspired by his contributions to the field of management. More important, the PSR–TQA system may give managers in the field of human services and education a concrete tool for implementing many TQM principles. It is our hope that this book provides such a concrete, adaptable, and usable tool for the field.

PSR–TQA provides a system within which an agency can strive for and achieve quality, even given the rapid turnover rate that most community-based service providers face. We hope you will be sufficiently motivated to implement a PSR–TQA system, either to begin or to continue your agency's efforts toward a system of total quality assurance. We are confident that once begun, the inherent reinforcer of continuously improving quality will be more than sufficient to maintain and further your effort.

We look forward to hearing from you about your successes.

· REFERENCES ·

Adams, G.L., Tallon, R.J., & Rimell, P. (1980). A comparison of lecture versus role-playing in the training of the use of positive reinforcement. *Journal of Organizational Behavior Management, 2*(3), 205–211.

Albin, J.M. (1992). *Quality improvement in employment and other human services: Managing for quality through change.* Baltimore: Paul H. Brookes Publishing Co.

Allyn, T., & Azrin, N. (1968). *The token economy: A motivational system for therapy and rehabilitation.* New York: Appleton-Century-Crofts.

Amabile, T.M. (1983). *The social psychology of creativity.* New York: Springer-Verlag.

Anderson, D.C., Crowell, C.R., Sponsel, S.S., Clarke, M., & Brence, J. (1983). Behavior management in the public accommodations industry: A three-project demonstration. *Journal of Organizational Behavior Management, 4*(1/2), 33–66.

Anderson, D.C., Crowell, C.R., Sucec, J., Gilligan, K.D., & Wikoff, M. (1983). Behavior management of client contacts in a real estate brokerage: Getting agents to sell more. *Journal of Organizational Behavior Management, 4*(1/2), 67–95.

Bacon, D.L., Fulton, B.J., & Malott, R.W. (1983). Improving staff performance through the use of task checklists. *Journal of Organizational Behavior Management, 4*(3/4), 17–25.

Billingsley, F.F., White, D.R., & Munson, R. (1980). Procedural reliability: A rationale and an example. *Behavioral Assessment, 2*(3), 247–256.

Braddock, D., & Mitchell, D. (1992). *Residential services and developmental disabilities in the United States: A national survey of staff compensation, turnover, and related issues.* Washington, DC: American Association on Mental Retardation.

Brethower, D.M. (1982). Linking two trends in management: Comments on Professor Kreitner's paper. *Journal of Organizational Behavior Management, 3*(3), 21–31.

Brown, K.M., Willis, B.S., & Reid, D.H. (1981). Differential effects of supervisor verbal feedback and feedback plus approval on institutional staff performance. *Journal of Organizational Behavior Management, 3*(1), 57–68.

Buhler, P. (1989). Rewards in the organization. *Supervision, 50*, 5–7.

Burg, M.M., Reid, D.H., & Lattimore, J. (1979). Use of a self-recording and supervision program to change institutional staff behavior. *Journal of Applied Behavior Analysis, 12*, 363–375.

Cautela, J.R., & Groden, J. (1978). *Relaxation: A comprehensive manual for adults, children, and children with special needs.* Champaign, IL: Research Press.

Cayer, M., Dumattia, D.J., & Wingrove, J. (1988). Conquering evaluation fear. *H R Magazine, 33*, 97–107.

Christian, W.P., & Hannah, G.T. (1983). *Effective management in human services.* Englewood Cliffs, NJ: Prentice Hall.

Christian, W.P., & Reitz, A.L. (1986). Administration. In F.J. Fuoco & W.P Christian (Eds.), *Behavior analysis and therapy in residential programs* (pp. 22–49). New York: Van Nostrand Reinhold Company, Inc.

Christian, W.P., & Romanczyk, R.G. (1986). Evaluation. In F.J. Fuoco & W.P Christian (Eds.), *Behavior analysis and therapy in residential programs* (pp. 145–193). New York: Van Nostrand Reinhold Company, Inc.

Commission on Accreditation of Rehabilitation Facilities. (1992). *Standards manual for organizations serving people with disabilities.* Tucson, AZ: Author.

Condry, J. (1977). Enemies of exploration: Self-initiated versus other-initiated learning. *Journal of Personality and Social Psychology, 35*, 459–477.

Craig, C.E., & Harris, R.C. (1973). Total productivity measurement at the firm level. *Sloan Management Review, 14*(3), 13–28.

Crosby, P.B. (1979). *Quality is free*. New York: McGraw-Hill.

Crowell, C.R., & Anderson, D.C. (1983). The scientific and methodological basis of a systematic approach to human behavior management. *Journal of Organizational Behavior Management, 4*(1/2), 1–31.

Dalton, B.A. (1992). *Outstanding integrative employment agencies: Creativity, leadership, and commitment* (Grant No. 90DD0157). Washington, DC: U.S. Department of Health and Human Services, Administration for Children and Families.

Deci, E.L., & Ryan, R.M. (1985). *Intrinsic motivation and self-determination in human behavior*. New York: Plenum.

Deming, W.E. (1975). On some statistical aids toward economic production. *Interfaces, 5*, 1–15.

Deming, W.E. (1986). *Out of crisis*. Cambridge: Massachusetts Institute of Technology, Center for Advanced Engineering Study.

Dierks, W., & McNally, K. (1987, March). Incentives you can bank on. *Personnel Administrator*, pp. 61–65.

Dietz, S.M., & Repp, A.C. (1973). Decreasing classroom misbehavior through the use of DRL schedules of reinforcement. *Journal of Applied Behavior Analysis, 11*, 395–412.

Doke, L.A., & Risley, T.R. (1972). The organization of day care environments: Required vs. optional activities. *Journal of Applied Behavior Analysis, 5*, 405–420.

Donnellan, A.M., LaVigna, G.W., Negri-Shoultz, N., & Fassbender, L.L. (1988). *Progress without punishment*. New York: Teachers College Press.

Donnellan, A.M., LaVigna, G.W., Zambito, J., & Thvedt, J. (1985). A time-limited intensive intervention program model to support community placement for persons with severe behavior problems. *Journal of The Association for Persons with Severe Handicaps, 10*(3), 123–131.

Drucker, P. (1974). *Management: Tasks; responsibilities; practices*. New York: Harper & Row.

Duerr, E.C. (1974). The effect of misdirected incentives on employee behavior. *Personnel Journal, 53*, 890–893.

Durand, V.M. (1990). *Severe behavior problems: A functional communication training approach*. New York: Guilford Press.

Dyer, K., Schwartz, I.S., & Luce, S.C. (1984). A supervision program for increasing functional activities for severely handicapped students in a residential setting. *Journal of Applied Behavior Analysis, 17*, 249–259.

Evans, I.M., & Meyer, L.H. (1985). *An educative approach to behavior problems: A practical decision model for interventions with severely handicapped learners*. Baltimore: Paul H. Brookes Publishing Co.

Evans, I.M., Kienast, P., & Mitchell, T.R. (1988). The effects of lottery incentive programs on performance. *Journal of Organizational Behavior Management, 9*(2), 113–135.

Falvey, M.A. (1989). *Community-based curriculum: Instructional strategies for students with severe disabilities* (2nd ed). Baltimore: Paul H. Brookes Publishing Co.

Feeney, E.J., Staelin, J.R., O'Brien, R.M., & Dickinson, A.M. (1982). Increasing sales performance among airline reservation personnel. In R.M. O'Brien, A.M. Dickinson, & M.P. Rosow (Eds.), *Industrial behavior modification* (pp. 141–158). New York: Pergamon.

Ferster, C.B., & Skinner, B.F. (1957). *Schedules of reinforcement*. New York: Appleton-Century-Crofts.

Fields, G. (1993, December 17). In '92, 750 were slain on the job. *USA Today*, p. 3A.

Ford, J.E. (1980). A classification system for feedback procedures. *Journal of Organizational Behavior Management, 2*(3), 183–191.

Frederiksen, L.W., Richter, W.T., Johnson, R.P., & Solomon, L.J. (1982). Specificity of performance feedback in a professional service delivery setting. *Journal of Organizational Behavior Management, 3*(4), 41–53.

Frederiksen, L.W., & Riley, A.W. (Eds.). (1983). Improving staff effectiveness in human service settings/organizational behavior management approaches. *Journal of Organizational Behavior Management, 5*(3/4).

Frederiksen, L.W., Riley, A.W., & Myers, J.B. (1985). Matching technology and organizational structure: A case study in white collar productivity improvement. *Journal of Organizational Behavior Management, 6*, 59–80.

Frost, J.M., Hopkins, B.L., & Conard, R.J. (1982). An analysis of the effects of feedback and rein-forcement on machine-paced production. *Journal of Organizational Behavior Management, 3*(2), 5–17.

Gaetani, J.J., Hoxeng, D.D., & Austin, J.T. (1985). Engineering compensation systems: Effects of commissioned versus wage payment. *Journal of Organizational Behavior Management, 7*(1/2), 51–53.

George, J.T., & Hopkins, B.L. (1989). Multiple effects of performance-contingent pay for wait-persons. *Journal of Applied Behavior Analysis, 22*, 131–141.

Gordon, T. (1970). *Parent effectiveness training.* New York: Peter H. Wyden.

Greene, B.F., Willis, B.S., Levy, R., & Bailey, J.S. (1978). Measuring client gains from staff-implemented programs. *Journal of Applied Behavior Analysis, 11*, 395–412.

Gresham, F.M., Gansle, K.A., & Noell, G.H. (1993). Treatment integrity in applied behavior anal-ysis with children. *Journal of Applied Behavior Analysis, 26*, 257–263.

Harris, B. (1980). *Improving staff performance through in-service education.* Boston: Allyn & Bacon.

Hogan, R., Curphy, G., & Hogan, J. (in press). Leadership effectiveness. *American Psychologist.*

Holden Lewin Productions. (Producer). (1987). *Supported employment: The right match.* [Video-tape]. Sacramento: California State Department of Rehabilitation.

Hopkins, B.L., & Mawhinney, T.C. (Eds.). (1992). Pay for performance: History, controversy, and evidence [Special issue]. *Journal of Organizational Behavior Management, 12*(1).

Hultman, K.E. (1986). Behavior modeling for results. *Training & Development, 40*, 60–63.

Hutchison, J.M., Jarman, P.H., & Bailey, J.S. (1980). Public posting with a habilitation team: Effects on attendance and performance. *Behavior Modification, 4*(1), 57–70.

Illgen, D.R., Fisher, C.D., & Taylor, M.S. (1979). Consequences of individual feedback on behavior in organizations. *Journal of Applied Psychology, 64*, 349–371.

Johnson, C.M., & Masotti, R.M. (1990). Suggestive selling by waitstaff in family-style restaurants: An experiment and multisetting observations. *Journal of Organizational Behavior Management, 11*(1), 35–54.

Jones, D.R. (1991). *Technical guide for implementing continuous quality improvement.* Austin: Texas Department of Mental Health and Mental Retardation.

Jones, H.H., Morris, E.K., & Barnard, J.D. (1986). Increasing staff completion of civil commitment forms through instructions and graphed group performance feedback. *Journal of Organizational Behavior Management, 7*(3/4), 29–43.

Kempen, R.W., & Hall, R.V. (1977). Reduction of industrial absenteeism: Results of a behavioral approach. *Journal of Organizational Behavior Management, 1*(1), 1–21.

Klaber, M.M. (1969). *Retardates in residence: A study of institutions.* West Hartford, CT: Hartford University.

Koestner, R., Ryan, R.M., Bernieri, F., & Holt, K. (1984). Setting limits on children's behavior: The detrimental effects of controlling versus informational styles on intrinsic motivation and creativity. *Journal of Personality, 52*, 233–248.

Kohn, A. (1988, January). Incentives can be bad for business. *Inc.*, pp. 93–94.

Komaki, J.L. (1983). Why we don't reinforce: The issues. *Journal of Organizational Behavior Man-agement, 4*(3/4), 97–100.

Komaki, J.L. (1986). Toward effective supervision: An operant analysis and comparison of managers at work. *Journal of Applied Psychology, 71*, 270–279.

Komaki, J.L., Waddell, W., & Pierce, M.G. (1977). The applied behavior analysis approach and individual employees: Improving performance in two small businesses. *Organizational Behavior and Human Decision Processes, 19*, 337–352.

Komaki, J.L., Zlotnick, S., & Jensen, M. (1986). Development of an operant-based taxonomy and observational index of supervisory behavior. *Journal of Applied Psychology, 71*, 260–269.

Komar, J.J. (1992, November/December). Make upgrading wages a priority. *AAMR News & Notes*, p. 3.

Kopelman, R.E. (1982). Improving productivity through objective feedback: A review of the evi-dence. *National Productivity Review, 83*, 43–55.

Kreitner, R., Reif, W.E., & Morris, M. (1977). Measuring the impact of feedback on the perfor-mance of mental health technicians. *Journal of Organizational Behavior Management, 1*(1), 105–109.

Lakin, K.C. (1988). Strategies for promoting the stability of direct care staff. In M.P. Janicki, M.W. Krauss, & M.M. Seltzer (Eds.), *Community residences for persons with developmental disabilities: Here to stay* (pp. 231–238). Baltimore: Paul H. Brookes Publishing Co.

LaVigna, G.W., & Donnellan, A.M. (1986). *Alternatives to punishment: Solving behavior problems with non-aversive strategies*. New York: Irvington.

LaVigna, G.W., Willis, T.J., & Donnellan, A.M. (1989). The role of positive programming in behavioral treatment. In E. Cipani (Ed.), *Behavioral approaches to the treatment of aberrant behavior* [AAMR Monograph Series] (pp. 59–82). Washington, DC: American Association on Mental Retardation.

LaVigna, G.W., Willis, T.J., Shaull, J.F., Abedi, M., & Sweitzer, M. (in press). Effective consultation for classroom and community settings. In E. Cipani & F. Spooner (Eds.), *Curricular and instructional approaches for persons with severe disabilities*. Boston: Allyn & Bacon.

Liberman, R.P., DeRisi, W.J., & Mueser, K.T. (1989). Social skills training for psychiatric patients. In A.P. Goldstein, L. Krasner, & S.L. Garfield (Eds.), *Psychology practitioner guidebooks*. Boston: Allyn & Bacon.

Locke, E.A., & Latham, G.P. (1984). *Goal setting: A motivational technique that works*. Englewood Cliffs, NJ: Prentice Hall.

Locke, E.A., Shaw, K.N., Saari, L.M., & Latham, G.P. (1980). Goal setting and task performance: 1979–1980. *Psychological Bulletin, 90*, 125–152.

Luthans, F., Paul, R., & Taylor, L. (1986). The impact of contingent reinforcement on retail salespersons' performance behaviors: A replicated field experiment. *Journal of Organizational Behavior Management, 7*(1/2), 25–35.

Luthans, F., & Thompson, K.R. (1987). Theory d and o.b. mod.: Synergistic of opposite approaches to performance improvement? *Journal of Organizational Behavior Management, 4*(1), 105–124.

Mankin, D., Bikson, T.K., & Gutek, B. (1985). Factors in successful implementation of computer-based office information systems: A review of the literature with suggestions for OBM research. *Journal of Organizational Behavior Management, 6*(3/4), 1–20.

Mawhinney, T.C. (1987). Section I: Fundamentals of statistical process control: Implications of and obstacles to its use in organizational behavior management. *Journal of Organizational Behavior Management, 9*(1), 1–4.

Mawhinney, T.C. (1992). Total quality management and organizational behavior management: An integration for continual improvement. *Journal of Applied Behavior Analysis, 25*, 525–543.

Mawhinney, T.C., Dickinson, A.M., & Taylor, L.A., III. (1989). The use of concurrent schedules to evaluate the effects of extrinsic rewards on "intrinsic motivation." *Journal of Organizational Behavior Management, 10*(1), 109–129.

McGraw, K., & Cullers, J. (1979). Evidence of a detrimental effect of extrinsic incentives on breaking a mental set. *Journal of Social Psychology, 15*, 285–294.

Mento, A.J., Steel, R.P., & Karren, R.J. (1987). A meta-analytic study of the effects of goal setting on task performance: 1966–1984. *Organizational Behavior and Human Decision Processes, 39*, 52–83.

Miller, L.M. (1977). Improving sales and forecast accuracy in a nationwide sales organization. *Journal of Organizational Behavior Management, 1*(1), 39–51.

Muckler, F.A. (1982). Evaluation productivity. In M.D. Dunnette & E.A. Fleishman (Eds.), *Human performance and productivity: Vol 1. Human capability assessment* (pp. 13–47). Hillsdale, NJ: Erlbaum Associates.

Murrell, S.A. (1973). *Community psychology and social system*. New York: Behavioral Publications.

Nadler, D.A. (1979). The effects of feedback on task group behaviors: A review of the experimental literature. *Organizational Behavior and Human Decision Processes, 23*, 309–338.

Nebeker, D.M., & Neuberger, B.M. (1985). Productivity improvement in a purchasing division: The impact of a performance-contingent reward system. *Evaluation and Program Planning, 8*, 121–134.

Parsons, M.B., Schepis, M.M., Reid, D.H., McCarn, J.E., & Green, C.W. (1987). Expanding the impact of behavioral staff management: A large-scale, long-term application in schools serving severely handicapped students. *Journal of Applied Behavior Analysis, 2*, 139–150.

Porter, L., & Lawler, E. (1968). *Management attitudes and performance*. Homewood, IL: Dorsey Press.

Potter, W. (1989, Winter-Spring). Preston Trucking: Moving forward with PM. *Performance Management Magazine*, pp. 3–6.

Pritchard, R.D., Jones, S.D., Roth, P.L., Stuebing, K.K., & Ekeberg, S.E. (1989). The evaluation of an integrated approach to measuring organizational productivity. *Personnel Psychology, 42*, 69–114.

Prue, D.M., & Fairbank, J.A. (1981). Performance feedback in organizational behavior management: A review. *Journal of Organizational Behavior Management, 3*(1), 1–16.

Quilitch, M.R. (1975). A comparison of three staff management procedures. *Journal of Applied Behavior Analysis, 8*, 59–66.

Quilitch, M.R. (1978). Using a simple feedback procedure to reinforce the submission of written suggestions by mental health employees. *Journal of Organizational Behavior Management, 1*(2), 155–163.

Redmon, W.K. (1992) Opportunities for applied behavior analysis in the total quality movement. *Journal of Applied Behavior Analysis, 25*, 545–550.

Reid, D.H., Parsons, M.B., & Green, C.W. (1989a.). *Staff management in human services*. Springfield, IL: Charles C Thomas.

Reid, D.H., Parsons, M.B., & Green, C.W. (1989b.). Treating aberrant behavior through effective staff management: A developing technology. In E. Cipani (Ed.), *Behavioral approaches to the treatment of aberrant behavior* [AAMR Monograph Series] (pp. 175–190). Washington, DC: American Association on Mental Retardation.

Reid, D.H., & Whitman, T.L. (1983). Behavioral staff management in institutions: A critical review of effectiveness and acceptability. *Analysis and Intervention in Developmental Disabilities, 3*, 131–149.

Rollins, T. (1988). Pay for performance: Is it worth the trouble? *Personnel Administrator, 33*, 42–46.

Shaull, J.F., LaVigna, G.W., & Willis, T.J. (1992). *Competency-based training program: A self-instructional training course for the certification of staff working with people challenged by developmental disabilities*. Los Angeles: Institute for Applied Behavior Analysis.

Skaggs, K.J., Dickinson, A.M., & O'Connor, K.A. (1992). The use of concurrent schedules to evaluate the effects of extrinsic rewards on "intrinsic motivation:" A replication. *Journal of Organizational Behavior Management, 12*(1), 45–83.

Skinner, B.F. (1938). *The behavior of organisms*. New York: Appleton-Century-Crofts.

Skinner, B.F. (1953). *Science and human behavior*. New York: Free Press.

Slater, P. (1980) *Wealth addiction*. New York: E.P. Dutton.

Sneed, T.J., & Bible, G.H. (1979). An administrative procedure for improving staff performance in an institutional setting for retarded persons. *Mental Retardation, 2*, 92–94.

Snyder, G., & Rourk, W. (1989, Winter-Spring). Chrysler at Belvedere: Changing the face of the auto industry. *Performance Management Magazine*, pp. 24–31.

Solomon, L.J. (1983). Considerations in laying off employees: A program description. *Journal of Organizational Behavior Management, 5*(1), 53–62.

State of the Art, Inc. (Producer). (1987). *Regular lives* [Videotape]. Alexandria, VA: PBS Video.

Stowe, J.E. (1989). [Review of *Out of the crisis*]. *Journal of Organizational Behavior Management, 10*(1), 205–207.

USA Today. (1993, May 15, p. B1).

Welsh, W.U., Ludwig, C., Radiken, J.E., & Krapfl, J.E. (1973). Effects of feedback on daily completion of behavior modification projects. *Mental Retardation, 11*, 24–26.

Wikoff, M., Anderson, D.C., & Crowell, C.R. (1983) Behavior management in a factory setting: Increasing work efficiency. *Journal of Organizational Behavior Management, 4*(1/2), 97–127.

Wilk, L.A., & Redmon, W.K. (1990). A daily-adjusted goal-setting and feedback procedure for improving productivity in a university admissions department. *Journal of Organizational Behavior Management, 11*(1), 55–75.

· Appendix A ·

ᴛʜᵉ**PSR**

PERIODIC SERVICE REVIEW AND OPERATIONAL DEFINITIONS FOR BEHAVIOR SERVICES GROUP HOMES

PERIODIC SERVICE REVIEW FOR BEHAVIOR SERVICES GROUP HOMES:

Score Sheet

Person's Name: _____   Date of Review: _____

Reviewer's Name: _____   Supervisor: _____

	Score	Possible	Comments
I. General Program Activities			
A. Daily Schedule of Activities			
1. Individual schedule posted			
2. Schedule spot check			
3. Staff schedule posted			
4. Staff schedule spot check			

	Score	Possible	Comments

B.   Skills Programs

    1.   Instructional protocols

    2.   Age-appropriate and functional

    3.   Datasheets

    4.   Summary graphs (optional)

    5.   Activity spot checks

    6.   Interobserver Reliability

       a.   Program

       b.   Independent

    7.   Procedural Reliability

       a.   Program

       b.   Independent

II.   Individual Behavior Support Plans

A.   Behavior Assessment

B.   Individualized Service Plan

C.   Quarterly Report

D.   Behavior Protocols and Checklists

E.   Program Implementation Knowledge

F.   Raw Data

G.   Reinforcement Charts

    1.   Current

    2.   Reliable

Score	Possible	**Comments**

H. Program Implementation

I. Competing Contingencies

J. Data Summary
    Procedures

    1. Daily data summary

       a. Current

       b. Accurate

    2. Weekly data
       summary

       a. Current

       b. Accurate

    3. Monthly data
       summary

       a. Current

       b. Accurate

    4. Behavior graphs

       a. Current

       b. Accurate

K. Reliability Checks

    1. Interobserver

       a. Program

       b. Independent

    2. Procedural

       a. Program

       b. Spot check

	Score	Possible	Comments

L.   Emergency Procedures

    1.   Available

    2.   Read by all

    3.   Accurate

    4.   Noted in raw data

III.   Staff Development

A.   Behavior Inservice
    Training

    1.   12-month record

    2.   Average once a
       month

    3.   Staff participants

    4.   Competency tests

    5.   Previous 4 weeks

B.   Scheduled Staff Meetings

IV.   Other Areas

A.   Communication Logs

B.   Outcome Evaluation

Total Earned	Total Possible	Percentage Score

SUMMARY SCORE

Comments/Recommendations/Objectives:

PERIODIC SERVICE REVIEW FOR
BEHAVIOR SERVICES GROUP HOMES:
Operational Definitions

I. **General Program Activities**
   A. **Daily Schedule of Activities**
      1. **Individual schedule posted.** Based on direct review of the individual's schedule, a + is given if the schedule is physically available, lists activities by the hour throughout the day, and lists data-based skills instruction programs, community access activities, and observational and procedural reliability checks.
      2. **Schedule spot check.** Based on direct observation by the behavior consultant, a + is given if, at the time of the observation, the program is being carried out by the staff member assigned to the individual, as indicated on the schedule.
      3. **Staff schedule posted.** Based on direct observation by the behavior consultant, a + is given if a staff schedule has been posted by the program supervisor by the time of the observation, if it identifies the staff who are responsible for providing services to specific individuals at all times of a shift, and if it is accurate for the current week.
      4. **Staff schedule spot check.** Based on direct observation by the behavioral consultant, a + is given if the staff-to-service recipient ratio is consistent with the program design at the time of the observation, and if the staff member for the selected individual is working with the right people, as indicated by the staff schedule.
   B. **Skills Programs**
      1. **Instructional protocols.** Based on a review of an individual's records and *four* randomly selected skill programs, a + is given for each skills instructional protocol completed by the program supervisor, which is up-to-date and available to staff within 5 minutes of a request.
      2. **Age-appropriate and functional.** Based on a review of an individual's records and the *four* randomly selected skills programs selected in B.1., a + is given for each targeted skill that meets the criteria for "meaningful" activities engaged in by others of the same chronological age.
      3. **Datasheets.** Based on a review of an individual's daily/weekly/monthly data summaries, and the *four* randomly selected skills programs selected in B.1., a + is given for each skill for which a datasheet is available, and where the data were updated by the assigned staff within one training session (as indicated on individual's schedule).
      4. **Summary graphs (optional).** Based on a review of an individual's daily/weekly/monthly graphs, and the *four* randomly selected skills programs selected in B.1., a + is given for each skill for which a graph is available, and where the graph was updated by the program supervisor by the end of the shift on the previous Friday.
      5. **Activity spot checks.** Based on direct observation by the program consultant of two randomly selected individuals observed consecutively for periods of 5 minutes, a + is given for each person if the activities throughout the entire observation period meet the criteria for chronological age–appropriate and functional activities.

6. **Interobserver Reliability**
   a. **Program.** Based on a review of observational reliability records, a + is given if the program supervisor has conducted at least one observational reliability check per individual during the quarter, and the results of the check have been entered as a percentage on the proper form, and this percentage is over 85%. The scores would be prorated for the months of the quarter. For the first month of the quarter, two checks would be expected; for the second month, four; and for the third month, six.
   b. **Independent.** Based on direct observation of one randomly selected skill program per month, of a randomly selected individual whose program is being run at the time that the PSR is conducted, a + is given if observational reliability exceeds 85%.
7. **Procedural Reliability**
   a. **Program.** Based on a review of procedural reliability records, a + is given if the program supervisor has conducted at least one procedural reliability check per person during the quarter. The scores would be prorated for the months of the quarter. For the first month of the quarter, two checks would be expected; for the second month, four; and for the third month, six.
   b. **Independent.** Based on direct observation of one randomly selected skill training program per month, of a randomly selected individual whose program is being run at the time that the PSR is conducted, a + is given if the training procedures used match those specified by the skills training program (i.e., exceed 85%).

II. **Individual Behavior Support Plans**
   A. **Behavior Assessment.** Based on a review of individual records, a + is given if the behavior consultant has completed an assessment, which is filed and available to staff within 15 minutes of a request, and is filed within 60 days of the person's arrival or within 60 days of anniversary of arrival.
   B. **Individualized Service Plan.** Based on a review of individual records, a + is given if the behavior consultant has completed an ISP, which is filed and available to staff within 15 minutes of a request, and is filed within 60 days of the person's arrival, or within 60 days of anniversary of arrival.
   C. **Quarterly Report.** Based on a review of individual records, a + is given if the most recent quarterly report has been completed by the program consultant, which is filed and available to staff within 15 minutes of a request, and is filed within 15 days of the end of the quarter period.
   D. **Behavior Protocols and Checklists.** Based on a review of an individual's records, a + is given for each step-by-step program description (identified in ISP, assessment, or quarterlies) completed by the program consultant, which is filed and available to staff within 15 minutes of a request.
   E. **Program Implementation Knowledge.** Based on an interview with a randomly selected staff member, and a randomly selected behavior from a randomly selected ISP, a + is given for each of the following criteria satisfied by the selected staff person.
   1. Define the target behavior (i.e., describe topography and cycle).
   2. Describe how the behavior is recorded (e.g., frequency, duration, ABC).
   3. Locate the proper recording sheet within 1 minute of a request
   4. Describe how the behavior is entered onto datasheet.
   5. Locate graph for behavior within 1 minute of a request.
   6. Describe how behavior is entered on graph.

7. Describe each positive program, direct treatment strategy, for selected behavior.

8. Describe reactive strategies for selected behavior.

F.   Raw Data.   Based on a review of individual raw datasheets cross-referenced with reinforcement charts, a + is entered if staff have entered all data within 30 minutes of a behavioral occurrence, and if all categories on data collection sheet are completed correctly.

G.   Reinforcement Charts

1. **Current.**   Based on a review of reinforcement tracking chart (or other) for a randomly selected behavior targeted on the person's ISP, a + is entered if reinforcement has been delivered in accordance with the specified schedule(s), and the assigned staff person has recorded the occasion within 30 minutes of the actual reinforcement delivery. A 0 is entered if no reinforcement tracking was in place for the randomly selected behavior.

2. **Reliable.**   Based on a cross-check of the reinforcement tracking chart with raw data for the randomly selected behavior described in G.1. above, for the previous consecutive 7 program days, a + is entered if reinforcement was delivered in accordance with prescribed schedule (e.g., DRO, DRL). An 0 is given if no tracking sheet is evident.

H.   Program Implementation.   Based on a review of the ISP, behavior assessment, quarterly reports, program addenda, review of the reinforcement tracking charts, and interviews with staff, a + is entered if all programs are currently being carried out by staff (not counted if formally discontinued).

I.   Competing Contingencies.   Based on a review of randomly selected data, logs, and incident reports, as well as interviews and observation for the period from the last PSR review, a + is entered if there is *no* evidence of unapproved program implementation by staff and program supervisors that might interfere with planned effects (e.g., informal contracts, special deals).

J.   Data Summary Procedures

1. **Daily data summary**

   a. **Current.**   Based on a review of the data summary sheet for the previous 7 days, a + is entered for each target behavior for which the data have been entered by staff and that are current within 1 day.

   b. **Accurate.**   Based on a comparison of raw datasheets and the data summary sheet for the previous 7 days, and based on a review of 10% of the transfers from raw data to the summary sheet made by the program supervisor, a + is entered if *all* the data checked on the data summary sheet are consistent with those found in the raw data.

2. **Weekly data summary**

   a. **Current.**   Based on a review of the data summary sheet for the previous calendar week, a + is given if all target behaviors have been summarized by the program supervisor (i.e., added and averaged) by the end of the shift on Monday.

   b. **Accurate.**   Based on a review of the data summary sheet for the previous calendar week, and based on a review of 50% of the weekly summaries, a + is given if all selected target behaviors have been correctly summed and averaged by the program supervisor.

3. **Monthly data summary**

   a. **Current.**   Based on a review of the data summary sheet for the previous complete calendar month, a + is given if all target behaviors have been summarized and averaged by the program supervisor within 3 days of the end of the program month.

    b. Accurate. Based on a review of the data summary sheet for the previous complete calendar month, and based on a review of 50% of the monthly summaries, a + is given if all selected target behaviors have been correctly summed and averaged by the program supervisor.

  4. Behavior Graphs

    a. Current. Based on a review of individual graphs, a + is entered for each behavior graph available, which matches assessment and addenda targets, is correctly and clearly labeled, and has been updated by the program supervisor to within 3 days of the review date.

    b. Accurate. Based on a subsample of 10 of the graphed points, a + is entered if the data are consistent with those contained on the data summary sheet.

K. Reliability Checks

  1. Interobserver

    a. Program. Based on a review of observational reliability records for the previous quarter, a + is recorded for each individual (six-resident home) for which an observational reliability check was conducted by the program supervisor for at least one behavior during the quarter, and for which the reliability coefficients were correctly calculated and were recorded on the proper form. The scores would be prorated for the months of the quarter. For the first month of the quarter, two checks would be expected; for the second month, four; and for the third month, six.

    b. Independent. Based on direct observation by the program consultant of a randomly selected individual engaging in a targeted behavior at the time of the PSR, a + is given if the behavior is recorded by the staff assigned or present on the proper form within 10 minutes of the cessation of the incident, and if observational reliability exceeds 85%.

  2. Procedural

    a. Program. Based on a review of individual records, a + is given if a check is carried out quarterly by the program supervisor on at least one implementation program per person. The scores would be prorated for the months of the quarter. For the first month of the quarter, two checks would be expected; for the second month, four; and for the third month, six.

    b. Spot Check. Based on direct observation by the program consultant of a randomly selected person available during the PSR process, a + is given if procedural reliability for a randomly selected program exceeds 85%.

L. Emergency Procedures. Based on a review of program records,

  1. Available. A + is given if a copy of emergency procedures for restraint, PRN medication, and injury are available within 15 minutes of a request.

  2. Read by all. A + is given if records show that procedures have been read by *all* staff on duty at time of the review.

  3. Accurate. A + is given if a review of one randomly chosen incident report from the previous 30 days agrees with written emergency procedures. An o is given if no procedures are available.

  4. Noted in raw data. A + is given if use of emergency procedures are noted on raw datasheets.

III. **Staff Development**
 A. **Behavior Inservice Training.**   Based on a review of training records for the home,
   1. **12-month record.**   A + is given if a 12-month record of behavior inservices has been provided by the program consultant and is available within 10 minutes of a request.
   2. **Average once a month.**   A + is given if the program consultant or designee has conducted inservices on the average of once a month.
   3. **Staff participants.**   A + is given for each participant from the total number of staff available, who attended the most recent inservice training.
   4. **Competency tests.**   A + is given for each participant at the most recent inservice training from the total number of staff available for whom a competency test is filed that exceeds 80%.
   5. **Previous 4 weeks.**   A + is given if an inservice was conducted by the program consultant or designee within the previous 4-week period.
 B. **Scheduled Staff Meetings.**   Based on a review of staff meeting notes for the previous 30-day period, a + is given if a staff meeting was conducted by the program supervisor or director during that period, and the notes indicate a discussion of skills programs, behavior programs, or related issues.

IV. **Other Areas**
 A. **Communication Logs.**   Based on a review of the communication log, a + is given if the notebook for posting changes to behavior and skill training programs is accessible within 15 minutes of a request, and all entries by the consultant for the previous 30 days have been initialed by the program supervisor.
 B. **Outcome Evaluation.**   Based on a review of the most recent quarterly report for a randomly selected client, a + is given for each quarterly objective met during the reporting period.

· Appendix B ·

ᵀʰᵉ**PSR**

PERIODIC SERVICE REVIEW AND OPERATIONAL DEFINITIONS FOR CLASSROOM USE

PERIODIC SERVICE REVIEW FOR CLASSROOM USE:
Score Sheet

Date: _____   Classroom: _____   Student: _____

	+ /o	Comments
I. General Concepts		
A. Philosophy		
B. Age-Appropriate/ Functional		
II. Administrative		
A. Student Notebooks		
B. Medical Records		
III. Individual Skill Programs		
A. Working Notebooks		
B. Schedule		
C. IEP		

	+ /o	Comments
D. ITP		
E. Lesson Plans		
F. Data		
G. Data Summaries/ Graphs		
H. Progress Reports		
I. Emergency Procedures		

	+ /o	
J. Reliability Checks		
1. Interobserver		
2. Procedural		

IV. Individual Behavior Programs

	+ /o	
A. Assessment Reports/ Intervention Plans		
B. Behavior Protocol/ Checklists		
C. Raw Data		
D. Reinforcement Charts		
E. Program Implementation		
F. Competing Contingen- cies not Present		

G. Data Summaries		
1. Charts		
2. Graphs		

	+ /o	**Comments**

H.   Reliability Checks

    1.   Interobserver

    2.   Procedural

  I.   Emergency Procedures

V.   Instruction

  A.   Individualized

  B.   Methods

  C.   Environments

  D.   Community Instruction

  E.   Communication

VI.   Staff Development

  A.   Workshops

  B.   Scheduled Staff Meetings

  C.   Inservice

  D.   Team Input

  E.   Classroom Team Meetings

  F.   Mainstream Staff

  G.   Mainstream Students

  H.   Specialist

VII.   Family Involvement

  A.   PPT

  B.   Communication

  C.   Meetings

  D.   Parent Committee

	+ /o	Comments
VIII. Coordination of Program		
A. Roles		
B. Responsibilities		
C. Team		

IX.   PSR Document

Total

Total Possible

PERCENTAGE SCORE

Report completed by: _____

PERIODIC SERVICE REVIEW FOR CLASSROOM USE:
Operational Definitions

The Periodic Service Review is used to measure the overall effectiveness of a special education program. Program effectiveness is measured monthly by this checklist to ensure that standards are being met. The areas to examine include the following.

I.	General Concepts	VI.	Staff Development
II.	Administrative	VII.	Family Involvement
III.	Individual Skill Programs	VIII.	Coordination of Program
IV.	Individual Behavior Programs	IX.	PSR Document
V.	Instruction		

I. **General Concepts**
  A. **Philosophy.**   The philosophy of the program is stated in the students' notebooks. The basis of the program is preparation for living, working, and enjoying life in an integrated environment.
  B. **Age-Appropriate and Functional Curriculum.**   Spot checks are done monthly to ensure that students are engaging in meaningful activities and that these are engaged in by others of the same age. Checks are also done to see if at least 20% of the curriculum is community based.

II. **Administrative**
  A. **Student Notebooks.**   Each student has an up-to-date notebook that includes pertinent forms, schedules, current individualized education program (IEP) and individualized treatment program (ITP), data forms, graphs, lesson plans, progress reports, behavior programs, emergency information, home/school communication, and a table of contents.
  B. **Medical Records.**   Available and up-to-date in the school file located in the guidance office. The information must include the name of the medication, dosage, when and where it is to be taken, and the possible side effects. Medication for seizure is also listed in the student's working notebook.

III. **Individual Skill Programs**
  A. **Working Notebooks.**   Each student has a working notebook located in the classroom and used by staff daily. It includes the following information: daily schedule, current IEP, lesson plans, datasheets and current behavior plan.
  B. **Schedule.**   Posted in the classroom is each student's daily schedule and the student's monitor for each period. The daily schedule should reflect scheduled lessons to be done that day.
  C. **IEP.**   Each student has an updated IEP located in the student and working notebooks. The IEP includes:
    1. **Identifying information**
    2. **IEP participants**
    3. **Present functioning level**
    4. **Goals**
    5. **Objectives**
    6. **Additional information**
  D. **ITP.**   Each student age 15 and older in special education has an up-to-date ITP in the student notebook.
  E. **Lesson Plans.**   Each objective has an updated lesson plan located in the working notebook. The plan may include:

    1. **Objective**
    2. **Discriminative stimuli**
    3. **Prompt (optional)**
    4. **Correct response**
    5. **Consequence**
       a. **Correct response**
       b. **Incorrect response**
    6. **Intertrial interval**
    7. **Data collection**
    8. **Program change criteria**
       a. **Pass**
       b. **Fail**
    9. **Special criteria (if necessary)**

F. Data. Current datasheets are located in the working notebooks. Data are collected within 5 minutes of lesson each time that lesson is taught. Completed datasheets are located in the student's notebook, and past semester datasheets are located in the student's file.

G. Data Summaries/Graphs. Raw data are summarized daily on a graph to show progress.

H. Progress Reports. Quarterly progress reports are completed and located in the student's notebook.

I. Emergency Procedures
    1. When emergency intervention is used, its use is documented and sent to the appropriate supervisor.
    2. A written plan is in the student and working notebooks for any medical problems.
    3. Emergency information is in the student and working notebooks.

J. Reliability Checks. Done at least monthly for each student.
    1. **Interobserver.** Behaviors recorded match operational definitions—score is 85% or more. One skill each month is randomly selected for the check.
    2. **Procedural.** Procedures followed match protocol/task analysis description. Score is 85% or more. One skill each month is randomly selected for the check.

IV. Individual Behavior Programs

A. Assessment Reports/Intervention Plans. For any existing program, there is a written assessment report and intervention plan following district protocols. Copies are entered in the student's notebook within 30 days of the start of the school year, the end of the quarter, or upon the student's enrollment. No aversives are to be written into the plan.

B. Behavior Protocol and Checklists. For each written intervention plan, there is a protocol and checklist in the working notebook.

C. Raw Data. Updated within 30 minutes.

D. Reinforcement Charts
    1. **Currency.** Updated within 30 minutes.
    2. **Reliability.** Reinforcement charts cross-check with datasheets.

E. Program Implementation. Behavior programs described and planned are currently being implemented.

F. Competing Contingencies not Present. No other program implemented for target behaviors other than those in plans (informal contracts, special deals).

G. Data Summaries
    1. **Charts.** Raw data summarized on weekly chart. Current within 1 week and matches raw datasheets.

      2. **Graphs.** One for each target behavior identified in assessment reports and addendum. Current within 1 week, clearly labeled and matching weekly charts.

   H. Reliability Checks. Done at least monthly for each student.

      1. **Interobserver.** Behavior recorded matches operational definitions. Score is 85% or more.

      2. **Procedural.** Procedures match protocols in working notebook. Score is 85% or more.

   I. Emergency Procedures

      1. When emergency behavior intervention is necessary, a written plan is entered in the working notebook.

      2. When special incidents occur, they are documented and sent to the appropriate supervisor.

      3. General emergency procedures are accessible to staff. All staff must initial the emergency procedures, to show they have read them. The procedures must be followed correctly and use of such procedures must be documented on raw datasheets. Report incidents as required.

V. Instruction

   A. Individualized. Objectives are individualized on the IEP and lesson plans.

   B. Methods. Both one-to-one and group instruction are used. Methods vary depending on student and skill being taught.

   C. Environments. Direct training occurs in actual situations in which target behaviors may occur.

   D. Community Instruction. There are a minimum of five community-based objectives for each student.

   E. Communication. The classroom is communication-based, and communication skills are incorporated within each student's lesson plans. The lessons are taught in real-life situations, rather than in isolated settings.

VI. Staff Development

   A. Workshops. Staff attend workshops and professional meetings pertinent to job duties within school system and out of district, a minimum of two per year.

   B. Scheduled Staff Meetings. Staff attends monthly school-based staff meetings, as documented.

   C. Inservice. Staff attend monthly special education meetings, as documented.

   D. Team Input. All objectives are developed by a team working with students that includes the teacher, assistants, speech therapist, and senior teacher. Minutes of the meeting are kept.

   E. Classroom Team Meetings. A weekly meeting to address student and classroom needs. Minutes of the meeting are kept.

   F. Mainstream Staff. By October 30th of each year, a presentation about people with disabilities is given to the mainstream staff. This is documented with a copy of the meeting agenda.

   G. Mainstream Students. By the spring, a presentation about people with disabilities is given to the mainstream students. This is documented by presentation notes.

   H. Specialist. Once per year, an outside specialist comes in to observe the program. This is documented by a report.

VII. Family Involvement

   A. Parent Participation. Families attend and are active participants during the development of the IEP. Questionnaires and rating scales are used to gather input from parents.

    B. **Communication.**   At least weekly communication between staff and families via phone, notes, and so forth, as documented in the working notebooks.

    C. **Meetings.**   Scheduled parent meetings throughout the year dealing with pertinent issues. A minimum of three meetings per year, as documented by minutes kept in a parent notebook.

    D. **Parent Committee.**   Parents working with parents on issues they deem important. This is documented by formal notice and minutes kept in a parent notebook.

VIII. **Coordination of Program**

    A. **Roles.**   There is a written definition of each team member's role. Copies are located in the central office and the classroom.

    B. **Responsibilities.**   Each role has a written list of responsibilities.

    C. **Team.**   Processes of team functioning are stated and followed. Copies are located in the central office and classroom.

IX. **PSR Document**

    A. **Effectiveness.**   There is an annual check and review of the effectiveness of this document.

· Appendix C ·

ᴛʜᵉPSR

PERIODIC SERVICE REVIEW AND OPERATIONAL DEFINITIONS FOR SUPPORTED EMPLOYMENT

PERIODIC SERVICE REVIEW FOR SUPPORTED EMPLOYMENT: Score Sheet

Participant's Name: _____   Date: _____

Specialist: _____   Rater: _____

	+/o	Comments
I. General Program Activities		
A. Daily Schedule for Consumers		
B. Daily Schedule for Program Specialists		
C. Substitute Instructions		
D. Job Description		
E. Curriculum Functional and Age-Appropriate— Spot Checks		
F. Standard Graphs*	/	

*This item should be prorated based on how many items met the criteria vs. the total number of items possible (e.g., 1/2 would mean one item out of two met the criteria).

	+/o	Comments

G.   Emergency Procedures

   1.   Behavior Problems

   2.   Special Incidents

   3.   Medical Problems

   4.   Emergency Contacts

II.   Individualized Service Plan

A.   List ISP Objectives
Programs Implemented

   1.   _____

   2.   _____

   3.   _____

   4.   _____

   5.   _____

   6.   _____

   7.   _____

   8.   _____

B.   List Programs

   1.   _____

     a.   Protocol

     b.   Datasheet

     c.   Graph

     d.   Reliability

       1)   Interobserver

       2)   Procedural

	+ /o	Comments
2. _____		
a. Protocol		
b. Datasheet		
c. Graph		
d. Reliability		
1) Interobserver		
2) Procedural		
3. _____		
a. Protocol		
b. Datasheet		
c. Graph		
d. Reliability		
1) Interobserver		
2) Procedural		
4. _____		
a. Protocol		
b. Datasheet		
c. Graph		
d. Reliability		
1) Interobserver		
2) Procedural		
5. _____		
a. Protocol		
b. Datasheet		
c. Graph		

	+/o	Comments
d. Reliability		
1) Interobserver		
2) Procedural		
C. Monthly Data Summary		
D. ISP Complete		
E. Objectives Met*		

III. Administrative

A. Participant Case File

B. Job Notebook

C. Case Notes

D. Employer Evaluation—
    Participant

E. Earnings

F. TJTC/SSI

G. Subminimum/productivity

IV. Staff Development

A. CBTs Complete

B. Staff Meetings/Inservices

C. Contact Meetings

D. Employer Evaluations—
    3s +

E. Professionalism

F. Attendance/Punctuality

	+/o	Comments
Total +s (add all +s and the numerator for prorated items)		
(add one bonus point to total +s if 75% or more objs. met on II.E)		
Total possible (count all +s, os, and denominator, for prorated items—do *not* add bonus)		
Percentage score (divide total +s by total poss.)		

Location of Rating _____

PERIODIC SERVICE REVIEW FOR SUPPORTED EMPLOYMENT:
Operational Definitions

Score + or o for opportunity on each item of PSR according to the criteria outlined below. Note any comments in space indicated.

I. **General Program Activities**
   A. **Daily Schedule for Consumers.**   Accessible (copy in job notebook) and followed; list of activities by times of day for 6-hour program day, including training toward all ISP objectives and community training.
   B. **Daily Schedule of Activities for Program Specialists.**   Accessible (copy in job notebook and STEP office) and followed; list of specific activities (including work, community, and social skills programming) by times of day for 6 direct service hours and for 1½ indirect service hour activities (including meetings, inservices, TJTC [Targeted Job Tax Credit] appointments).
   C. **Substitute Instructions.**   Detailed instructions for substitutes in office file and on site. Updated within 1 week of changes.
   D. **Job Description.**   List of tasks and job duties in job notebook.
   E. **Curriculum Functional and Age-Appropriate During Spot Checks.**   Spot checks are done monthly to ensure that participant is engaging in meaningful activities engaged in by others of same age.
   F. **Standard Graphs Complete.**   Participant has monthly job tenure and earnings graph, which are clearly labeled and detailed with work demographics. Updated within 3 working days of close of month. (This item can be prorated out of 2.)
   G. **Emergency Procedures**
      1. **Behavior Problems.**   When emergency behavior intervention is necessary, a written plan is in job notebook and participant file and is followed correctly.
      2. **Special Incidents.**   When these occur, they are handled appropriately, including documentation to supervisors and other agencies.
      3. **Medical Problems.**   Where medical problems exist, such as seizures, there is a written plan on what might occur and what to do.
      4. **Emergency Contacts.**   Procedures are documented: numbers and names of whom to call in an emergency, hospital preference, drug allergies, and MediCal or other health insurance are on face sheet in job notebook and in participant file. Also, participant carries identification card, and documentation exists that he or she knows what to do in an emergency.

II. **Individualized Service Plan**
   A. **Program Implementation for each ISP Objective.**   Behavior and skills programs described in ISP are currently being implemented. To score on PSR, list key word or phrase to denote ISP objectives (e.g., tenure, productivity, task, speed, breaks, grooming, purchase, bus). Fill in a + or an o in the score box for each.
   B. **List Programs.**   List by key words (e.g., work checklist, DRO, DRIP, PET, TA) in spaces 1–5. Fill in a + or an o in score box. For a program with multiple TAs, you may prorate.
      1. a. **Protocol.**   For each program, there is a written plan describing how it is implemented.
         b. **Datasheet.**   For each program, there are corresponding data that are accurate, reliable, and updated at end of day or sooner.
         c. **Graph.**   Generally, one per ISP objective, match objectives, current within 1 week, clearly labeled, accurate, and reliable.

          d. **Reliability Checks.** At least quarterly, another staff member observes identified behaviors and programming and takes data.

             1) **Interobserver.** Behaviors recorded match operational definitions—score is 85% or more reliability between two observers.

             2) **Procedural.** Procedures followed with protocol description—score is 85% or more.

    C. **Monthly Data Summary.** Sheet in job workbook summarizing monthly data for each ISP objective, updated by the fifth day of each month, and is accurate.

    D. **ISP Complete.** STEP ISP and quarterly (triannual) updates complete and timely (during birth month, within 60 days of entering program, or by 10th of month after quarter [triannual period] ends).

    E. **Objectives Met.** Prorated number of ISP objectives met on last report (e.g., 3/4). In the case of job coaches getting people who were previously assigned to other job coaches, they can select another option to the way this item is scored. That is, for the first month the job coach has the new participant, an NA (not applicable) can be scored. For subsequent months, until a new ISP (or quarterly update) is written, objectives met can be scored on the basis of the past month's data toward the ISP objectives (on data summary sheet).

III. **Administrative**

    A. **Participant Case File.** File in central office is neat, organized, and updated (include all necessary information, such as STEP intake packet signed and completed, updated intake packet from regional center, case notes, earnings records, Social Security information, SIRs, employer evaluations, STEP ISPs).

    B. **Job Notebook.** Job notebook is accessible in field, neat, organized, and updated (includes identifying information, current data on ISP objectives, graphs, attendance, earnings, SIR forms). Follows model notebook outline available in local office.

    C. **Case Notes.** Anecdotal log notes about progress, problems, or concerns recorded once a week, then filed in case file within 5 days of close of month.

    D. **Employer Evaluation.** Completed monthly by employer and discussed with participant, then placed in case file.

    E. **Earnings.** Monthly earnings and hours recorded accurately on correct form and updated within 1 day. Earnings totaled at end of month, copies of paychecks included and turned in punctually on last day of month.

    F. **TJTC/SSI.** Targeted job tax credit forms filed in timely manner with receipt and interviews completed in timely fashion. Monthly paycheck information submitted to Social Security by end of month.

    G. **Subminimum/Productivity.** State and federal subminimum wage certificate and renewals and required supporting documentation filed in timely manner (for new certificates, before job begins). Also includes checking that job sites have received certificate and have the federal certificate posted and state certificate in employee's personnel file. Productivity time and motion studies to be completed at least once every 3 months, and wages paid to be commensurate with results of studies.

IV. **Staff Development**

    A. **CBTs Complete.** Competency-based training complete or prorated by tenure, 7 during pretraining, 1 during each 2 subsequent weeks, 13 by 3 months, all by 6 months.

    B. **Staff Meetings/Inservices.** Staff member attends mandatory monthly staff meeting and quarterly inservice.

    C. **Contact Meeting.** Staff member attends weekly (or otherwise specified) meeting with contact person and follows through on recommendations.

    D. **Employer Evaluations.** Staff member scored 3s and above on last evaluation by employer and no major complaints since last check.

    E. **Professionalism.** During spot check, staff member appropriately attired for work-sites, exhibits positive attitude, acts in accordance with client rights and client advocacy. To score + on this category, there must have been no major job site or supervisory problems or conflicts in this category between checks.

    F. **Attendance/Punctuality.** Staff member follows protocol for absences or lateness (i.e., appropriate notice so coverage can be arranged). To score +, arrived on time and attended work each day since last check (except for prespecified time off or emergency).

Total +s   After coding all items, count all +s (and top number for prorated items). Add one bonus point to Total + s if 75% or more objectives were met on item 5 under ISP.

Total Possible: Count total possible score, that is, all + s and Os (and bottom number for prorated items) from main section. (Do *not* count the bonus item here.)

Percentage Score: Divide total + s by total possible for % score. Remember to note any comments in the blank space provided.

· Appendix D ·

ᵗʰᵉ*PSR*

PERIODIC SERVICE REVIEW AND OPERATIONAL DEFINITIONS FOR SUPPORTED LIVING

PERIODIC SERVICE REVIEW FOR SUPPORTED LIVING:
Score Sheet

The Periodic Service Review (PSR) is a service evaluation instrument designed to assess the consistency of the support provided to an individual consumer, the ability of the staff to implement recommendations regarding individual services, and the overall quality of the services provided.

It is important to remember that the PSR looks at the overall services for a consumer, and that a particular staff member may not be responsible for every item evaluated. When opportunities for improvement are identified, it will be noted who is responsible to ensure this improvement. The responsible staff member must take advantage of the opportunity in a timely manner, or ask the supervisor for help.

Consumer _____   Date _____

CTS* _____   Senior CTS _____

CTS _____   Service Supervisor _____

CTS _____   Service Manager _____

Overnight Support _____   Overnight Support _____

---

*CTS, Community training specialist.

	Score	Person Responsible	Target Date

I. General Service Activities

   A. Individual Schedule

   B. Staff Schedule

   C. Substitute Instructions

   D. Standard Graphs Complete

   E. Spot Checks: Age Appropriate
      and Functional

   F. No Aversives Used

   G. Special Incidents

   H. First Week Protocol

   I. Time Spent in Community

   J. PET

II. Service Delivery

   A. List Implemented Support Plans

   B. List Support Plans

      1. _____

         a. Protocol

         b. Datasheet

         c. Graph

         d. Reliability

            1) Interobserver

            2) Procedural

      2. _____

         a. Protocol

         b. Datasheet

         c. Graph

	Score	Person Responsible	Target Date

d.   Reliability

    1)   Interobserver

    2)   Procedural

3. _____

   a.   Protocol

   b.   Datasheet

   c.   Graph

   d.   Reliability

    1)   Interobserver

    2)   Procedural

4. _____

   a.   Protocol

   b.   Datasheet

   c.   Graph

   d.   Reliability

    1)   Interobserver

    2)   Procedural

5. _____

   a.   Protocol

   b.   Datasheet

   c.   Graph

   d.   Reliability

    1)   Interobserver

    2)   Procedural

6. _____

Score	Person Responsible	Target Date

   a.   Protocol

   b.   Datasheet

   c.   Graph

   d.   Reliability

Score	Person Responsible	Target Date

      1)   Interobserver

      2)   Procedural

7. _____

Score	Person Responsible	Target Date

   a.   Protocol

   b.   Datasheet

   c.   Graph

   d.   Reliability

Score	Person Responsible	Target Date

      1)   Interobserver

      2)   Procedural

8. _____

Score	Person Responsible	Target Date

   a.   Protocol

   b.   Datasheet

   c.   Graph

   d.   Reliability

Score	Person Responsible	Target Date

      1)   Interobserver

      2)   Procedural

9. _____

Score	Person Responsible	Target Date

   a.   Protocol

   b.   Datasheet

   c.   Graph

	Score	Person Responsible	Target Date

d. Reliability

   1) Interobserver

   2) Procedural

10. _____

   a. Protocol

   b. Datasheet

   c. Graph

   d. Reliability

     1) Interobserver

     2) Procedural

C. Monthly Data Summary

D. ISP Complete

E. Objectives Met

F. Social Integration

G. Community Integration Plan

III. Health and Safety

A. Medication Provided Appropriately

B. Medication Stored Appropriately

C. Medication Chart

D. Medication Count Sheet

E. Disposal of Medication

F. Medication Treatment Plan

G. Medication Protocol

H. Fire Drills

	Score	Person Responsible	Target Date
I. Escape Routes			
J. Fire Extinguisher			
K. Earthquake Drills			
L. Earthquake Preparedness Kit			
M. Emergency Contact Drill			
N. Menu Documented			
O. Menu Followed			
P. Medical/Dental Evaluations			
Q. Medical Contacts			

IV. Finances and Budgeting

	Score	Person Responsible	Target Date
A. Financial Responsibility Policy			
B. Reconciliation of Personal Monies			
C. Bills Paid			

V. Positive Futures Plan

	Score	Person Responsible	Target Date
A. Personal Profile Session			
B. Futures Planning Session			
C. Circle of Support Logistics			
D. Circle of Support Content			

VI. Staff Development

	Score	Person Responsible	Target Date
A. CBTs Complete			
B. Staff Meetings/Inservices			
C. Contact Meetings			
D. House Meetings			
E. Consumer Evaluations			

	Score	Person Responsible	Target Date
F. Professionalism			
G. Attendance/Punctuality			
H. Consumer Case File			
I. Case Notes/Log			
J. Support Plan Notebook			
K. Personal Telephone Calls			
L. Field Visit by Management			

Total Score Achieved

Total Score Possible

Percentage Score

Comments:

PERIODIC SERVICE REVIEW FOR SUPPORTED LIVING:
Operational Definitions

I. **General Service Activities**
   A. **Individual Schedule.** Daily or weekly by times or days, kept by consumer in day planner or personal appointment book, at discretion of the individual. Verified by spot checks (includes scheduled instructional sessions).
   B. **Staff Schedule.** Kept in central office and in the apartments, and followed. Any changes are verified with the assigned contact person ahead of time.
   C. **Substitute Instructions.** Detailed and updated instructions for substitutes outlining what specific support services the staff must provide, including any protocols that must be implemented, any medication that must be provided, and so forth are kept in the office file and on site and are updated within 1 week of changes.
   D. **Standard Graphs Complete.** Consumer has monthly apartment tenure and community integrated hours graphs, which are clearly labeled and detailed with demographics. Updated within 3 working days of close of month (this item can be prorated out of 2).
   E. **Spot Checks: Age Appropriate and Functional.** During spot check, consumer is engaged in age-appropriate and functional activities.
   F. **No Aversives Used.** Staff are positive with consumers at all times, as observed during spot checks and from the absence of negative reports from consumers.
   G. **Special Incidents.** When these occur, they are handled appropriately, including documentation to supervisors and other agencies, and documentation to office within 24 hours.
   H. **First Week Protocol.** First week protocol completed within the first week and filed in consumers' files.
   I. **Time Spent in Community.** Staff spend the allotted amount of time with the individual in the community. This specific amount of time is decided by each individual, within 30—60 days of receiving services, and it is noted in the ISP.
   J. **PET.** Consumers attend at least two social skills instructional sessions per week, or as otherwise provided for in their service plans. This is documented.

II. **Service Delivery**
   A. **List Support Plans Implemented.** There should be a support plan/teaching method for each ISP objective. To score PSR, list key word or phrase (e.g., cooking, cleaning, grooming, shopping, budgeting).
   B. **List Support Plans.** List by key word (e.g., work checklist, DRO, DRIP, PET, TA). Mark + or 0 in appropriate score box.
      a. **Protocol.** For each support plan, there is a written protocol. That is, a written step-by-step description on how service is to be provided.
      b. **Datasheet.** For each support plan, there are corresponding data that are accurate, reliable, and updated, as per protocol, at the end of day or sooner.
      c. **Graph.** Generally, one graph per ISP objective, current within 1 week as per protocol, clearly labeled, accurate, and reliable.
      d. **Reliability.** At least quarterly, another staff observes consumer behaviors, delivery of support plan(s) for both skills and behavior support, and takes data.

        1) **Interobserver.**   Behaviors recorded match operational definitions, and task analysis scored according to hierarchy of prompt or otherwise as reflected in each protocol. A + is earned when 85% or more reliability between two observers is achieved.

        2) **Procedural.**   Procedures followed with protocol description—score is 85% or more.

  C. **Monthly Data Summary.**   Sheet in notebook summarizing monthly data for each ISP objective, updated daily.

  D. **ISP Complete.**   SCIP ISP and quarterly updates complete and timely (during consumer birth month, within 60 days of entering service, or by 10th of month after quarter ends).

  E. **Objectives Met.**   Prorated number of ISP objectives met on last report (e.g., 3/4).

  F. **Social Integration.**   Individual has been attending activity as addressed on community integration protocol (CIP) regularly. This is verified by individual report and spot check if necessary. CIP may not be necessary for every consumer, as per manager's disclaimer.

  G. **Community Integration Plan.**   Within 60 days of enrollment, every person has active support plan for increasing interactions with people other than staff, and/or for participation in community and socially integrated activities, or as dictated by the person's interests, abilities and, personal goals and objectives, or manager writes a disclaimer.

III. Health and Safety

  A. **Medication Provided Appropriately.**   Each medication has a written order signed by a physician (oral or telephone orders must be documented appropriately and signed by a physician within 72 hours). Physician's order is consistent with medication chart and medication label.

  B. **Medication Stored Appropriately.**   Medication is stored in a safe, discrete place in a storage box. It is locked, if necessary.

  C. **Medication Chart.**   Medication chart is filled out correctly and up to date to the last time medication was taken by the individual.

  D. **Medication Count Sheet.**   The medication count sheet is filled out correctly on a weekly basis and is up to date.

  E. **Disposal of Medication.**   Any medication disposal since the last PSR was done correctly, and was documented appropriately.

  F. **Medication Treatment Plan.**   A medication treatment plan is filled out correctly for each medication prior to administration.

  G. **Medication Protocol.**   Any individuals who have a plan for taking their medication (i.e., self-medication) have a protocol, which is being followed.

  H. **Fire Drills.**   Fire evacuation drills are carried out monthly and documented on data summary.

  I. **Escape Routes.**   Two escape routes per bedroom/apartment are documented and posted, or available in consumer apartment.

  J. **Fire Extinguisher.**   Participants are able to locate and use fire extinguisher. Fire extinguisher is in working order, recharged as necessary, and kept in an accessible area.

  K. **Earthquake Drills.**   Earthquake drills are carried out monthly and documented on data summary.

  L. **Earthquake Preparedness Kit.**   Earthquake preparedness kit is complete (within 30 days of moving) and readily available.

M. Emergency Contact Drill.   Monthly beeper and 911 drills are carried out and documented, demonstrating consumer competence. This must be done during all shifts.

N. Menu Documented.   Each individual has a written menu and follows sound dietary guidelines. It is not required to have a written menu if a consumer does not need support in this area. Lack of need should be documented.

O. Menu Followed.   The menu is followed, and it is checked once per month. There should be at least 90% compliance. Any changes to the menu are documented.

P. Medical/Dental Evaluations.   Within 30 days of receiving services and annually, medical and dental appointments are carried out and documented on the physician recommendation form. If an individual has had a medical or dental examination within 3 months prior to receiving SCIP services, only annual appointments must be done. Medical recommendations are followed 100% of the time.

Q. Medical Contacts.   Each person has the name of a doctor, dentist, and hospital to be used for medical problems, and these are reflected on the face sheet.

IV. Finances and Budgeting

    A. Financial Responsibility Policy.   All individuals, their parents, or other responsible parties have read and signed financial responsibility policy upon intake.

    B. Reconciliation of Personal Monies.   Weekly reconciliation prepared and accountable within $1.00 on appropriate form.

    C. Bills Paid.   Bills are paid by due date on bill, and neither late charges nor service interruptions have been incurred within month. If this is a specific issue for a person, a written plan is in place and implemented.

V. Positive Futures Plan

    A. Personal Profile Session.   Session is completed before individual begins receiving SCIP services.

    B. Futures Planning Session.   Session is completed within first 30 days of an individual receiving services.

    C. Circle of Support Logistics.   Groups meet at least once per quarter, unless special circumstances arise. Invitations and coordination are done by focus person or support staff. Minutes of circle of support will be typed and made available to all parties within 1 week after the meeting.

    D. Circle of Support Content.   A task grid is generated and at least 75% of tasks are accomplished by the next meeting. One task should always be to seek out a friend.

VI. Staff Development

    A. CBTs Complete.   Competency-based training complete or prorated by tenure, 7 during pretraining, 1 during each 2 subsequent weeks, 13 by 3 months, all by 6 months. (In Los Angeles, all must be completed in 3 months.)

    B. Staff Meetings/Inservices.   Staff attends mandatory monthly staff meeting and quarterly inservice.

    C. Contact Meetings.   Staff attend weekly (or otherwise specified) meeting with supervisory contact person and follows through on recommendations (e.g., no past-due assignments).

    D. House Meetings.   Held monthly. Attended by service manager and/or supervisor every other quarter. Minutes summarized by contact person and shared at weekly management meeting.

    E. Consumer Evaluations.   Staff and services are rated monthly and are scored at least satisfactory by individual and/or staff are working on resolving any difficulties in relationship or dissatisfaction with services.

    F. Professionalism.   During spot check, staff are appropriately attired for work, exhibit positive attitude, and act in accordance with individuals' rights and advocacy.

To score, there must have been no major problems or conflicts in this category between checks.

G. Attendance/Punctuality. Staff follow protocol for absences or lateness (i.e., appropriate notice so coverage can be arranged). To score a +, staff must have arrived on time and attended work each day since last check (except for prespecified time off or emergency).

H. Consumer Case File. File in central office is neat, organized, and updated by fifth of the month (include all necessary information such as SCIP intake packet signed and completed, updated intake packet from regional center, case notes, Social Security information, SIRs, CTS evaluations, SCIP ISPs).

I. Case Notes/Log. Anecdotal log notes about individual progress, problems or concerns written once a week (staff log written daily), then filed in case file or log book within 5 days of close of month.

J. Support Plan Notebook. Notebook accessible in field/apartment, neat, organized, and updated (includes identifying information, current data on ISP objectives, graphs, attendance, SIR forms). Follows model notebook outline.

K. Personal Telephone Calls. Personal telephone calls using telephone of service recipient should not be necessary. If they must be made, nonemergency calls should be cleared first with supervisor and logged by him or her. Emergency calls should be cleared within 24 hours and documented in log.

L. Field Visit by Management. The service manager or supervisor has visited this person's home at least twice per month. An ISP meeting cannot count as a visit unless the management staff stayed half an hour or longer before or after the meeting. This is documented in the case file.

· Appendix E ·

The PSR

SOCIAL/COMMUNITY INTEGRATION AND PARTICIPATION (SCIP)
COMMUNITY INTEGRATION PROTOCOL

I. **Identify Applicable Social Interest.** Identify a group, club, or class that interests the person. This can be done through discussions with the individual, through reviewing the positive futures plan, through speaking with the person's significant others, and/or by observation.

II. **Ecological Inventory.** The support staff should attend at least one session of the group, club, or class for which the client has shown interest during his or her indirect service hours. He or she should pay close attention to such things as common behavior, attire, idiosyncrasies of the group, and so forth. If appropriate, speak to someone in charge to find out more details, and explain why you are there, what your goals are, and how that person can help. The support staff might also want to speak to a group member to find out more about the group. In addition, photographs may be taken so that the person knows what to expect when he or she attends. A discrepancy analysis should be completed to disclose those aspects of the identified activity for which support or training may be necessary, as well as transportation and financial analyses.

III. **First Client Contact.** Now the support staff should begin to talk with the person about the activity and begin to plan the first contact. There are a number of ways this first contact may be carried out. One or more of the following may be used.

    A. **Potentiating Activities.** It may be helpful for the person to experience the situation through such means as watching a videotape, reading a book on the topic, discussing the activity, or watching another engage in the activity.

    B. **Personal Effectiveness Training.** The activity may be reviewed during social skills instruction groups, with emphasis on role-playing.

    C. **Imagery-Based Role-Playing.** This technique uses role-playing and consists of imagining a scenario and rehearsing appropriate responses.

D. Relaxation Training. Because the person may be nervous about attending the activity, it may be necessary for him or her to engage in some relaxation exercises before the activity.

E. Worry Inventory. The support staff may need to sit down with the person and identify all the concerns the individual has about the activity, then come up with solutions. (Social skills instruction and imagery-based practice may be used to address concerns.)

F. Inservice. It may be necessary for the support staff or management staff to speak to the group ahead of time to explain any special concerns or issues about the person. This is also the perfect opportunity for the members to get answers to questions they may have.

G. Instructional. The person may need instructions about the activity and what he or she should do, wear, how to behave, and so on. These instructions may be oral or written.

H. Obtaining Appropriate Materials. The person may need to purchase, borrow, or locate from among his or her personal possessions, certain items needed to fit in at the activity (e.g., Western clothes for swing dancing, clay for ceramics class).

I. Define Role. The person may need help in defining beforehand the specific role he or she will play in the activity (e.g., if the person is joining a softball team, he or she will have to decide which position the person can play and wants to play).

J. Medical Issues or Release. Certain medical issues may need to be addressed before the person can attend the activity. Additionally, a medical release from a doctor may need to be obtained.

K. Pep Talk. The person may benefit from a pep talk immediately before the activity begins to help motivate him or her, and to alleviate any last-minute fears.

L. Buddy-Person Active. The support staff member may accompany the person to the activity. While there, the support staff member may also be an active participant (such as square dancing along with the person on a double date) or he or she may be a passive observer, attending for support only.

M. Nonsupport Staff Buddy. The person may be paired with another person to attend the activity.

N. Peer Buddy. The person may be paired with a peer to attend the activity.

O. Passive Observation. At the first visit, the person may choose merely to sit back and observe. The support staff member may accompany the person or the individual may choose to go alone.

P. Shaping. The person may need to be exposed to the activity incrementally. For example, one day he or she may take the bus past the site of the activity; the next time the person may go inside, look around, and then leave; next, the individual might stay for the entire activity but only as an observer.

Q. Pretraining. This cannot exceed 2 weeks, and should consist of practicing the actual activities to reach the minimum competency level of the rest of the group. It may also consist of things that must be done or learned to enable the person to perform the activity. For example, in order for the individual to begin playing on a community softball team, he or she may need to build up his or her endurance to that level of activity, or he or she may need to learn the vocabulary appropriate to the activity.

R. Reinforcement Schedule. It may be helpful to establish a reinforcement schedule so the person can earn something tangible for attending. This should be faded out as the natural reinforcement of the activity becomes stronger.

S. Permanent Product Assignment. A person may need the motivation of bringing back a tangible item from an activity to show that he or she attended. This also may serve as a reinforcing souvenir and reminder (e.g., the person may bring back a bowl constructed in ceramics class).

    T.   **Other.**   The support staff should be alert for any specialized circumstances that may need to be addressed for any particular activity.

IV. **Troubleshooting/Plan Revision.** After the first contact, the support staff and his or her supervisor should look at the progress that was made, the problems that arose, and what is still missing. They should then go back through Step III and revise the plan for the second contact. This step should be implemented after every contact until the person is fully integrated in the activity.

V. **Parallel Training.** At any time that a person attends a specific activity, the individual may need some help outside the group in order to keep pace with the other members. This may consist of, tutoring, modeling, practicing, social skills instruction, a behavior support plan, and so forth.

VI. **Fading.** As the person becomes more fully integrated in the activity, a formal plan of fading staff participation should be implemented. This plan will depend on the specific steps used in Step III. The person will be considered independent after he or she has attended the activity five times with no intervention, including preactivity prompts. It should be noted that fading will not necessarily be a goal for all people; some may need staff help indefinitely.

VII. **Follow-Up Plan.** Once the person is considered independent on an activity, a maintenance plan should be implemented. This will depend on the specific individual and the specific activity; in any case, it may consist of monthly calls to a group member or leader, or quarterly permanent product assignment, and so on.

· Appendix F ·

The PSR

BEHAVIOR ASSESSMENT REPORT AND SUPPORT PLAN
EVALUATION INSTRUMENT AND WRITING GUIDE

BEHAVIOR ASSESSMENT REPORT AND SUPPORT PLAN:

Evaluation Instrument and Writing Guide/Score Sheet

Person's Name _____ Protocol Number _____

Scorer's Name _____ Total Percentage Score _____

	Score	Comments
I. General Format		
A. Format		
1. Title		
2. Headings		
3. Report Date		
4. Referral Date		
5. Author's Name and Title		

	Score	Comments
B. Identifying Information		
1. Person's Name		
2. Person's Date of Birth		
3. Person's Present Address		
4. Referring Agency or Person		

II.   Reason(s) for Referral

A.   Source of Referral
(Agency and/or Person)

B.   Referral Behaviors

C.   Key Social Agent's Reasons for
Referral and Possible
Discrepancies

III.   Data Source

IV.   Description of Services

A.   Service Settings

B.   Types of Services

C.   Date Provided

D.   Duration

V.   Background Information

A.   Learner Description

1.   Age

2.   Sex

3.   Diagnosis

4.   Appearance

5.   Ambulation

6.   Use of Hands and Arms

	Score	Comments
7. Physical Disabilities		
8. Cognitive Abilities		
9. Expressive Language		
10. Receptive Language		
11. Adaptive Skills		
12. Domestic Skills		
13. Leisure Skills		
14. Community Skills		

B. Living Arrangements

    1. Location

    2. Name and Relationship

    3. Residence Type

    4. Residence Description

    5. Family Members

C. Day Setting

    1. General Statement
       (Yes/No)

    2. Name

    3. Location

    4. Type

    5. Evaluation

D. Health and Medical Status

    1. General Health

	Score	Comments

2. Seizure Activity (Yes/No)

    a. Type

    b. Frequency

    c. Most Recent Incidence

3. Medication (Yes/No)

    a. Type

    b. Dosage

    c. Schedule

    d. Purpose

E. Previous or Current Services

    1. General Statement

    2. Name of Service Provider

    3. Reason for Service

    4. Outcome of Service

VI. Functional Analysis

A. Behavior 1 _____
                     (fill in)

    1. Description of the Problem
        Behavior

        a. Topography

        b. Onset/Offset

        c. Course/Precursors

        d. Strength

        e. Severity

	Score	Comments

2. History of the Problem

   a.   Onset

   b.   Duration

   c.   Changes

3. Environmental Analysis

4. Antecedent Analysis

   a.   Settings/Location

   b.   Persons

   c.   Time

   d.   Activities

   e.   Immediate Events

5. Consequence Analysis

   a.   Reactions

   b.   Management

      1)   Methods

      2)   Effects

   c.   Maintaining Events

6. Impressions and Analysis of
    Meaning

   a.   List of Hypotheses

   b.   Strategy Summary

B. Behavior 2 _____
                    (fill in)

   1. Description of the Problem
       Behavior

      a.   Topography

      b.   Onset/Offset

	Score	Comments

c. Course/Precursors

d. Strength

e. Severity

2. History of the Problem

   a. Onset

   b. Duration

   c. Changes

3. Environmental Analysis

4. Antecedent Analysis

   a. Settings/Location

   b. Persons

   c. Time

   d. Activities

   e. Immediate Events

5. Consequence Analysis

   a. Reactions

   b. Management

      1) Methods

      2) Effects

   c. Maintaining Events

6. Impressions and Analysis of Meaning

   a. List of Hypotheses

   b. Strategy Summary

	Score	Comments

VII.   Motivational Analysis

    A.   Method of Analysis

    B.   List Potential Reinforcers

    C.   Prioritize Potential Reinforcers

VIII.   Mediator Analysis

    A.   Description of Agents

    B.   Estimate of Abilities

IX.   Recommended Support Plan

    A.   Long-Range Goals

    B.   Short-Term Behavioral
        Objectives

        1.   Label Target Behavior

        2.   Decrease, Maintain, or
            Increase

        3.   Degree of Change

        4.   Time Interval

    C.   Data Collection

        1.   Methods

            a.   Behavior 1

            b.   Behavior 2

        2.   Reliability

            a.   Behavior 1

            b.   Behavior 2

	Score	Comments

D.   **Intervention Procedures**

　　1.   Environmental Changes

　　2.   Positive Programming

　　　　a.   General Skills

　　　　b.   Functionally Equivalent
　　　　　　Skills

　　　　c.   Functionally Related
　　　　　　Skills

　　　　d.   Coping Skills

　　3.   Focused Support

　　　　a.   Behavior 1

　　　　b.   Behavior 2

　　4.   Reactive Strategies

　　　　a.   Behavior 1

　　　　b.   Behavior 2

　　5.   Staff Development

X.   Comments and Recommendations

A.   Anticipated Difficulties

B.   Additional Resources and/or
　　Services Requested

C.   Strategies for Evaluating
　　Outcome

　　Summary Score

　　Percentage Score (PSR)

BEHAVIOR ASSESSMENT REPORT AND SUPPORT PLAN:

Evaluation Instrument and Writing Guide/Operational Definitions

I. **General Format**
   - A. **Format**
     1. **Title.** A + is given if the report is properly titled at the top of the first page. It should, at a minimum, contain the words "Behavior Assessment Report."
     2. **Headings.** A + is given if all the following sections are headed properly (i.e., IB, II, III, IV, V, VI, VII, IX, and X).
     3. **Report Date.** On the first page, include date of report (i.e., date final typed).
     4. **Referral Date.** See item 3 above.
     5. **Author's Name and Title.** The author's name, title, and affiliation should appear at the end of the report.
   - B. **Identifying Information**
     1. **Person's Name**
     2. **Person's Date of Birth**
     3. **Person's Present Address**
     4. **Referring Agency or Person.** The agency should be named, and if there is a service coordinator or counselor, this person's name should be provided.

II. **Reason(s) for Referral**
   - A. **Source of Referral.** Provide a brief statement identifying the agency and/or person making the referral.
   - B. **Referral Behaviors.** The specific behaviors or reasons precipitating the referral should be described.
   - C. **Key Social Agent's Reasons for Referral and Possible Discrepancies.** This should be a brief statement of the key social agent's reasons for requesting services. If the referral was made by an agency separate from the key social agent, some determination should be made concerning the agreement between them as to the reasons for the referral.

III. **Data Source.** This section should identify and list the methods used in conducting the assessment. This could include direct observation, interviews, questionnaires, review of evaluation reports prepared by other professionals, previous program data, and so forth.

IV. **Description of Services**
   - A. **Service Settings.** This section should list the settings where the assessment was done (e.g., home, school, worksite).
   - B. **Types of Services.** The names of the programs visited should be listed. The type of service provided (e.g., interview with parents, direct observation in classroom) should be indicated.
   - C. **Date Provided.** The date of service and the duration of service per date of delivery should be provided.
   - D. **Duration.** Times and dates should be indicated. Also included should be telephone conferences, plan development, and report-writing time.

V. Background Information
   A. Learner Description
      1. **Age**
      2. **Sex**
      3. **Diagnosis**
      4. **Appearance.**   Describe the person's physical characteristics and appearance. At the minimum, describe height and weight.
      5. **Ambulation**
      6. **Use of Hands and Arms**
      7. **Physical Disabilities.**   Provide a brief statement about the presence/absence of any physical disabilities.
      8. **Cognitive Abilities.**   The formal level of functioning and the source of the diagnosis should be provided. Any relevant formal testing results should be described. A brief statement regarding the person's abilities to read, write, and manipulate numbers should be made.
      9. **Expressive Language.**   The person's ability to communicate via vocalizations, sign language, pictures, and/or gestures should be stated. A general sense of his or her ability to make needs known should be provided.
      10. **Receptive Language.**   The person's ability to comprehend language should be described. This should include a description of the person's ability to understand simple to complex requests and conversation.
      11. **Adaptive Skills.**   A brief statement should be made about the person's level of independence in these skills.
      12. **Domestic Skills.** See item 11.
      13. **Leisure Skills.** See item 11.
      14. **Community Skills.** See item 11.

   B. Living Arrangements
      1. **Location.**   This should include a description of the general location where the client resides (e.g., city, rural, suburb).
      2. **Name and Relationship.**   Include the name(s) of the persons living with the client and their relationship to the client. If the person does not live in the parental home, give the name of the caregiver and his or her title or function (e.g., foster parent).
      3. **Residence Type.**   For example, board-and-care, specialized group home, independent living apartment, or supported living.
      4. **Residence Description.**   A brief description of the ecology of the residence, including number of other residents, size of residence, cleanliness, crowding conditions, and so forth.
      5. **Family Members.**   If the person does not live at home, contact with any (other) family members should be noted.

   C. Day Setting
      1. **General Statement (Yes/No).**   Provide a general statement as to whether the person receives services during the day. If not, why? If the individual is not receiving services, items 2–5 below need not be scored.
      2. **Name.**   Enter the name of the program.
      3. **Location.**   General locaton of the program should be noted—institution as opposed to community, name of city.
      4. **Type.**   For example, workshop, special education class, development center, or supported work.
      5. **Evaluation.**   Briefly describe the adequacy of the services to meet the person's needs.

D. Health and Medical Status
 1. **General Health.**   Provide a brief description of the person's general health. If the person is in poor health, describe the problems and the treatment.
 2. **Seizure Activity (Yes/No).**   Indicate the presence or absence of seizures, both in the past as well as currently. (If the person currently has seizures, fill in items a–c, below. If absent, mark a–c N/A.)
    a. Type
    b. Frequency
    c. Most Recent Incidence
 3. **Medication (Yes/No).**   State whether the person is receiving medication.
    a. **Type**
    b. **Dosage**
    c. **Schedule**
    d. **Purpose.**   For example, behavior control, seizures, enuresis, hypertension. If the medication is for behavior, its effects should be described briefly.

E. Previous or Current Services
 1. **General Statement.**   Indicate whether or not the person has received services for current behavior problems or previous behavioral treatment. (If the person has not received services, enter N/A in items 2–4, below.)
 2. **Name of Service Provider**
 3. **Reason for Service**
 4. **Outcome of Service**

VI. Functional Analysis

A. Behavior 1 _____
                                       (fill in)
 1. **Description of the Problem Behavior**
    a. **Topography.**   Describe the physical characteristics (i.e., visual, auditory, olfactory, tactile) of the behavior
    b. **Onset/Offset.**   Describe the first occurrence of the topography and its cessation—behavior continues for 5 seconds; topography absent for 5 minutes.
    c. **Course/Precursors.**   State the presence or absence precursors. If they are present, describe order of their occurrence.
    d. **Strength.**   The present rate of the behavior should be described. Rate is defined as frequency during a unit of time. If other measures are appropriate, they should be presented (e.g., duration).
    e. **Severity.**   If appropriate, the impact of the behavior (e.g., damage, injury) on the environment and/or the person should be noted.
 2. **History of the Problem**
    a. **Onset.**   State the point of onset. If it is unknown, then state this.
    b. **Duration.**   Describe the duration.
    c. **Changes.**   A statement should be made regarding any recent changes in the rate or severity of the behavior. If there has been a recent exacerbation or a decrease, a statement should be made about the factors contributing to these changes.
 3. **Environmental Analysis.**   Environmental factors that might have an impact on the behavior should be described. These include such factors in the physical environment as overcrowding, noise, location of facility, number of people in the environment, and sudden environmental changes. These can also include such programmatic characteristics as lack of schedule of activities, lack of functional programming, instructional technology, and nature of materials used in instruction. Furthermore, these can include such interpersonal factors

as quality and quantity of interactions with others, opportunities for interactions with others, expectations of others, and philosophy of those around the person.

4. **Antecedent Analysis**
   a. **Settings/Location.** Describe the settings and/or locations (e.g., bedroom, bathroom) where the behavior is most or least likely to occur. If there is no apparent difference, this should be noted.
   b. **Persons.** Describe the characteristics of people in whose presence the behavior is most or least likely to occur. For example, is the behavior more likely in the presence of men or women? If there are no differences, this should be noted.
   c. **Time.** Note the times of the day, week, and month when the behavior is most or least likely to occur. If there are no differences, this should be noted.
   d. **Activities.** Describe the specific activities during which the behavior is most or least likely to occur. For example, the behavior may be more frequent when doing the dishes or when showering. If there are no differences, this should be noted.
   e. **Immediate Events.** If the occurrence or the nonoccurrence is immediately preceded by the onset or cessation of an environmental event (e.g., a demand, a person walking into the room, noise) these specific events should be described. If there are no identifiable events, this should be noted.

5. **Consequence Analysis**
   a. **Reactions.** Describe the others' reactions to the behavior. That is, given that the behavior has occurred, what is the immediate response of others —including nonstaff members?
   b. **Management**
      1) **Methods.** Briefly describe the formal methods used to manage the behavior (e.g., timeout, reinforce alternatives, ignore). This may be cross-referenced to item V.E. Previous or Current Services. In addition, describe the effectiveness of the strategies.
      2) **Effects.**
   c. **Maintaining Events.** Describe the events that maintain the target behavior (e.g., positive/negative reinforcement). This information is in item VI.A.6. below. Credit should be given if this is the case.

6. **Impressions and Analysis of Meaning**
   a. **List of Hypotheses.** List hypotheses regarding the possible functions served by the behavior. These might include communication, initiation/maintenance of social interaction, stress reduction, increase/decrease of sensory input, acquisition of events from the environment, escape/avoidance of unpleasant events in the environment.
   b. **Strategy Summary.** A brief statement or list of possible intervention programs should be presented.

B. **Behavior 2** _____
(fill in)

1. **Description of the Problem Behavior**
   a. **Topography.** Describe the physical characteristics (i.e., visual, auditory, olfactory, tactile) of the behavior
   b. **Onset/Offset.** State the first occurrence of the topography and cessation of topography; behavior continues for 5 seconds; topography absent for 5 minutes.

      c. **Course/Precursors.** State the presence or absence precursors. If there are precursors, these should be described in order of their occurrence.

      d. **Strength.** Describe the present rate of the behavior. Rate is the frequency during a unit of time. If other measures are appropriate, they should be included (i.e., duration).

      e. **Severity.** The impact of the behavior (e.g., damage, injury) on the environment and/or the person should be noted.

2. **History of the Problem**

      a. **Onset.** If this is not known, this should be stated.

      b. **Duration**

      c. **Changes.** Describe any recent changes in the rate or severity of the behavior. If there has been a recent exacerbation or a decrease, describe the factors contributing to these changes.

3. **Environmental Analysis.** Describe environmental factors that might have an impact on the behavior. These can include such physical factors as overcrowding, noise, location of facility, number of people in the environment, and sudden environmental changes. These can also include such programmatic characteristics as lack of a schedule of activities, lack of functional programming, instructional technology, and the nature of the materials used in instruction. Moreover, these can be such interpersonal factors as quality and quantity of interactions with others, opportunities for interactions with others, expectations of others and philosophy of those around the person.

4. **Antecedent Analysis**

      a. **Settings/Locations.** Describe the settings and/or locations (e.g., bedroom, bathroom) where the behavior is most or least likely to occur. If there is no apparent difference, this should be noted.

      b. **Persons.** Describe the characteristics of people in whose presence the behavior is most or least likely to occur. For example, does the behavior occur most or least in the presence of men or women? If there are no differences, this should be noted.

      c. **Time.** Describe the times of the day, week, and month when the behavior is most or least likely to occur. If there are no differences, this should be noted.

      d. **Activities.** Describe the specific activities during which the behavior is most or least likely to occur. For example, the behavior may be more frequent when doing dishes or when showering. If there are no differences, this should be noted.

      e. **Immediate Events.** If the target behavior's occurrence or nonoccurrence is immediately preceded by the onset or offset of an environmental event (e.g., a demand, a person walking into the room, noise), these specific events should be described. If there are no identifiable events, this should be noted.

5. **Consequence Analysis**

      a. **Reactions.** Describe the reactions of others to the behavior. That is, given that the behavior has occurred, describe the immediate response of others—including nonstaff members.

      b. **Management**

         1) **Methods.** Describe the formal methods used to manage the target behavior (e.g., timeout, reinforce alternatives, ignore). This may be cross-referenced to item V.E. Previous or Current Services.

2) Effects. Describe the effectiveness of the treatment strategies.

    c. Maintaining Events. Describe the events that maintain the target behavior (e.g., positive/negative reinforcement). This information can be found in item VI.B.6. Impressions and Analysis of Meaning, below. Credit should be given, if this is the case.

  6. Impressions and Analysis of Meaning

    a. List of Hypotheses. Describe hypotheses as to the possible functions served by the behavior. These might include communication, initiation/maintenance of social interaction, stress reduction, increase/decrease of sensory input, acquisition of events from the environment, escape/avoidance of unpleasant events in the environment.

    b. Strategy Summary. List possible intervention programs.

VII. Motivational Analysis

A. Method of Analysis. For example, interview, observation, free access test, questionnaire.

B. List Potential Reinforcers

C. Prioritize Potential Reinforcers

VIII. Mediator Analysis

A. Description of Agents. Describe the key social agents (i.e., parents, teachers, aides, etc.) responsible for support services.

B. Estimate of Abilities. Describe the strengths and weaknesses of these potential mediators, with specific attention to how these might have an impact on the course of intervention. This should lead to a realistic estimate of the potential mediators' abilities to perform programs, given the demands of time, energy, emotions, and the constraints imposed by the specific service settings.

IX. Recommended Support Plan

A. Long-Range Goals. Briefly describe the long-range goal(s) for the support plan in terms of quality of life measures; for example, living in the least restrictive settings, increasing contact with the population that have no disabilities, increasing independence, maximizing opportunities to interact with persons without disabilities in everyday situations with minimal supervision.

B. Short-Term Behavioral Objectives. For each target behavior, time-limited, measurable objectives should be present. Each objective should contain *all* of the following.

  1. A label for the target behavior

  2. A description of whether the target behavior is to be decreased/maintained/increased

  3. A statement in measurable terms (frequency, rate, percentage occurrence, duration) of the degree of change expected (25 times a week to 10 times a week; 10 minutes a day to 5 minutes a day)

  4. A statement of interval of time during which the change is expected to occur (1 month, 1 quarter)

The short-term objective should not exceed a 3-month period.

C. Data Collection

  1. Methods. Present methods of observation and data collection for each target behavior described above. The method described should be adequate and appropriate, given the topography and frequency of the target behavior, as well as the available staffing resources.

  2. Reliability. Methods of determining the accuracy and reliability of the observational data should be described for each target behavior described. The methods should be appropriate, given the behaviors described and their relative frequencies.

D. **Intervention Procedures**
1. **Environmental Changes.** Specific recommendations should be made for alterations to the person's physical, programmatic, and/or interpersonal environments for the purpose of providing the most support for achieving the overall goals and objectives. If there are no needs in this area, a statement in this regard should be made. Appropriateness of the recommendations should be evaluated.
2. **Positive Programming**
   a. **General Skills.** If appropriate, a statement should be made regarding systematic instruction in the areas of adaptive skills, vocational activities, domestic activities, community functioning, and/or leisure time/recreational activities. The tasks, skills, and activities should be functional, chronological age appropriate, and should be performed under the conditions where they would naturally be used.
   b. **Functionally Equivalent Skills.** If appropriate, given the functional analysis, specific behaviors should be taught that provide the person with more appropriate/effective ways of achieving the legitimate function served by the target behaviors and identified in the functional analysis. For example, if the behavior is designed to communicate, then the program should include alternative communication strategies.
   c. **Functionally Related Skills.** If appropriate, given the functional analysis, specific skills should be taught that are related to, but not functionally equivalent to the target behaviors described above. Examples might include teaching choice making, teaching a person to use a schedule or activity sequence board, teaching independent food preparation and shopping, teaching discriminations, and so forth.
   d. **Coping Skills.** In the previous sections, the person is taught to be more skillful in his or her interactions with the environment. The person is taught to be more independent, and to achieve needs more effectively and more appropriately. In this section, the person is taught to *tolerate* or *cope with* areas of the natural environment that cannot or will not be changed, especially those events that have been identified as discriminative for the target behaviors. Thus, if appropriate given the functional analysis, a statement should be made describing the instruction that will occur. This might include relaxation training, desensitization, tolerance training, emotive imagery, graduated extinction, vicarious extinction, and counter-conditioning strategies.
3. **Focused Support.** If appropriate, given the functional analysis described above and other environmental and medical issues, specific strategies should be described that are designed to produce rapid changes in each target behavior (e.g., DRO, DROP, ALT-R, DRL, stimulus satiation, stimulus control, combined schedules, DRH, instructional control). Each procedure should be appropriate given the overall goals and objectives and the frequencies and intensities described in the functional analysis. In evaluating the procedures, special attention should be given to selection of interval sizes in DRO(P) programs, selection of criteria for the DRL, the 100% rule, or approximation, given the use of an ALT-R schedule, and reinforcement characteristics, given the free access rule. Full consideration should be given to the basic rules of good contingency management in evaluating this area (e.g., contingency, timeliness of reinforcement schedule of delivery).

4. **Reactive Strategies.**   Specify strategies for managing each target behavior consistent with the Institute for Applied Behavior Analysis (IABA) emergency management guidelines.

5. **Staff Development.**   Describe specific strategies for teaching the mediators how to carry out the above described support plans. These strategies might include inservice training, competency-based training, role-playing, modeling, in-home consultation with direct procedure-by-procedure instruction.

X.   Comments and Recommendations

A. **Anticipated Difficulties.**   Describe the level of anticipated cooperation or motivation of the mediators and/or the presence or absence of any issues that might impede progress. If there are no anticipated problems, then state that this is so.

B. **Additional Resources and/or Services Requested.**   Describe any other services that the person may require. Any recommendations regarding further behavioral consultation, intensive intervention, and so forth should be made. If no further services are requested, state this with a brief explanation.

C. **Strategies for Evaluating Outcome.**   If services are to be provided, a timeframe for evaluating the effectiveness of and need for continuing services should be provided. This might include monthly or quarterly reports.

· Appendix G ·

The PSR

FIDELITY CHECKLIST
AND SAMPLE
INSTRUCTIONAL MODULES

FIDELITY CHECKLIST:
Evaluations of Teaching Style

Rater: Check each item that reflects observed instructor behaviors during leadership of skills-training session(s). Each instructor behavior listed should be demonstrated at least once during the session under observation.

Prepares for lesson:

_____ Arranges seats in circle or so that all participants face each other

_____ Establishes appropriate pace

Relates positively:

_____ Motivates participants (e.g., "This has really worked for me, and I think it might work for you, too.")

_____ Demonstrates interest in participant (e.g., "I've missed your comments. Have you been ill?")

_____ Displays empathy (e.g., "That must have been a rough time in your life.")

_____ Reinforces positively approximately 80% of the time

_____ Repeats participant's response or comments during review

---

Adapted by Catherine Phipps (Institute for Applied Behavior Analysis staff member) from Liberman, DiRisi, and Mueser (1989).

Stresses learning:

_____ Is enthusiastic about module or skill being taught

_____ Asks participant to answer in his or her own words

_____ Asks for definition of vocabulary

_____ Before moving on to another participant, encourages participant (e.g., "Tell the group a little more about that.")

_____ Checks back with participant who was initially unclear or gave incorrect response to make sure he or she understood

_____ Gives examples of concepts being taught

_____ Asks participants a specific question when no one volunteers a question

_____ Clarifies what participant *does* know, if participant gives an incorrect response

Prompts participant:

Gives oral prompts

_____ Repeats question

_____ Asks participants to complete a sentence

_____ Asks a yes/no question

_____ Other

Gives gestural prompts

_____ Holds up an object

_____ Points to a chart or object

_____ Acts out an emotion or situation

_____ Other

Encourages participation:

_____ Makes participant the expert (e.g., "What was that like for you?")

_____ Asks group, "How many agree?" or "How many disagree?"

_____ Asks participant why he or she agrees

_____ States participant's name after question has been stated (e.g., "What do you think of that, John?")

_____ States, "I would like a comment from everyone on this."

_____ Asks, "Do you want to add anything?"

_____ Gives positive feedback for participant's contribution or effort, whether it was correct or incorrect (e.g., "Not quite, but thank you for volunteering.")

_____ Prompts participants to listen to another participant (e.g., "Listen to what John thinks, and then I'll come back to you.")

_____ Returns to participant after listening to another participant ("So, what did you think about John's comment?")

_____ When participant responds, "I don't know," to a question, instructor asks, "What part do you remember?"

Fosters listening and participant's responsibility for own learning:

_____ Refrains from repeating participant's correct response for the group, and instead asks participant to ask others to paraphrase or repeat the response

_____ Encourages participant to ask other participants for clarification of what they mean

_____ Encourages participant to ask other participants to speak up if he or she cannot hear

Manages behavior:

_____ Ignores minor disruptions

_____ Asks inattentive or disruptive participant a question to redirect his or her attention to group process

_____ Asks participants to "Tell (name) what you liked about his or her role-playing."

_____ Directs participants, when necessary, to direct comments to participants who just completed role-playing

_____ Directs participants, when necessary, to be specific about what they liked about the role-playing (e.g., Instead of accepting "I liked it," or "He was good," asks, "What do you like?" or "What was good about it?")

_____ Uses the list of communication skills

_____ Asks participants for suggestions after giving positive feedback (e.g., "What would you suggest (name) do to improve her role-playing?")

_____ Prompts participants to begin sentence with "I suggest . . . "

_____ Redirects questioning during role-playing so that participants can answer correctly

_____ Re-does role-playing when less than 80% accurate

_____ Helps participants to identify components of good communication skills, using list of communication skills

Evaluation of Fidelity to Modules

Checklist of Instructor's behaviors

Rater: Check each item that reflects observed instructor behaviors during modules. Make ratings while observing an instructional session in action.

Laying the groundwork:

_____ Introduces self and other staff members

_____ Asks participants to introduce themselves

_____ Asks participants to tell where they live, favorite hobbies, and so forth

> _____ Asks each participant a question or two about the introduction or

> _____ Makes a comment about the introductions or

> _____ Makes a connection between one participant's introduction and another participant's introduction or interest

_____ Acknowledges each participant after he or she has spoken by asking the group to applaud and welcome that person to the group

_____ Presents overview of module (aim, context, skills)

_____ Presents goal of module

_____ Presents goal of skills areas

> _____ Discusses benefits of reaching the goals

_____ Stresses importance of attendance and punctuality, location, days, and times of the group's sessions

_____ Displays posters with goals, skill areas, communication skills, problem solving, and/or resources (possibly done with pictures)

Introduction to skills areas:

_____ Reviews previous session's content

_____ Asks, "What is the goal of the skill area?"

_____ Asks, "What is the goal of the entire module?"

_____ Describes the structure of the group for that session (e.g., participants will participate in role-playing, discussions)

Role-playing:

_____ Asks goal of module

_____ Asks benefits of reaching the goals

_____ Emphasizes value of role-playing

_____ Asks participants if they have any questions

_____ Asks, "What is my role?"

_____ Asks, "What is your role?"

_____ Asks, "What is your task in the scene?"

_____ Designates area and chairs for role-playing

_____ Positions participants so that role-playing is visible to all

_____ Role-plays with each participant

_____ Applauds performance

_____ Comments about own performance

_____ Asks participants to comment on their performances

_____ Gives entire group positive feedback on their good performances

_____ Asks participants, to "Tell (name) what you like about his or her role-play ."

_____ Directs participants, when necessary, to direct comments to the participants who just completed role-playing

_____ Directs participants when necessary, to be specific about what they like about the role-playing (e.g., Instead of accepting "I liked it" or "He was good," asks, "What do you like?" and/or "What was good about it?")

_____ Uses the list of quality skills

_____ Asks participants for suggestions after giving positive feedback (e.g., "What would you suggest (name) do to improve her role-play?")

_____ Prompts participants to begin sentence with "I suggest . . . "

_____ Redirects questioning during role-playing so that participants can answer correctly (e.g., if participant answers that yelling at your manager was wrong, instructor can ask, "What makes yelling at your manger wrong?" Then "So, if I yell at my manager I could get fired?")

_____ Re-does role-playing when less than 80% accurate

_____ Helps participants identify components of good communication skills, using list of quality skills

Homework assignment:

_____ Asks goal of module

_____ Asks benefits of reaching the goal of module

_____ Explains homework assignment to participants

_____ Asks participants if they have any questions

_____ Asks participants, "What resources will you need to complete this assignment?"

_____ Asks participants to repeat instructions

_____   Asks, "How will completing this assignment benefit you?"

_____   Has participants perform exercise

_____   Requests participants to bring back proof of homework completion

_____   Discusses homework with each participant

_____   Reviews material covered in entire module

Instructor Fidelity Evaluation for Modules

Summary Report Form

Name of Observer: _____   Date/Time: _____

Names of Participants: _____

_____

_____

_____

Name of Module: _____

Positive Feedback Regarding the Module and Instructor:

Opportunities for Improvement Regarding the Module and Instructor:

Comments and Recommendations:

SAMPLE INSTRUCTIONAL MODULES
Sample Module 1/Saying No

INTRODUCTION TO SKILLS AREA 1: Saying No

Content:

In this skills area, the participant will learn three skills that will help him or her to say *no* assertively to requests or demands.

1. **Restate the objectionable request.**   The participant should restate the request so he or she can be sure that he or she understood.
2. **State negative response clearly.**   The participant should say the negative response clearly. This may consist of "No," "I can't," "I don't want to," and so forth. It may be necessary to restate this several times.
3. **Clearly explain the reason.**   The participant should give the reason he or she is responding negatively to the request. He or she may pose an alternative solution.

Quality:

Throughout this and all other modules the following skills will be taught to enhance the quality of the communication.

1. Eye contact
2. Gestures
3. Posture
4. Appropriate distance
5. Voice tone

Instructor should say the following to introduce the topic.

"Sometimes people will ask you to do things that you don't want to do. Today we are going to begin to work on learning to respond to people when they ask you to do something you don't want to do. Learning these skills will help prevent others from taking advantage of you."

Assessment scenes

1. You have plans to go to the bank and do your weekly grocery shopping after work. I am an acquaintance, and I ask you if you will take me to the mall when you get off work. You do not have time to take me to the mall and to do your banking and shopping.

    What is your role?   I need to go banking.
    What is my role?   You want to go to the mall.
    What is your task?   I am going to say no.

    Instructor begins role-playing saying, "Can you take me to the mall?"

2. You have just made a withdrawal from the bank. I am a stranger. As you are leaving, I come up to you and ask if you can give me money for food because I am hungry.

    What is your role?   I made a withdrawal.
    What is my role?   You are a stranger.
    What is your task?   I am going to say no.

    Instructor begins role-playing saying, "Will you give me some money? I am hungry and need to buy food."

3. I work with you. I tell you that I got kicked out of my apartment and need a place to stay. You tell me that I can't stay with you. I tell you that I am really desperate and ask again if I can move in with you for a while.

    What is your role?   I work with you.
    What is my role?   You ask to move in with me.
    What is your task?   I am going to say no.

    Instructor begins role-playing saying, "I really need to move in with you."

Instructional scenes

1. You bought tickets to go to a concert on Saturday night with your best friend. I am a different friend, and I ask you if you want to come over to my house for a barbecue on Saturday night.

    What is your role?   I have tickets for a concert.
    What is my role?   You ask me to go to a barbecue.
    What is your task?   I am going to say no.

    Instructor begins role-playing saying, "Can you come over to my house for a barbecue on Saturday night?"

2. You are lying on the beach, listening to music on your portable radio. Pretend I am a 10-year-old child, and I ask if I can buy your radio for $5.00.

    What is your role?   I am on the beach.
    What is my role?   You ask to buy my radio.
    What is your task?   I am going to say no.

    Instructor begins role-playing saying, "Can I buy your radio for $5.00?"

3. I am your roommate, and I have already spent my weekly allowance. I need to buy a present for my mother's birthday, and I ask to borrow $30.00. You tell me I can't. I tell you that my mother will really be upset if I don't buy her a present and that I really need the money.

What is your role?	I am your roommate.
What is my role?	You need to borrow money.
What is your task?	I am going to say no.

Instructor begins role-playing saying, "I really need to borrow $30.00 for a gift for my mother."

Generalization scenes

1. You are at the bank with your staff support. While withdrawing your weekly money, she says she is broke and asks you if she can borrow $10.00. She says she will pay you back the next day when she gets her paycheck. What do you say?
2. You are at home watching TV. Your roommate comes into the room and asks you to drive him to his softball game, which is 20 miles away. You tell him you will if he pays for the gas. He says he has no money now, but he will probably be able to pay you in a few days. What do you say?
3. You are cleaning the parking lot at your job. Your friend drives up and tells you he has free movie passes for a movie that will start in 20 minutes. He tells you to go tell your boss that you don't feel well so you can leave and go to the movies with him. What do you say?

Individualized scenes

Here the instructor needs to make up three scenes that are specific for the particular participant working on the module. These scenes should be made up beforehand and written below:

1. _____

_____

_____

_____

_____

2. _____

_____

_____

_____

_____

3. _____

_____

_____

_____

_____

Sample Module 2/Asking for Help

INTRODUCTION TO SKILLS AREA 2: Asking for Help

Content:

In this skills area, the participant will learn three skills to help him or her ask for help effectively.

1. **Politely say, "Excuse me," and get the person's attention.**
2. **Ask clearly for help. This should include saying "please."**
3. **State the problem.** You should be able to tell the person why you need help.

Instructor should include the following before introducing the topic.

"Today we are going to practice asking for help when you are unable to complete a task. By learning this skill, you will be assured of getting assistance when you need it, and thus avoiding frustration."

Assessment scenes

1. You are buttering garlic bread at work, and you run out of butter. You do not know where it is stored. What do you do?
2. You are making cookies in your apartment. You realize you added salt instead of sugar to the batter. What do you do?
3. You are at work. Your manager asks you to clean the bathroom, and you do not know how. What do you do?

Instructional scenes

Instructor says: "There are three things you should include when you ask for help." (Instructor recites three skill areas.)

1. You are at the bank, and you cannot find any deposit slips. What do you do?
2. You are lost in the community, nowhere near a telephone, and you see a policeman. What do you do?
3. You are in your apartment, and your instructor asks you to make hamburgers for dinner. You do not know how. What do you do?

Generalization scenes

1. You are at the library and are asked to find a book on a certain subject. You do not know how to find it. What do you do?
2. You are waiting for your job coach at a prearranged time. The job coach does not show up. Someone you know walks by. What do you do?
3. Your job coach asks you to take the bus independently to a new mall. What do you do?

Individualized scenes

Here the instructor needs to make up three scenes that are specific for the particular participant working on the module. These scenes should be made up beforehand and written below:

1. _____

_____

_____

_____

_____

2. _____

_____

_____

_____

3. _____

_____

_____

_____

_____

· Appendix H ·

ᴛʰᵉ*PSR*

INDIVIDUAL PERFORMANCE STANDARDS AND OPERATIONAL DEFINITIONS FOR BEHAVIOR SPECIALISTS

INDIVIDUAL PERFORMANCE STANDARDS FOR BEHAVIOR SPECIALISTS:

Score Sheet

Name: _____ Date: _____

Department: _____ Position: _____

Supervisor: _____

	Score	Comments and Explanations
I. Administrative Area		
A. Individual Casebook		
B. Contract Hours		
C. Service Hours		
D. Timesheets		
E. Contact Logs		
F. Regional Center Contact		
G. Behavior Assessment Report (Timelines)		

	Score	Comments and Explanations

H. Quarterly and Termination
    Reports (Timelines)

Total Score

Total Possible

II. Clinical Practice

A. Behavior Assessment Guide

B. Behavior Assessment Report
    (Quality)

C. Quarterly and Termination
    Reports (Quality)

D. Case Notes

E. Data Summary

F. Training of Key Social Agents

G. Observational and Procedural
    Reliability

H. Periodic Service Review (Group
    Home)

Total Score

Total Possible

III. Evaluation Area

A. Outcome Evaluation

B. Consumer Evaluation

Total Score

Total Possible

IV. Specialist Training and Supervision

Score	Comments and Explanations

    A. Specialist Training

    B. Group Supervision

    C. Individual Supervision

       Total Score

       Total Possible

V. Reporting Requirements

    A. Special Incidents

VI. Summary Scores

Score	Possible	% Score

    A. Administrative

    B. Clinical

    C. Evaluation

    D. Training/Supervision

    E. Reporting

       Overall

Comments/Recommendations/Objectives

INDIVIDUAL PERFORMANCE STANDARDS FOR BEHAVIOR SPECIALISTS:

Operational Definitions

I. **Administrative Area**
   A. **Individual Casebook.** Based on a review of the individual casebook for a randomly selected individual in the specialist's active caseload, a + is given if the casebook is available and up-to-date as of the time of the review.
   B. **Contract Hours.** Based on a review of the specialist monthly timesheets for the previous calendar month, a + is given if services provided for all individuals are within the parameters of the formal authorization, including number of hours provided and period of service.
   C. **Service Hours.** Based on a review of specialist monthly timesheets for the previous 3-month period, a + is given if a full-time behavior specialist has provided a monthly average of at least 145 billable service hours (unless otherwise specified in writing by the supervisor). For a behavior specialist who is an independent contractor, a + is given if the specialist provides services for a minimum of three individuals per month.
   D. **Timesheets.** Based on a review of specialist monthly timesheets for the previous calendar month, a + is given: 1) if the timesheets were complete and turned in by the first day of the month following the service month; or 2) if the first day of the month falls on a weekend or holiday, timesheets were complete and turned in by the last working day of the service month.
   E. **Contact Logs.** Based on a review of the contact logs and the specialist monthly timesheets for the previous calendar month, a + is given for each service recipient for whom ALL the following criteria have been met: 1) contact log was completed and turned in with the specialist monthly timesheets; 2) each contact includes date of service, time in, time out, and the location where the service was provided; and 3) each contact is verified with the signature of the client or a key social agent.
   F. **Regional Center Contact.** Based on a review of the regional center contact log for one randomly selected individual from the specialist's active caseload, a + is given if at least one telephone contact has been made with the case manager during the assessment period, and during each contracted service period (usually a 3-month quarter).
   G. **Behavior Assessment Report (Timelines).** Based on a review of the report tracking log for the previous 60 days, a + is given for each report turned in to be typed within 30 days of assignment by the supervisor, or within a timeframe otherwise specified in writing by supervisor.
   H. **Quarterly and Termination Reports (Timelines).** Based on a review of the report tracking log for the previous 60 days, a + is given for each quarterly report turned in to be typed 3 weeks prior to the end of the period of authorization, and for each termination report turned in within 30 days of the end of the contract for services.

II. **Clinical Practice**
   A. **Behavior Assessment Guide.** Based on a review of a randomly selected individual whose assessment was completed within the previous 60 days, a + is given: 1) if the assessment guide is available, and 2) if the assessment guide is complete.
   B. **Behavior Assessment Report (Quality).** Based on a review of a randomly selected individual whose assessment was completed within the previous 60 days, a

+ is given if the assessment and intervention plan achieves a minimum of 85% on the evaluation instrument.

C. **Quarterly and Termination Reports (Quality).**   Based on a review of a randomly selected individual whose quarterly or termination report was completed within the previous 60 days, a + is given if the report achieves a minimum of 85% on the evaluation instrument.

D. **Case Notes.**   Based on a review of the individual casebook for a randomly selected individual in the specialist's active caseload, a + is given if the progress notes are current (include the most recent visit) and include a minimum of the following: list of target behaviors, current rates of occurrence, statement of current programs or recommendations being implemented, evaluation of progress, and recommendations.

E. **Data Summary.**   Based on a review of the Individual casebook for a randomly selected individual in the specialist's active caseload, a + is given if data for each target behavior have been summarized on the data summary sheet and are current by the end of the preceding calendar week (providing a session was conducted during that week).

F. **Training of Key Social Agents.**   Based on a review of the behavioral assessment report, quarterly reports, and ongoing progress notes for a randomly selected individual in the specialist's active caseload, a + is given if a randomly selected intervention procedure has been documented as being taught and if key social agents have been documented as carrying out the procedure with 85% reliability.

G. **Observational and Procedural Reliability.**   Based on a review of the reliability summary sheet in the individual casebook for a randomly selected individual in the specialist's active caseload, a + is given if, during the previous month of service, at least one observational and one procedural reliability check was conducted, *and* if the results meet or exceed 85%. (*Note:* Observational reliability will depend on the form of data collection used. In cases where oral reports are the primary source of data, observational reliability may not be appropriate.)

H. **Periodic Service Review (Group Home).**   Based on a review of the group home PSR summary sheet for the previous calendar month, a + is given for *each* group home for which a PSR checksheet has been completed and turned in.

III. **Evaluation Area**

A. **Outcome Evaluation.**   Based on a review of the most recent quarterly report for a randomly selected individual from the specialist's active caseload, a + is given if 80% of the quarterly behavior objectives have been achieved.

B. **Consumer Evaluation.**   Based on a review of the consumer evaluation sheet conducted for a randomly selected individual from the specialist's active caseload each month, a + is given if all the items scored are rated by the consumer as 3 or above.

IV. **Specialist Training and Supervision**

A. **Specialist Training.**   Based on a review of individual training records, a + is given if the specialist has completed *all* training required to that point in time.

B. **Group Supervision.**   Based on a review of the staff meeting attendance record for the previous month, a + is given if the specialist attended *all* scheduled meetings. The specialist is expected to attend 1 hour of group supervision for every 20 hours of direct service, or no less than one meeting per month. This is done on an unpaid basis.

C. **Individual Supervision.**   Based on a review of supervision contact sheets for the previous calendar month, a + is given if the specialist has received 1 hour of face-to-face supervision for every 20 hours of direct service, or as otherwise specified by the supervisor.

V.   Reporting Requirements

   A.   Special Incidents.   It is the responsibility of the behavior specialist to report in a timely fashion any suspected incident of physical or emotional abuse, neglect, or violation of the person's rights. Based on a review of available documentation (e.g., assessment, quarterlies, special incident reports, and case notes) and/or information provided during supervision meetings, for a randomly selected individual in the specialist's active caseload, a + is given if all incidents have been reported (oral and in writing) to the appropriate agencies (e.g., regional center, licensing, protective services) within the legally specified time requirements, and a special incident report has been reviewed and signed by the supervisor. If there are no events requiring a report, this item is scored N/A.

VI.   Summary Scores

   A–E.   In these sections, the summary scores of all the preceding areas are entered in turn and then totalled to produce an overall score reflecting the behavior specialists' performance against their individual performance standards.

· Appendix I ·

The**PSR**

PERIODIC SERVICE REVIEW AND INDIVIDUAL PERFORMANCE STANDARDS FOR A BEHAVIOR SERVICES UNIT

PERIODIC SERVICE REVIEW FOR A BEHAVIOR SERVICES UNIT:
Score Sheet

Date of Evaluation: _____

Evaluator: _____

Responsibilities	Achieved	Possible
I. Administrative and General		
A. Job Performance Standards		
1. Monthly Individual Reviews		
2. 85% Performance Level		
B. Client Case Files		
1. Deinstitutionalization Candidates		
2. Community Cases Caseload		
C. Periodic Service Reviews		

II. Deinstitutionalization Project

	Achieved	Possible

A. Community Integration

1. Initial Placement

2. Maintenance

B. Assessment and Intervention Plan

1. Complete

2. Timely

C. Approval of Intervention Plan

1. Individualized Program Plan (IPP)

2. Program Review Committee (PRC)

D. Key Social Agent (KSA) Procedural Reliability

1. Achieved

2. Maintained

E. Communication

1. State Hospital Meetings

2. Provider Meetings

3. Provider Evaluations

F. Reports

1. Quarterly Progress Reports

    a. Complete

    b. Timely

    c. Submitted and Filed

2. Termination Reports

    a. Complete

    b. Timely

    c. Submitted and Filed

	Achieved	Possible
3. Follow-Up Reports		

G. Database

	Achieved	Possible
1. Baseline Data		
2. Ongoing Data		
3. Quality of Life		

III. Intensive Intervention

	Achieved	Possible
A. Consent for Treatment		
B. Intensive Intervention Agreement		

C. Procedural Reliability

	Achieved	Possible
1. Achieved		
2. Maintained		

D. Communication

	Achieved	Possible
1. Weekly Meetings		
2. Provider Evaluations		

E. Fading

	Achieved	Possible
1. Target Date		
2. Fading Process		

F. Provider Periodic Service Review

	Achieved	Possible
1. Developed		
2. Staff Responsible		
3. Maintained		

IV. Community Behavior Services

A. Referrals

	Achieved	Possible
1. Logged		
2. Initial Information Gathered		

	Achieved	Possible

3.   State Hospital Deflection

4.   Advisory Committee Review

5.   Assignment

B.   Assessment and Intervention Plan

	Achieved	Possible

1.   Completed

2.   Timely

C.   Intervention Plan Approval

	Achieved	Possible

1.   IPP

2.   PRC

D.   KSA Procedural Reliability

	Achieved	Possible

1.   Achieved

2.   Maintained

E.   Reports

1.   Quarterly

	Achieved	Possible

   a.   Complete

   b.   Timely

   c.   Submitted and Filed

2.   Termination Reports

	Achieved	Possible

   a.   Complete

   b.   Timely

   c.   Submitted and Filed

	Achieved	Possible

3.   Follow-Up Reports

	Achieved	Possible

F.   KSA Evaluations

G.   Database

	Achieved	Possible
1. Baseline Data		
2. Ongoing Data		
3. Quality of Life		

	Achieved	Possible
H. Consent for Treatment		
I. Intervention Agreement		
J. Periodic Service Review		

Total score possible _____

Total score achieved _____

Percentage score   _____

Comments/Issues/Recommendations:

PERIODIC SERVICE REVIEW
FOR A BEHAVIORAL SERVICES UNIT:
Operational Definitions

I. **Administrative and General**
    A. **Job Performance Standards**
        1. Each staff member is evaluated monthly on individual performance standards, as documented by individual performance graphs.
        2. Each staff member maintains performance levels of 85% or better.
    B. **Client Case Files**   Files in unit office are neat, organized, updated, and include everything on standard table of contents. Follow model case file. Evaluation is based on a random sample of three people each month from each of the following categories.
        1. Deinstitutionalization candidates
        2. Community caseload
    C. **Periodic Service Reviews**   Service programs are maintained at the average 85% level or better, as measured by their own periodic service review, based on summary graph of all services. If not established through intensive intervention, service meetings are tracked on separate graphs for the first 6 months of behavior services unit participation.

II. **Deinstitutionalization Project**
    A. **Community Integration**
        1. **Initial Placement.**   Deinstitutionalization candidates are placed in community settings and programs, as determined by comparing formal project placement schedule with updated list of current placement for all identified clients. Score + if all candidates who should have been placed were by the target date and an o if not.
        2. **Maintenance.**   All people placed in the community are being maintained in initial placement or other community placement identified as less restrictive or more appropriate. Score o if person was or is back in a state hospital or in another psychiatric hospital, as determined by review of updated list of current placements.
    B. **Assessment and Intervention Plan**
        1. **Complete.**   Assessment reports and intervention plans satisfy the behavior services unit format and content requirements, as documented by an 85% score or better on the behavior services unit evaluation review for all deinstitutionalization candidates.
        2. **Timely.**   Assessment reports and intervention plans for deinstitutionalization candidates are complete and available for formal staffing prior to placement, based on review of report date and date on staffing meeting minutes. Score based on reports due that month. Reports due for previous months must also be complete to receive a + .
    C. **Approval of Intervention Plan**
        1. The complete proposed intervention plan along with draft protocols is reviewed, modified (if applicable), and approved by the person's individualized program plan (IPP) team prior to implementing the plan. Score based on comparison of date on IPP, which includes the intervention plan with the date of implementation of the plan.

   2. If applicable, the intervention plan and protocols approved by the IPP team are reviewed and approved by the program review committee (PRC) prior to implementing the plan. Make any needed changes based on PRC recommendations within 1 week of the PRC meeting. Submit final plans and protocols to the case manager, state hospital, and the provider, and file in the client's file. Score based on comparison of the date on the PRC approval form with the date of implementation of the plan.

D. **Key Social Agent (KSA) Procedural Reliability**
   1. **Achieved.** KSAs achieve 90% procedural reliability on all elements of intervention plan within 30 days of placement for those individuals who do not receive intensive intervention services, or within 30 days of transition from intensive intervention. This is based on formal procedural reliability checklist. Plans that should have been fully implemented during the previous month should also have achieved 90% on procedural reliability scores to receive a +
   2. **Maintained.** KSAs maintain an 85% or better procedural reliability score for all program elements as determined by monthly procedural reliability checks for each element as documented on control sheet.

E. **Communication**
   1. **State Hospital Meetings.** Monthly meeting held between behavior services unit management team and state hospital representative for the purpose of updating state hospital on the status of project and individual candidates as documented by formal meeting minutes showing that meeting protocol was followed.
   2. **Provider Meetings.** Weekly meetings are held by the behavior services unit supervisor with each provider, represented by both management and direct care staff, as documented by formal meeting minutes showing that meeting protocol was followed. Upper management of provider agency will be included in these meetings monthly for the first quarter of placement and quarterly thereafter.
   3. **Provider Evaluations.** These are completed monthly by the immediate supervisor at the provider agency. Score + if 3s or better on all items and no complaints to the behavior services unit since the last PSR evaluation.

F. **Reports**
   1. **Quarterly Progress Reports**
      a. **Complete.** Quarterly progress reports satisfy behavior services unit format and content requirements, as documented by 85% score or better on behavior services unit evaluation review for all deinstitutionalization caseload based on last scheduled reports.
      b. **Timely.** Quarterly progress reports are submitted for typing within 2 weeks of end of service quarter.
      c. **Submitted and Filed.** Final versions of quarterly progress reports are typed, submitted, and filed within 30 days of end of service quarter. Submission should be to state hospital, service providers, and case managers in addition to submission to the behavior services unit supervisor.
   2. **Termination Reports**
      a. **Complete.** Termination reports satisfy behavior services unit format and content requirements, as documented by 85% score or better on behavior services unit evaluation review for all deinstitutionalization caseload.
      b. **Timely.** Termination reports are submitted for typing or editing within 2 weeks of the termination date.

c. Submitted and Filed. Final versions of termination reports are typed, submitted, and filed within 30 days of the termination date. Submission should be to state hospital, service providers, and case managers in addition to the behavior services unit supervisor.

    3. Follow-Up Reports. Follow-up reports are completed within 30 days, 6 months, 12 months, and 18 months following termination date in accordance with the behavior services unit follow-up protocols. Score + if report is complete and is filed in all applicable client files.

  G. Database

    1. Baseline Data. One full week of baseline data on all targeted behaviors are collected and summarized on a graph prior to placement when feasible, but no longer than within 1 week of placement. Formal interobserver reliability checks are to be conducted for each target behavior showing 85% reliability or better. Score based on all candidates placed in current month.

    2. Ongoing Data. Ongoing data are maintained for all targeted problems with at least one formal reliability check each month per target behavior with reliability at 85% or better as documented on data-tracking chart.

    3. Quality of Life. Quality of life indicators are tracked based on recording of:

      a. Number of environments (off grounds of the residence) obtained by the individual daily

      b. Number of hours spent in different community settings (not counting day program) daily

      c. Number of people the individual has interactions with daily who are neither disabled nor paid to interact with him or her

      d. Daily mood ratings documented at weekly team meetings

      e. Weekly dollars earned

    Specific quality of life measures are established for each individual in the program setting Periodic Service Reviews. Score quality of life database + if individual data have been maintained completely for the month.

III. Intensive Intervention

  A. Consent for Treatment. All items on the informed consent checklist are discussed by the behavior specialist with the individual, responsible person, and key social agents. Agreement is reached on each item and signatures are obtained prior to initiation of intensive intervention services. The consent form is maintained in the client's master record. This item is scored by a comparison of the signature dates on the consent form with the date intensive intervention services begin for all cases initiated for the month.

  B. Intensive Intervention Agreement. The intensive intervention agreement is reviewed and signed by the director of the provider agency (or KSA if appropriate) and the behavior services unit manager prior to initiation of intensive intervention services. The agreement is maintained in the behavior services unit individual master record. This item is scored by a comparison of the signature dates on the agreement with the date intensive intervention services began for all cases initiated for the month.

  C. Procedural Reliability

    1. Achieved. Intensive intervention staff achieve 90% procedural reliability within 7 days of program implementation based on a formal reliability check. A + is given if the plans that have been implemented during the previous month reveal scores of 90% or better on procedural reliability checks performed for responsible staff.

2. **Maintained.** Intensive intervention staff maintain 90% procedural reliability based on a formal reliability check conducted monthly.

D. **Communication**

Intensive intervention staff meet weekly with KSA to discuss individual progress, KSA satisfaction with intensive intervention services and any issues or problems. These meetings are documented in the case file. Results of these meetings are reported to the supervisor at weekly staff meetings.

E. **Fading**

1. **Target Date.** The target date for fading of intensive intervention services is established as a part of the intensive intervention agreement and is documented in the intensive intervention case record.

2. **Fading Process.** The fading process is completed within 30 days after the target date. All KSAs responsible for the individual's program achieve 90% procedural reliability and interobserver reliability on formal reliability checks on all aspects of the individual's service plan.

F. **Provider Periodic Service Reviews**

1. **Developed.** A periodic service review is developed for each site in which intensive intervention services are provided that reflects the intensive intervention service plan. Intensive intervention staff maintain an 85% level or better, based on weekly formal performance checks.

2. **Staff Responsible.** Agency staff are trained to assume responsibility for all items on the PSR within 30 days after the target fading date. All agency staff responsible for the individual's service plan achieve 85% level or better based on formal reviews.

3. **Maintained.** Agency staff maintain an 85% level or better based on monthly formal PSR checks.

IV. **Community Behavior Services**

A. **Referrals**

1. **Logged.** All new referrals are logged within 1 working day of receiving the referral. Score + if all known referrals are documented in the log, o if a known referral has not been logged.

2. **Initial Information Gathered.** The referral information form is completed based on initial information from appropriate KSA within 1 week of receipt of the referral. Score by comparing date of referral in log with date on referral information form.

3. **State Hospital Deflection.** Those individuals currently living in the community who previously resided at the state hospital within the past 3 years are considered a part of the deinstitutionalization project. These people will be given priority for behavior services unit service if they are at risk for return to state hospital. The names of these people will be recorded and maintained in the referral file.

4. **Advisory Committee Review.** The committee will meet every 2 weeks to review and prioritize community referrals for the behavior services unit. Decisions made by the committee will be kept in meeting minutes that will be filed in the behavior services unit referral file. The committee will only provide disposition for as many referrals as time is available. In the event that the behavior services unit determines that it is unable to initiate new services due to present caseload, regular committee meetings will be suspended until time is available.

5. **Assignment.** Assignment of cases from the advisory committee is made within 2 working days to an available behavior specialist, as evidenced by the date of initiation of an intervention activities checklist on the case.

B. Assessment and Intervention Plan

    1. Completed. Comprehensive behavior assessments and intervention plans will be developed using the standard behavior services unit format, as evidenced by an 85% or better on the behavior services unit assessment checklist on one random service recipient per month.

    2. Timely. Assessment reports and intervention plans will be submitted for typing and/or editing within 30 days of assignment or within timeframes otherwise specified.

C. Intervention Plan Approval

    1. IPP. The complete proposed service plan along with draft protocols is reviewed, modified (if applicable) and approved by the individual's IPP team prior to implementing the plan. Score based on comparison of date on IPP that includes the intervention plan with the date of implementation of the plan.

    2. PRC. If applicable, the intervention plan and protocols approved by the IPP team is reviewed and approved by the PRC prior to implementing the plan. Make any needed changes based on PRC recommendations within 1 week of the PRC meeting. Submit final plans and protocols to the case manager, state hospital, and the provider, and file in the case file. Score based on comparison of the date on the PRC approval form with the date of implementation of the plan.

D. KSA Procedural Reliability

    1. Achieved. KSAs achieve 90% procedural reliability on all elements of intervention plans within 30 days of program implementation based on formal reliability checks. Plans that should have been fully implemented during the previous month should also have achieved 90% on procedural reliability scores to receive a $+$.

    2. Maintained. KSAs will maintain an 85% or better procedural reliability score for all program elements as determined by monthly procedural reliability checks for each element as documented on control sheet.

E. Reports

    1. Quarterly

        a. Complete. Quarterly progress reports satisfy behavior services unit as documented by an 85% score or better on the behavior services unit evaluation review.

        b. Timely. Quarterly progress reports are submitted for typing 2 weeks prior to the end of service quarter as evidenced by an 85% score on the tracking cover sheet.

        c. Submitted and Filed. Final versions of quarterly progress reports are typed, submitted, and filed within 30 days of the end of the service quarter. Submission should be to the case manager, responsible person, and service providers in addition to submission to the behavior services program supervisor.

    2. Termination Reports

        a. Complete. Termination reports satisfy behavior services unit format and content requirements as documented by 85% score or better on behavior services unit evaluation review for all behavioral services recipients.

        b. Timely. Termination reports are submitted for typing or editing within 2 weeks of the termination date.

        c. Submitted and Filed. Final versions of termination reports are typed, submitted, and filed within 30 days of the termination date. Submission should be to the responsible person, service providers, and case managers in addition to the behavior services program supervisor.

3. **Follow-Up Reports.** Follow-up reports are completed within 30 days, 6 months, 12 months, and 18 months following termination date in accordance with the behavior services unit follow-up protocols. Score + if report is complete and is filed in all applicable case files.

F. **KSA Evaluations.** KSAs will be asked to complete a social validity questionnaire for each individual receiving services monthly for the duration of intervention services from the behavior services unit. Behavior services unit staff will receive a 3 or better on each item on the social validity check.

G. **Database**

1. **Baseline Data.** One full week of baseline data on all targeted behaviors are collected and summarized on a graph prior to program implementation. Formal interobserver reliability checks are conducted for each target behavior showing 85% reliability or better. Score based on all individuals placed in current month.

2. **Ongoing Data.** Ongoing data are maintained for all targeted problems with at least one formal reliability check each month per target behavior with reliability at 85% or better, as documented on data-tracking chart.

3. **Quality of Life.** Quality of life indicators are tracked based on recording of:

   a. Number of environments (off grounds of the residence) accessed by the person daily

   b. Number of hours spent in different community settings (not counting day program) daily

   c. Number of people the person has interactions with daily who are neither disabled nor paid to interact with him or her

   d. Weekly mood ratings documented at weekly team meetings

   e. Weekly dollars earned

   Score quality of life database + if individual data have been maintained completely for the month.

H. **Consent for Treatment.** All items on the informed consent checklist are discussed by the behavior specialist with the individual, responsible person, and key social agents. Agreement is reached on each item and signatures are obtained prior to initiation of behavior services unit services. The consent form is maintained in the master record. This item is scored by a comparison of the signature dates on the consent form with the date behavior services unit services began for all cases initiated for the month.

I. **Behavior Services Intervention Agreement.** This is reviewed and signed by the service provider representative (or KSA, if appropriate) and the behavior specialist prior to initiation of intervention services. The agreement is maintained in the case file. This item is scored by a comparison of the signature dates on the agreement with the date intervention services began for all cases initiated for the month.

J. **Periodic Service Review.** A periodic service review is developed for each site in which services are provided that reflects the service plan. Agency staff are trained to assume responsibility for all items on the PSR, achieve an initial 90% level within 30 days of implementation, and maintain an 85% level or better based on monthly formal PSR checks.

INDIVIDUAL PERFORMANCE STANDARDS/BEHAVIOR SERVICES UNIT MANAGER:

Score Sheet

Name: _____

Date of Evaluation: _____

Evaluator: _____

Responsibilities	Achieved	Possible

I. Meetings

   A. Weekly Unit Meetings

   B. Provider Agency Management

   C. Monthly with State Hospital

II. Budget and Contracts

   A. Identify Providers and Establish Contracts for Services for Deinstitutionalization Candidates

   B. Contract for Support Services

   C. Track Expenditures

   D. Process Billings

III. Supervision

   A. Personnel

   B. Timesheets

   C. Staff Travel

   D. 1:1 Supervision of Supervisor

   E. Serve as Program Supervisor

IV. Monitoring

   A. PSR for Program Supervisor

   B. PSR for Behavioral Services Unit

	Achieved	Possible
C. Service Providers Summary Graph		
D. Monthly Reports to Area Program Manager (APM)		

V. Referral Process

A. Referral Packets Complete		
B. Call Advisory Committee Meetings		
C. Cancel Advisory Committee Meetings		
D. Assign Cases		

VI. Direct Service

Total score possible _____

Total score achieved _____

Percentage score   _____

Comments/Issues/Recommendations:

INDIVIDUAL PERFORMANCE STANDARDS/BEHAVIOR SERVICES UNIT MANAGER:
Operational Definitions

I. **Meetings**
   A. Conduct weekly unit meetings including the following agenda items
      1. Administrative and informational items
      2. Discussion of status of all unit cases
      3. Full staffing of one case
      4. Presentation of training/professional development topic by one member of the unit staff one meeting per month
      Score + if meeting minutes reflect all agenda items discussed.
   B. Meet monthly with the administration of agencies providing service to unit clients to review progress and discuss any problems. Score + if meeting minutes reflect the above discussion.
   C. Meet monthly with state hospital staff to provide updated information on planned movement of deinstitutionalization candidates and to discuss any problems. Score + if meeting minutes reflect the above discussion.

II. **Budget and Contracts**
   A. Identify providers for deinstitutionalization candidates and work with contracts staff to establish contracts or contract amendments. Ensure that residential and day-care service plans are finalized at least 30 days prior to each person's target discharge date. Score + if provider is identified and contract or amendment is in process.
   B. Identify providers and contract for support services for the behavior services unit, including management and psychological and psychiatric consultation. Score + if contracts are in place for all needed services.
   C. Track expenditures for behavior services unit services and submit an expenditure report to the area program manager within 2 weeks of the end of each month. Score + if date on expenditure report is within 2 weeks of the end of the month.
   D. Process billings from consultants within 2 days of receipt of statements at the behavior services unit office. Score by comparing date billing received with date billing forwarded to appropriate person.

III. **Supervision**
   A. Perform personnel-related responsibilities including hiring and possible disciplinary actions for program supervisor within policy and timeliness. All personnel actions are maintained in behavior services unit personnel files. Score + if dates on all personnel paperwork fall within timelines.
   B. Ensure that program supervisor timesheets are completed correctly, sign timesheets of subordinate staff, and deliver timesheets to the appropriate authority prior to noon on the final day of each pay period.
   C. Approve the use of private vehicles or state vehicles for official purposes. Approve travel claims, ensuring the accuracy of all travel claimed. Score + if no travel claims are returned for correction during the month.
   D. Provide 1:1 supervision of program supervisor at least 2 hours per week.
   E. Serve as program supervisor for those cases in which the unit program supervisor is providing direct services. Score based on achievement of 85% or better on applicable sections of the program supervisor's performance standards.

IV. Monitoring

A. Conduct PSR of program supervisor performance monthly.

B. Conduct PSR for behavior services unit monthly, graph and post results in behavior services unit office within 2 weeks of the end of each month.

C. Graph and post summary graph of service provider PSR scores monthly. Except for those providers who are not receiving intensive intervention services and have provided services to behavior services unit clients for fewer than 6 months—the PSR for these providers will be graphed separately.

D. Provide monthly progress reports to the area program manager within 2 weeks of the end of each month that contain the following information:

    1. Number of individuals served by type of setting

    2. Number of current active cases

    3. Number of follow-up cases

    4. Number of closed cases

    5. Number of referrals received

    6. Number of deinstitutionalization candidates placed in the community

    7. Number of people referred and waiting for service

    8. Graph of unit PSR results

V. Referral Process

A. Ensure that referral packets are complete within established timeliness.

B. Calculate availability of time to accept new cases and call meeting of advisory committee when unit has the capacity to accept new cases.

C. Cancel meeting of advisory committee when unit does not have the capacity to accept new cases at least 1 week prior to a scheduled meeting.

D. Assign top priority cases to the available and appropriate behavior specialist for assessment and intervention plan services within 2 days of the committee meeting.

VI. Direct Service.
Provide the services of a behavior specialist to a minimum of one case at all times. Score + if 85% level or better achieved on the behavior specialist performance review.

INDIVIDUAL PERFORMANCE STANDARDS/BEHAVIOR SERVICES SUPERVISOR:

Score Sheet

Name: _____

Date of Evaluation: _____

Evaluator: _____

Responsibilities	Achieved	Possible

I. Administration

A. Attendance Sheets

B. Personnel

C. Timesheets

D. Staff Travel

II. Meetings

A. Weekly Unit Meetings

B. Monthly State Hospital Meetings

C. Provider Meetings

   1. Weekly for State Hospital Caseload

   2. Monthly for Community Caseload

III. Supervision

A. Provide 1:1 Supervision

   1. 2 Hours Weekly for Intensive Intervention Team (IIT)

   2. 1.5 Hours Weekly for Behavior Specialist

B. Evaluate Performance Reviews

C. Field Visits

D. Provider Evaluations—Social Validity

	Achieved	Possible
E. Reports		
1. Assessment and Intervention Plan		
2. Quarterly Reports		
3. Termination Reports		

F. On-Call Supervision		

IV. Direct Service

Total score possible _____

Total score achieved _____

Percentage score _____

Comments/Issues/Recommendations:

INDIVIDUAL PERFORMANCE
STANDARDS/BEHAVIOR SERVICES SUPERVISOR:
Operational Definitions

I. **Administration**
   A. Receive attendance sheets from subordinate staff and verify appropriate use of service hours by comparing attendance sheet information with client authorization. Attendance sheets are initialed by the supervisor and are maintained in the behavior services unit files. Score + if all current attendance sheets are present in file.
   B. Perform personnel-related responsibilities, including hiring and possible disciplinary actions for subordinate staff within policy and timelines. All personnel actions are maintained in behavior services unit personnel files. Score by a cross-check of timelines and dates on personnel actions.
   C. Ensure that staff timesheets are completed correctly, sign timesheets of subordinate staff, and deliver timesheets to the appropriate authority prior to noon on the final day of each pay period.
   D. Approve use of private vehicles or state vehicles for official purposes. Approve travel claims, ensuring the accuracy of all travel claimed. Score + if no travel claims are returned for correction during the month.

II. **Meetings**
   A. Attend weekly behavior services unit meetings. Submit names of individuals to be staffed to the unit manager no later than 2 days prior to the meeting. Score + if meeting minutes indicate presence (or excused absence) *and* if case name submitted as per above.
   B. Attend monthly meetings with state hospital representatives. Present current status of each person on the state hospital list. Score + if meeting minutes indicate presence (or excused absence) *and* if current information is presented on each person.
   C. Attend meetings with provider agencies providing service to behavior services unit clients to review progress and identify and resolve any problems
      1. Weekly for intensive intervention and deinstitutionalization caseload
      2. Monthly for other community caseload
      Score + if meeting minutes indicate presence and discussion as above.

III. **Supervision**
   A. Provide 1:1 supervision of staff as follows
      1. Two hours weekly for each intensive intervention specialist
      2. One and a half hours weekly for each behavior specialist
      Score + if results of each 1:1 meeting with staff are discussed with unit manager weekly.
   B. Conduct formal checks on performance for all subordinate staff monthly. Score + if scores on all staff are submitted to unit manager 1 week before the end of each month.
   C. **Field Visits.** Conduct at least one on-site observation of services being provided by each subordinate staff and document on the field observation checklist. Score + if results of each observation are discussed with unit manager monthly.
   D. **Social Validity Checks.** Receive social validity checks from each provider (or KSA) monthly, discuss results with staff involved, and take corrective action as needed. Validity checks are maintained in behavior services unit files. Score + if results of each validity check are discussed with unit manger monthly.

      E. **Reports.** Review, edit, return for revision, and approve the following reports from persons providing behavior specialist services

         1. **Assessment and Intervention Plan.** One random report per month

         2. **Quarterly Reports.** One random report per quarter

         3. **Termination Reports.** One random report per quarter

      F. **On-Call Supervision.** Be available by telephone or beeper for emergency supervision based on schedule. Score + if no reports received of unavailability during scheduled on-call hours.

IV. **Direct Service.** Provide the services of a behavior specialist to a minimum of one case at all times. Score + if 85% level or better achieved on the behavior specialist performance review.

INDIVIDUAL PERFORMANCE STANDARDS/BEHAVIOR SPECIALIST:

Score Sheet

Name: _____

Date of Evaluation: _____

Evaluator: _____

Responsibility	Achieved	Possible
I. Develop Behavior Assessments and Intervention Plans		
II. Submit Plans on Timely Basis		
III. Write Quarterly Progress Reports		
IV. Submit Quarterly Reports on Timely Basis		
V. Write Termination Reports		
VI. Submit Termination Reports on Timely Basis		
VII. Provide Service as Authorized		
VIII. Submit Attendance Sheets		
IX. Attend Weekly Unit Meetings		
X. Attend 1:1 Meetings with Supervisor		
XI. Billable Service—Contract		
XII. 120 Hours Direct Service		
XIII. Evaluate Assessment Reports for Other Specialists		
XIV. Data Summary		
XV. Monthly Progress Summary		
XVI. Train Staff and KSAs		
XVII. Procedural Reliability		

	Achieved	Possible
XVIII. Monthly Contact with Case Manager		
XIX. Maintain Case Record		
XX. Competency-Based Training		
XXI. Periodic Service Review		
XXII. Notification of Abuse, and so on		
XXIII. 85% on Monthly Field Observation Checklist		

Total score possible _____

Total score achieved _____

Percentage score _____

Comments/Issues/Recommendations:

INDIVIDUAL PERFORMANCE STANDARDS/BEHAVIOR SPECIALIST:
Operational Definitions

I. Develop comprehensive behavior assessments and intervention plans using the standard behavior services unit format as evidenced by an 85% score on the behavior services assessment checklist on one randomly selected service recipient per month.

II. Write and turn in for typing and/or editing behavior assessments and intervention plans within 30 days of assignment by supervisor, or within timeframes otherwise specified by supervisor in writing, as evidenced by an 85% score on the tracking cover sheet.

III. Write progress reports for each on a quarterly basis using the standard behavior services format as measured by an 85% score on the behavior services quarterly checklist on one randomly selected individual client.

IV. Write and turn in for typing and/or editing a quarterly progress report for each person within 2 weeks prior to the end of the quarter and authorization, as evidenced by an 85% score on the tracking cover sheet.

V. Write a termination report as needed using the behavior services standard format as evidenced by an 85% score on the behavior services termination checklist on one randomly selected person.

VI. Write and turn in for typing and/or editing a termination report within 30 days after intervention services have ceased, as evidenced by an 85% score on the tracking cover sheet.

VII. Provide only those services within the parameters of the formal authorization regarding both the number of hours and the length of service, as evidenced by a 100% cross-check of attendance sheets and authorization.

VIII. Submit completed and accurate attendance sheets no later than the first day of the month following the service month.

IX. Attend weekly behavior services unit meetings. Score + if meeting minutes indicate the presence (or excused absence).

X. Attend individual sessions on the required basis of 1 hour of face-to-face supervision per 20 hours of direct service per month, as measured by supervisor documentation.

XI. Behavior specialists hired on a contract basis will be responsible for providing a minimum of three cases of billable services per month, as indicated by monthly billing sheet. (*Note*—Nonapplicable at this time).

XII. Behavior specialist hired on a full-time basis will be responsible for providing at least 120 hours of direct service per month, as indicated on attendance sheet.

XIII. Evaluate one report of another specialist per month using standard evaluation form, as indicated by copy of completed review checklist turned into supervisor.

XIV. Summarize individual data on a monthly basis, as evidenced by direct observation of case file per month updated within 1 week.

XV. Complete a monthly progress summary for each individual on your caseload and submit each to the case manager within 5 working days of the end of the month. A copy will be retained in the behavior services unit master record. This will be measured by direct observation of master record on one randomly selected person per month.

XVI. Train designated key social agents to implement intervention procedures to a procedural reliability and interobserver reliability score of 90% within 30 days of implementation, as indicated on the behavior performance competency checklist (BPCC) of one randomly selected person.

XVII. Conduct procedural reliability checks as prescribed on key social agents trained. Ensure maintenance of a score of 85%, as indicated on the procedural reliability checklist based on one randomly selected person per month.

XVIII. Document at least one telephone contact per month to the case manager, as evidenced by written documentation on the client contact log based on one randomly selected person per month.

XIX. Maintain all required documentation for client file as evidenced by one randomly selected case file per month.

XX. Complete competency-based training as required. (*Note*—Nonapplicable at this time).

XXI. A Periodic Service Review is developed for each service site. Service providers are trained to assume responsibility for all items on the PSR, to achieve an initial 90% level within 30 days of implementation, and to maintain an 85% level or better, based on monthly formal PSR checks.

XXII. Notify appropriate agencies, in accordance with legal requirements, of suspected abuse, neglect and/or violation of client rights, and document such incidents in client contact log and/or case notes, and in 1:1 supervisory meetings. This item to be measured by observation of written documentation in one randomly selected case record. Score + if an incident is documented and a report made or there is documentation of why incident was not reported. Score o if no documentation exists for a known incident, and N/A if there are no incidents known or documented.

XXIII. Maintain at least an 85% score on the monthly field observation checklist as completed by the supervisor during the field visit.

INDIVIDUAL PERFORMANCE
STANDARDS/INTENSIVE INTERVENTION SPECIALIST:
Score Sheet

Name: _____

Date of Evaluation: _____

Evaluator: _____

Responsibility	Achieved	Possible
I. Arrives on Time		
II. Notifies Supervisor of Absences		
III. Maintains Daily Data		
IV. Data Summary Sheet		
V. Daily Graphs		
VI. Procedural Reliability		
VII. Interobserver Reliability		
VIII. Activity Schedule		
IX. Competency-Based Training		
X. Weekly Team Meetings		
XI. Rules/Standards of Host		
XII. Notifies Supervisor of Conflicts		
XIII. Incident Reports		
XIV. Ethical Standards		
XV. Social Validity		
XVI. Appearance		
XVII. Notification of Abuse, and so on		
XVIII. Periodic Service Review		
XIX. Trains Staff and KSAs		

	Achieved	Possible
XX. Attendance Sheets		
XXI. Timesheets		

Total possible points _____

Total points achieved _____

Percentage score _____

Comments/Issues/Recommendations:

INDIVIDUAL PERFORM NCE
STANDARDS/INTENSIVE INTERVENTION SPECIALIST:
Operational Definitions

I. Arrive within 5 minutes of scheduled time at least 80% of working days in a month. Arrive between 5 and 15 minutes no more than the remaining 20% of the time. Remain until end of assigned shift. Items are scored by direct observation and review of sign-in sheet maintained at the intensive intervention site.

II. Notify supervisor of absences
   a. No later than 1 hour before start of shift, when absent due to illness. In addition, notify appropriate person at intensive site within the same time period. Score based on cross-check with sign-in sheet and supervisor's documentation of calls.
   b. At least 2 weeks in advance of requested use of annual leave in excess of 2 days.
   c. At least 24 hours in advance of other known absences.

III. Maintain all data daily, as prescribed by behavior specialist per task based on one randomly selected individual per week.

IV. Maintain data summary sheet, as prescribed by behavior specialist based on one randomly selected person per week.

V. Graph all data daily at end of shift, as prescribed by behavior specialist based on one randomly selected person per week.

VI. Adhere to programs as designed by behavior specialist and meets procedural reliability criteria of 90%, as measured weekly for one randomly selected service recipient per provider.

VII. Meet 85% of criteria of interobserver reliability monthly, or as otherwise prescribed for all individuals documented in each case file.

VIII. Carry out schedule of activities at 85% level or better based on one randomly selected person per month. Schedule is posted in the program setting, and activities are documented in an activity log maintained in the program setting.

IX. Complete competency-based training as specified (Note—nonapplicable at this time).

X. Attend weekly provider meetings with supervisor, host facility supervisor, and staff (or KSAs), and, if applicable, fellow intensive staff, as documented in meeting minutes.

XI. Adhere to rules and standards of dress and behavior of host facility/environment, unless directed otherwise, as measured on monthly social validity checks completed by the host agency/family.

XII. Notify supervisor of conflicts or concerns with host staff/family within 24 hours of end of shift. This item is scored + if no issues are raised at the weekly provider meeting that the supervisor has not been notified of by the intensive intervention staff, except for those issues of which staff were not aware.

XIII. Complete unusual incident reports when necessary as prescribed, and notifies the supervisor orally by the end of shift. All other incidents are reported to the supervisor within 24 hours. Written incident reports must be submitted to the host facility supervisor by the end of the next working day for review and filing in the master record. This item is rated + if an incident is documented and a report is made, o if there is no documentation of a known incident, and N/A if no incidents are reported or documented.

XIV. Maintain ethical standards of confidentiality and client dignity. Do not disclose identifying information, confidential reports of client likeness without express written permission of supervisor and responsible person, in accordance with applicable laws.

This item is rated + if required approvals are obtained prior to disclosure, o if disclosure is reported without required approvals, and N/A if no disclosures are made.

XV. Maintain a 3 or higher on each criterion measured on the monthly social validity checks, as submitted by the host facility/family to the behavior services unit supervisor.

XVI. Upon arrival at host/facility home, ensure that individual receiving services is dressed and neatly groomed in an age-appropriate manner and notes discrepancies in the case notes section of the case file. Appearance is evaluated by weekly observation by supervisor.

XVII. Notify appropriate agencies, in accordance with legal requirements, of suspected abuse, neglect, and/or violation of client rights. Notify supervisor of all such notification by end of shift and document such incidents in case notes. This item is measured by observation of written documentation in one randomly selected client's case record. Score + if incident is documented and report made, or there is documentation of why incident was not reported, o if there is no documentation of a known incident, and N/A if no incidents are known or documented.

XVIII. A Periodic Service Review is developed for each service site. Service providers are trained to assume responsibility for all items on the PSR, to achieve an initial 90% level within 30 days of implementation, and to maintain an 85% level or better based on monthly formal PSR checks.

XIX. Train designated key social agents to implement programs at 90% criteria of procedural reliability and interobserver reliability, as specified in the intensive intervention fading plan that is maintained at the program site. Documentation of training is maintained on behavior performance competency checklist.

XX. Submit completed and accurate attendance sheets no later than the first working day of the month following the month of service. All attendance sheets must reflect only authorized hours.

XXI. Submit complete and accurate timesheets no earlier than the Wednesday and no later than the Thursday prior to the end of each pay period.

· Appendix J ·

The **PSR**

COMPETENCY-BASED TRAINING
OUTLINE OF COMPETENCIES AND CRITERIA

The topics are denoted by Roman numerals, the competencies by capital letters, and the criteria by Arabic numerals.

I. **Orientation**
   A. Demonstrates familiarity with 1) service population and characteristics, 2) funding agencies, and 3) own agency.
      1. Given an objective true and false test about service population and characteristics, trainee scores at least 90%.
      2. Trainee correctly identifies funding sources (or agencies) for his or her program.
      3. Given the assignment, "Name three services provided by your agency," trainee responds correctly.

II. **Administrative Requirements**
   A. Identifies job description, chain of command, and general agency policies.
      1. Given a written test, trainee can state three aspects of his or her job duties.
      2. Given the question, "Identify the chain of command leading from your position to the head of your agency," trainee can correctly do so.
      3. Given a list, trainee can correctly identify all situations that could lead to dismissal from her or his job.
      4. Given a written test, trainee correctly describes agency's grievance procedures.
      5. Trainee correctly describes what to do if she or he is going to be absent due to illness.
      6. Trainee correctly describes procedure for requesting vacation time.

    B. Demonstrates familiarity with special incident reporting procedures.

       1. Given a written test about what situations require special incident reporting, who writes them and when, and who receives them and when, trainee scores 100%.

       2. Given a list including 10 or more situations and vignettes, trainee accurately chooses those situations that would require a special incident report.

       3. Having read the adult abuse reporting requirements, trainee signs a statement to be filed in his or her personnel file that he or she understands responsibilities under state law, and will comply with the provisions.

III. Full Inclusion and Social Role Valorization (has corresponding videotaped material)

    A. Is familiar with and understands the principles of full inclusion and social role valorization and is able to identify it as the program philosophy.

       1. After viewing a videotape and asked, "What is the philosophy of your program?" trainee describes the principles of full inclusion and social role valorization.

       2. Given a set of pictures, trainee is able to pinpoint at least five areas that conflict with the principles of full inclusion and social role valorization, and can recommend specific changes for each area to bring it into compliance.

       3. Given an actual special service or other program setting, trainee is able to identify at least three areas that conflict with the principles of full inclusion and social role valorization, and can recommend specific changes for each area to bring it into compliance.

       4. Given a list of goals for adult services, trainee is able to check those items that are in compliance with the principles of full inclusion and social role valorization with 100% accuracy.

IV. Ethical Issues

    A. Understands and can state clearly that the client has the following rights: 1) to have his or her name concealed from persons who are not authorized to have such information, and 2) to have his or her records concealed from others, unless the client or his or her legal conservators give written permission for specific others to view those records.

       1. Given three vignettes, trainee is able to identify instances where the client's right to confidentiality was compromised.

    B. Understands and can describe that the client, his or her parent, or other legally responsible party, has the right to refuse any treatment or to withdraw from treatment, and that the client has the right to be free from coercion (i.e., not forced into treatment).

       1. Given three vignettes, trainee can identify and briefly describe the ethical issue that is being addressed, and whether it is being violated.

    C. Understands that the client has the right to be informed, and should be, of all aspects of treatment, including goals, methods, procedures, and possible benefits and drawbacks associated with the program.

       1. Given three vignettes, trainee is able to identify the particular ethical issue being addressed, and can describe whether the client's rights are being violated.

    D. Understands that training or treatment should be provided only by individuals who have been trained in the use of the specific methods, have experience using the procedures, and have adequate supervision.

       1. Given two vignettes, trainee can identify the particular ethical issue being addressed, and can identify whether the client's rights are being violated in this area.

    2. Given a list of training procedures, trainee can discriminate whether he or she is qualified to carry out the procedures.

E. Understands that the client has a right to treatment that does not inflict pain, cause distress, or severely restrict.

    1. Given a list of 11 procedures, trainee is able to identify correctly those that create pain, cause distress, or are restrictive.

F. Understands that clients have a right to be treated by staff as peers and equals; and that they have the right to be treated with the utmost dignity, free from ridicule.

    1. Given three vignettes, trainee can identify whether the clients are being treated with dignity, or whether their rights in this area are being violated.

G. Understands client rights as stipulated by law.

    1. Having read the regulations, and having passed all other competencies in this topic, trainee signs an agreement for his or her personnel file indicating that he or she has read and understands the rights of persons with developmental disabilities and will act accordingly.

V. Public Relations

A. Can describe his or her role regarding the public as an agent of the program.

    1. Given a test, trainee can name three roles he or she will have in representing the program to the public, such as liaison, educator, public relations person, or model of how to treat people with developmental disabilities.

    2. Given a role-playing situation, trainee will respond to being approached by a citizen in the community and asked why the person being supported is not in an institution. The response should include explanations of client rights and the legal mandate for community integration. It can also include the issues of client education, cost effectiveness, and inclusion.

VI. Managing Client Records

A. Is able to maintain client attendance records (also for supported employment—earnings and job tenure records).

    1. Given the end of 2 calendar months, trainee correctly fills out all parts of client attendance.

    2. Given the end of 2 calendar months, trainee correctly fills out all parts of client earnings (for supported employment program).

    3. Given the end of 2 calendar months, trainee correctly fills out all parts of client job tenure record (for supported employment program).

B. Is able to demonstrate understanding of the individualized service plan (ISP).

    1. Given a written test, trainee can answer the questions: 1) What is an ISP? 2) Who writes the ISP? 3) When? 4) What kind of goals are part of an ISP? 5) How and when do you monitor goals and objectives?

C. Reviews, understands, organizes, and maintains client program notebooks.

    1. Having read the program notebooks for all assigned clients and given a client program notebook, trainee correctly states what information goes in each section.

    2. Given the program notebooks for assigned clients, trainee is able to put five documents in the correct sections.

    3. Given two spot checks over at least a 2-month period, trainee maintains program notebooks in good condition.

D. Reviews, understands, organizes, and maintains client case files.

    1. Having read the case files for all assigned clients and given a case file, trainee correctly states what information goes in each section.

    2. Given the case files for assigned clients, trainee is able to put five documents in correct places.

3. Given two spot checks over at least a 2-month period, trainee maintains client case files in good condition.

E. Understands why a consistent team approach is important and the factors that contribute to it.

1. Given a multiple choice test about why a consistent team approach is important and the factors that contribute to it, trainee scores 90% or more.

2. Given three vignettes, trainee can correctly identify at least two issues of organization that may have contributed to the problem.

F. Is able to organize and schedule duties to meet job requirements.

1. Given sample data, trainee is able to complete a daily schedule of activities for clients and for self.

2. Given 2 calendar months, trainee correctly completes and turns in a daily schedule of activities (for direct and indirect service hours).

G. Understands and accurately performs job duties.

1. Trainee describes the Periodic Service Review, mentioning the general areas it measures and how a score is determined.

2. Trainee scores 80% or higher on the Periodic Service Review.

VII. Basic Principles of Behavior

A. Is able to describe the three-part contingency of antecedent–behavior–consequence and to label each element.

1. Given an objective test, trainee correctly identifies the three-part contingency, a definition for each of the three parts, and the meaning of contingency.

2. Given five written vignettes, trainee is able to describe each using the three-part contingency of antecedent–behavior–consequence.

B. Trainee is able to distinguish between the characteristics of operant and respondent behavior, and identify examples of each.

1. Trainee is able to define operant and respondent behavior, and describe the differences between the two.

2. Given a list of 10 behaviors, trainee correctly distinguishes between operant and respondent behavior.

C. Trainee is able to identify and define consequential operations.

1. Trainee correctly defines the following items: positive reinforcement, negative reinforcement, recovery from punishment, punishment I, punishment II, and extinction.

2. Trainee is able to identify the specific criteria that distinguish reinforcement from punishment.

3. Given 16 behavioral vignettes, trainee is able to correctly match each with the correct consequential operation.

D. Understands discriminative stimulus.

1. Trainee is able to complete an objective test about discrimination.

VIII. Instructional Strategies (has corresponding videotaped material)

A. Identifies and distinguishes between the instructional strategies of shaping and chaining (forward, backward, and global).

1. Trainee scores 90% on an objective test on shaping and chaining (forward, backward, and global).

B. Is familiar with, can discriminate among, and can demonstrate various types of prompting (oral, gestural, model, and physical).

1. From videotaped vignettes of hierarchy of prompt and discrete trial instructional strategies, trainee accurately records what prompts were effective in getting the learner to respond to each step of the task analysis.

2. In role-playing an instructional situation, trainee demonstrates all prompts in hierarchy.

    C. Is familiar with the assessment techniques of ecological inventory and discrepancy analysis, and with the three stages of learning (task acquisition, productivity, and skills maintenance).

        1. Trainee scores 90% or higher on an objective test.

        2. Given a sample task, trainee creates a written task analysis.

    D. Understands adaptations, when they might be used, and why.

        1. Trainee scores 90% or higher on a true/false test on adaptations.

        2. Given four vignettes, trainee correctly states which adaptations might benefit the learner.

    E. Can identify relevant and well-written goals and objectives for instructional plans, and knows how they are developed.

        1. Given an objective test on instructional plans, trainee scores 90% or higher.

        2. Trainee can correctly identify from a list of objectives those that are well-written and relevant.

    F. Can devise a simple objective and instructional program.

        1. Trainee correctly fills out a blank teaching protocol.

    G. Trainee is proficient at instructing learners using both a hierarchy of prompting and discrete trial data-based teaching strategy.

        1. In a role-playing situation, trainee correctly implements a hierarchy of prompting strategy.

        2. In a role-playing situation, trainee correctly implements a discrete trial data-based teaching strategy.

        3. In a real-life situation, trainee correctly implements a discrete trial data-based teaching strategy.

IX. Positive Reinforcement

    A. Understands that there is a range of reinforcers that could be used in a behavior modification or training program and understands how to identify reinforcers.

        1. When asked to describe possible reinforcers to be used for intervention plans, trainee's specific examples include reference to at least three different categories of reinforcers.

        2. When asked how to identify reinforcers, trainee describes three methods including reinforcement inventories, asking the individual what he or she likes, asking significant others, watching what the individual does, and trying different methods.

    B. Discriminates among different types and schedules of reinforcement.

        1. Given six situations, trainee can match them to the type of reinforcement schedule used.

    C. Understands how to ensure effectiveness of reinforcement procedures.

        1. Given 10 vignettes, trainee correctly identifies whether the rules governing the effectiveness of reinforcement, including deprivation, satiation, free access, immediacy, and consistency, were followed.

    D. Understands the role, key characteristics, and advantages of such mediating systems as token economies and contingency contracts.

        1. Trainee scores at least 90% on objective examination.

X. Data Recording (has corresponding videotaped material)

    A. Is able to describe the major reasons or rationale for measuring behavior.

        1. Trainee describes three rationale for measuring behavior.

    B. Is able to define behavior operationally to include a description of the behavior in *observable* terms, and the *cycle* (onset–offset) of the behavior.

        1. Given a list of seven definitions, trainee identifies those that are defined operationally, and is able to describe how those that are not correctly defined should be modified.

2. Given a videotaped vignette, trainee is able to write two operational definitions for the behavior problems portrayed.

C. Can identify and discriminate each of the described data-recording techniques, including frequency count, duration, whole and partial interval time sampling, permanent product, and anecdotal data recording.

   1. Given 10 vignettes of data-recording techniques, trainee correctly identifies/discriminates each technique.

D. Can accurately take data, using a variety of data-recording techniques.

   1. Given five videotaped vignettes, trainee is able to collect data with 90% reliability, using each of the following data-recording techniques (antecedent–behavior–consequence, interval, momentary time sampling, frequency, permanent product, and duration).

E. Is able to summarize data on a data summary sheet for each data collection method (frequency, duration, and interval) for specified units of time.

   1. Given a series of varied data, trainee correctly translates to a data summary sheet.

   2. Given several series of data, trainee calculates rate per month, average daily frequency, percentage of occurrences, duration, and weekly average.

F. Is able to label the axes of a graph (horizontal vs. vertical), and describe the dimensions represented by each.

   1. Given a list of 10 terms, trainee can match each to the correct axis of the graph.

G. Is able to plot three types of data (frequency, duration, and percentage) on a graph for each of the following time periods (day, week, and month); and is able to label the axes of graph correctly.

   1. Given four sets of data, trainee correctly plots data points on graphs for the prescribed time period, including labeling the axes of one of the graphs.

H. Understands the purpose of observational reliability.

   1. Trainee can provide a description of the reasons for conducting reliability checks, such as for consistency of data collection and evaluating results of treatment.

I. Is able to conduct a reliability check and calculate a reliability index using each of the following methods: antecedent–behavior–consequence, frequency recording, duration recording, interval recording, momentary time sampling, and permanent product.

   1. Given videotaped vignettes, trainee conducts a reliability check, using the above methods and gives feedback to peer with 90% accuracy (pair with **X.D.1.**).

XI. Behavior Assessment Report and Support Plan

A. Demonstrates understanding of baseline assessment period, staff's role in it, and its purpose.

   1. Given a written test about baseline assessment, trainee answers all questions correctly.

B. Understands the behavior assessment report and the purpose of each section.

   1. Given a sample behavior assessment report, trainee describes the purpose of each section and answers the following questions. "What functions do the target behaviors serve for the person? Name the target behaviors and data collection strategies. Name the support services and briefly describe how each is carried out."

  C. Identifies staff responsibilities mandated by the behavior assessment report.
    1. When asked, trainee states that staff are responsible for reading behavior assessment reports and protocols, collecting data, and implementing the procedures as written.
    2. Given three sample situations describing confusion in a behavior support plan, trainee states correctly how to resolve the problem (i.e., that he or she would look at the protocol, and if he or she were still unsure, he or she would ask the supervisor or behavior consultant for clarification).
  D. Identifies procedure for changing behavior support plans.
    1. When asked how support plans are changed, trainee states by approval of the behavior consultant, and that all changes to the protocol are made in writing.
    2. When asked what he or she would do in three situations about problems with the implementation of support plans, trainee response indicates understanding that staff cannot change plans on their own; protocols must be amended in writing by the behavior consultant for the entire support team.

XII. **Positive Programming** (has corresponding videotaped material)
  A. Understands positive programming (its definition, purpose, and when it takes place).
    1. Given a true/false test about positive programming, trainee scores 90% or above.
  B. Understands the relationship between behavior problems and communication, and is familiar with strategies for communication training.
    1. When given three vignettes about problem behaviors, trainee is able to describe possible messages being conveyed.
    2. Trainee scores 80% or better on an objective examination that covers development of communication skills, alternatives, and augmentative systems in behavior management.
  C. Understands the role environmental variables can play in behavior problems and in the solution of those problems.
    1. Given five vignettes, trainee is able to list environmental factors that might be affecting the problems, and makes specific suggestions for environmental manipulations that should be attempted.
  D. Is familiar with personal profiles/positive futures planning and self-advocacy support groups.
    1. In an objective test about personal profiles/positive futures planning and self-advocacy support groups, trainee scores 80% or more.
  E. Understands the relationship between social skills deficits and behavior problems.
    1. When given a written test, trainee can select the correct responses to, "Define social skills," "How do social skills relate to behavior problems?", and "Give examples."
    2. For each of three descriptions of problem behaviors, trainee can list at least two specific social skills that might decrease the target behaviors.
  F. Is familiar with personal effectiveness training as a strategy for teaching specific social skills.
    1. Given the opportunity to observe a real or videotaped personal effectiveness training group, trainee describes three parts of the social skills training process.

G. Demonstrates familiarity with relaxation procedures.
   1. Given a videotaped relaxation group, trainee practices relaxation along with the group.
   2. Trainee scores at least 90% on a matching test about relaxation training.

XIII. Reducing Behavior Problems (has corresponding videotaped material)
A. Is familiar with at least 10 alternatives to punishment for reducing behavior problems.
   1. Given a list of supports, trainee is able to match them to the corresponding procedural designation.
B. Understands what information is useful in deciding which strategies to select for individual support plans.
   1. Given three vignettes, trainee is able to identify which items of information from a list could be useful in deciding which strategy to select.
C. Demonstrates familiarity with and proper implementation of active listening strategies.
   1. Given three dialogs, trainee correctly selects active listening statements.
   2. After seeing a videotape of active listening strategies, trainee can actively listen for at least 3 minutes in a role-playing situation.
D. Knows what options are available to staff if a target behavior occurs.
   1. Given a written test, trainee correctly identifies at least four options for responding to target behaviors.
E. Knows the proper use of physical intervention for client behavior problems.
   1. After viewing a videotape, trainee scores 90% on a test about emergency physical interventions with service recipients.

XIV. Evaluation and Troubleshooting
A. Evaluates behavior trends by reading graphs.
   1. Given four graphs, trainee identifies whether the behavior is increasing, decreasing, or stable, and makes a statement about impact of services (desired effect, undesired effect, or no effect).
B. Compares data with objectives to evaluate progress.
   1. Given a list of objectives and several months of data, trainee can identify correctly whether each objective was met or unmet.
C. Can devise action plans based on evaluating data.
   1. Given a multiple-choice test, trainee can answer each question correctly, and can then choose the correct plan of action for each example.
D. Understands rationale for procedural reliability and can implement support plans with 90% or more reliability.
   1. Given a true/false test about the definition of and rationale for procedural reliability, trainee scores 90% or more.
   2. Given a behavior protocol, trainee can achieve 90% or higher reliability on the behavior programming competency checklist for orally describing the procedure.
   3. Given a behavior protocol and a simulated situation, trainee can role-play a behavioral procedure with 90% reliability.
   4. Given a behavior or teaching protocol, trainee can achieve 90% or higher procedural reliability in a natural setting with a service recipient.
   5. Having run a procedural reliability check on another person, trainee can accurately calculate a procedural reliability score and give feedback to the other person in a simulated or actual situation.

    E. Defines what is meant by *troubleshooting* support plans, identifies variables to examine, and can apply knowledge to case vignettes.

        1. Given the questions, "What does troubleshooting mean? Is this a normal part of behavior support plans?" trainee response includes *de-bugging* concept, evaluating where improvements can be made, and that trouble-shooting is a normal part of behavior support plans.

        2. Given a list of items, trainee can select which variables may influence individual response to behavioral services.

        3. Given two case summaries, trainee can identify at least two variables for each that might have influenced outcomes.

        4. Given three troubleshooting vignettes, trainee correctly identifies what must be done to remedy the problems.

    F. Is familiar with third-party evaluation and program outcome objectives.

        1. In a multiple-choice test about other types of evaluation and troubleshooting, trainee scores at least 90%.

XV. **Generalization and Maintenance**

    A. Understands the importance of programming for generalization and maintenance, and can identify strategies for promoting them.

        1. Given a multiple-choice test about generalization and maintenance and why they are important for people with developmental disabilities, trainee scores at least 85%.

        2. From 10 vignettes, trainee identifies those that provide examples of generalization and maintenance, and matches them to specific strategies.

XVI. **Supported Employment**

    A. Is familiar with the supported work model.

        1. Trainee scores 95% or above on an objective test about supported work.

    B. Understands the job specialist's role and duties.

        1. Trainee scores 95% on objective test.

    C. Demonstrates community relations.

        1. Given a role-playing situation, trainee responds correctly to the following.

            a. An employee who works at your company approaches you and asks you to describe your program and what it does for participants.

· Appendix K ·

The PSR

ACTIVE LISTENING PROTOCOL

I. **When**
   A. **Style.** Active listening[1] is not only a strategy, but a nonjudgmental style to be used in all your interactions with the people with whom you work.
      1. When something good happens
      2. When someone is providing information
      3. When someone is trying to problem solve or make a decision
   B. **Person-Specific (Reactive Strategy).** Active listening is also a strategy to be used reactively when someone is visibly upset; he or she may show a wide spectrum of behaviors from mild concern to extreme anger or frustration.

II. **Listening**
   A. **General Guidelines**
      1. Before speaking with the person, the staff should try to understand what the person is feeling or what his or her message means.
      2. Staff should then put what they understand the person to be saying into his or her own words in order to verify his or her understanding of what the person is feeling (i.e., reflect back what he or she is saying in staff's own words).
      3. *Do not* evaluate, give an opinion, advise, analyze, or question (see roadblock section for more details).
      4. Staff should feed back only what they feel the person's message meant—nothing more, nothing less.
   B. **Examples**
      1. *Person says*, "I hate my job. I want to quit!"
         Staff says, "It sounds like you are unhappy with your job, and you don't want to work there anymore."
      2. *Person says*, "I've had it with my roommate, Susan. She's such a slob!"
         Staff says, "It seems you are fed up with Susan and that you think she is very messy!"
         Staff should, in general, match the emotional level of the person expressing his or her feelings. For example, if the person has an excited tone of voice, the

---

[1]For more about active listening, please refer to PET: Parent Effectiveness Training, by Thomas Gordon (Peter H. Wyden, Inc. 1970).

staff should also have an excited tone of voice. However, use your best judgment, as you get to know someone better. Some people might escalate if you match their emotional level, in which case you should maintain a calm demeanor, while continuing to reflect their feelings.

III. Staging

    A. General.   When using active listening as a reactive strategy, try your best to get to an area free from distractions.

    B. Home.   Rather than trying to actively listen to a person who is upset in front of his or her roommates, try to get him or her to a quiet room, such as the bedroom.

    C. Community.   When using active listening as a reactive strategy in the community, again, try to go to an area that is both uncrowded and uncluttered. For example, if you are in the grocery store, try to walk to the parking lot, or at least to an uncrowded part of the store.

IV. Avoiding Roadblocks

    A. General.   Remember, active listening is only feeding back to the person what you think he or she is saying—nothing more, nothing less. Try to avoid the following responses or roadblocks to active listening identified by Gordon (1970).

        1. Ordering, directing, commanding
        2. Warning, admonishing, threatening
        3. Exhorting, moralizing, preaching
        4. Advising, giving solutions or suggestions
        5. Lecturing, teaching, giving logical arguments
        6. Judging, criticizing, disagreeing, blaming
        7. Praising, agreeing
        8. Name calling, ridiculing, shaming
        9. Interpreting, analyzing, diagnosing
      10. Reassuring, sympathizing, consoling, supporting
      11. Probing, questioning, interrogating
      12. Withdrawing, distracting, humoring, diverting

V. Monitoring.   During the active listening process, try your best to track the progress you are making (i.e., is the person beginning to calm down or continuing to escalate?). The indicators are specific to each individual.

    A. Oral Indicators.   Voice tone should start becoming closer to a normal volume, and the speed with which the person is speaking should become closer to a normal pace. Enter any person-specific indicators.

    B. Physical Indicators.   Person seems to become calmer (less frenetic body movements) and begins to look physically more relaxed and less tense (body not as stiff and rigid). Enter any person-specific indicators.

VI. Make Transitions Appropriately

    A. Timing.   The timing as to when to switch from active listening to another mode, such as relaxation or problem solving, is vital to the success of the reactive strategy. Some specific signs indicate the person may be ready to move on.

        1. The person's affect comes down; the voice has a normal tone, and he or she talks at a normal pace.
        2. There are physical signs of relaxation; the person is not moving about restlessly, shoulders are relaxed, and so forth.
        3. Staff has made sure that all the nuances of the message the person is trying to communicate have been reflected. It is important not to stop at generic reflection, such as, "You sure are angry."
        4. Finally, the person may indicate he or she is ready to move on. He or she may say something such as, "Well, what should I do about It?" Alternatively, he or she may begin to take deep breaths, initiating a relaxation process.

5. Staff should review with the person the issues brought out during the active-listening process. This could be done in a list fashion such as, "Let me make sure I understand all we talked about. You said you were upset because your roommate came in your room without permission and because you do not want to cook dinner tonight. Is there anything I missed?" The person should then indicate if he or she feels understood and is ready to move on.

B. Next Strategy.   Once you have been through the above process, move on to the next strategy listed on the person's protocol, such as relaxation training or problem solving.

VII. Reinstate Active Listening.   If you move on to a new strategy, and the person begins to escalate, return to active listening. Remember, it can take a long time for a person to feel that all his or her concerns have been heard, so take your time, and be patient. You may need to listen to the same concerns over and over.

VIII. Fail Criteria.   If staff has been actively listening using this protocol for at least 15 minutes, and there are absolutely no physical or oral indicators that the person is calming down, you may need to stop active listening and move on to an alternative reactive strategy (see below).

IX. Fail Strategy.   If active listening has failed in this instance (see above definition), move to the alternative reactive strategy listed in the person's protocol (e.g., stimulus change, relaxation training).

· Appendix L ·

The PSR

PERIODIC SERVICE REVIEW FOR SUPPORTED EMPLOYMENT MANAGEMENT TEAM

Score Sheet

Date: _____ Score: _____

County: _____

I. Staff

A. Meetings

	Achieved	Possible

1. Coordinate scheduled monthly all-staff meeting.

2. Hold ongoing individual or group contact meetings with program specialists and employment maintenance specialists at least bi-monthly.

3. Direct management meeting bi-monthly (senior program specialists, supervisors, manager).

4. Report to assistant or director of supported employment services weekly appraising of program progress and problems.

5. Annual retreat planning and participation.

	Achieved	Possible

B. Training

1. **Competency-Based Training (CBT).** Staff are completing CBT according to schedule; have completed all (if over 6 months), completed all but three (if 3 months), prorated (one per 1½ weeks) if less than 3 months, unless a written plan is in place or for special circumstances.

2. **Advanced CBT.** Management (and other) staff are completing according to manager's assignments.

3. **Respond and Grade Staff CBT.** 1 week turn-around time.

4. Present in-services at least quarterly.

C. Evaluations

1. Complete within 2 weeks of due date (end of 3 months for new employees, annually thereafter).

2. Follow policies for disciplinary action, raises, and promotions.

D. Hiring

1. If staff openings, ad placed in newspapers, two candidates interviewed weekly.

2. For each staff hired, agency policies followed regarding reference checks, orientation, and forwarding of information to master personnel files.

E. Substitutes. Absent staff covered by appropriately trained and recruited staff.

F. Keep Ratio. Overall ratio within two service recipients of 1:3 ratio with all service recipients appropriately covered (daily).

II. Employment Sites

A. Procurement. Develop new jobs at rate of at least two per quarter.

	Achieved	Possible

B.   Targeted Job Tax Credit (TJTC).   Filed prior to client starting, use checklist, and follow up promptly with Employment Development Department (EDD) appointments (within 1 month after eligible).

C.   Set Up New Sites

   1.   Completed checklist for new jobs within 1 week of start date.

   2.   Applicable federal and state department of labor certificates filed with corresponding documentation prior to job starting.

D.   Coordinate Sites.   At least monthly management on-site check-in (documented).

E.   Jobs Filled.   All available jobs filled or plans in progress.

F.   Back-Ups Identified.   One viable back-up per group with availability verified at least once every 6 months (unless excused by assistant or director of supported employment services).

G.   Employment Factor.   No more than 8% unemployed.

H.   Safety Committee.   Safety committee meets quarterly and recommendations are carried out.

III.   Service Participants

A.   Program Capacity.   Each program at specified capacity.

B.   Intakes.   Referral packets acknowledged in writing within 1 week of receipt.

C.   Intake Interviews.   Four per month with completed packets, or waiting list of 15.

D.   Participant Solicitation.   Generates sufficient client referrals to meet criteria for intake interviews (see above).

Achieved	Possible

E. Individualized Service Plans. Submitted to regional center and/or department of rehabilitation within 2 weeks of deadline (initials, 30 days; annuals, month of birth); staffing to finalize written ISPs held at least annually during client birth month.

F. Quarterlies/Monthlies. Submitted within 2 weeks of deadline (end of month specified).

G. Objectives Met. Seventy-five percent or more client objectives are met quarterly.

H. Reliability. Procedural reliability monthly for one participant per job coach; interobserver reliability monthly for one participant per job coach.

IV. Public Relations

A. Presentations and Tours. Average three per year to agencies, parent groups, community groups, case managers, and so forth, and recorded on list.

B. Parents/Care Providers. Contact at least once per quarter per participant, or more often, if stipulated.

C. Regional Center/Department of Rehabilitation

 1. One contact per quarter per participant with case managers and/or Vocational Rehabilitation (VR) counselor.

 2. One contact per quarter with Regional Center (RC) vocational liaison.

V. Troubleshooting

A. Participant Problems

 1. Lack of progress on behavior or skill goals is noted and documented to management.

 2. Meeting to discuss plan within 2 weeks of above.

Achieved	Possible

B. Parent/Care Provider Problems. Communicated to management via incident report and/or telephone call, and appropriate action taken.

C. Employer Problems. Noted to management, and action taken within 1 week.

VI. Data Management and Reporting

A. Earnings and Attendance. Compiled by the third of each month for participants; for staff, attendance and pay raises reported accurately and timely.

B. Social Security Submission. Written earnings record submitted to Social Security by the sixth day of the quarter (month).

C. Billing. Submitted no later than the fifth of the month.

D. Office Data Management System

1. Operations board and map accurate and updated within 3 days of changes.

2. Master annual calendar of events posted and followed (includes at least the following: staff, management, IABA management meetings; inservices; annual questionnaires; presentations/tours; outside evaluation).

3. Notebooks accurate and updated for the following: federal and state subminimum wage; TJTC; CBT (basic and advanced); PSR; contact meeting minutes.

4. Case files organized (intake, ongoing, termination), and confidentiality policies followed.

5. Forms for staff and management labeled, in appropriate order, and in marked file cabinets, and inventory of hard copies or computer disks maintained.

6. Files maintained for job sites, participant separation, individual earnings, staff meeting minutes.

	Achieved	Possible

7. Lists of current participants, current staff, terminated clients, and terminated staff are accurate and updated within 1 week.

VII. Program Evaluation

A. Periodic Service Reviews

1. One per month per coach.

2. One per quarter for management.

3. Annual review of all PSRs, including formal feedback from staff.

4. PSR reliability checks cross-county and within county, each at least twice a year (one per year for management).

B. Employer Evaluations. One per month per coach.

C. Statistics Summary. Statistics for PSR summarized and forwarded by the third of the month; by the 10th of the month, earnings, hours worked, enrollment, and PSR mean posted.

D. Budget. Helps plan annual budget, reviews monthly cost figures, and stays within planned allowance (unless deviation approved by assistant or director of supported employment services).

E. Questionnaires. At least yearly to participants, care providers/parents, employers, staff, RC service coordinators/VR counselors, with results summarized.

F. Annual Review and Goal Setting. Using all information listed here under Periodic Service Review, plus staff tenure, staff separation, job tenure, participant separation, and termination statistics, sets annual goals for improvement and expansion.

Achieved	Possible

G. Outside Evaluation.   Once every 2 years.

Totals

Percentage (PSR) Score

· Index ·

The**PSR**

ᵀʰᵉ PSR